Lucy Waverman's SEASONAL CANADIAN COOKBOOK

COOKING TECHNIQUES, TIME-SAVING TIPS, MOUTH-WATERING RECIPES AND UNIQUE MENUS FOR EVERY SEASON'S HARVEST

Harper & *Collins*

TORONTO

First published in 1989 by
Harper & Collins Publishers Ltd.
Suite 2900, Hazelton Lanes
55 Avenue Road
Toronto, Canada
M5R 3L2

Canadian Cataloguing in Publication Data

Waverman, Lucy.
   The seasonal Canadian cookbook

Includes index.
ISBN 0-00-215978-3

1. Cookery. I. Title.

TX715.W38 1989   641.5'64   C89-094027-4

Text illustrations: Jack McMaster
Typesetting: Jay Tee Graphics Ltd.
Printed in Canada

Some of the recipes in this book originally appeared in the Toronto *Sun*, *Canadian Living Magazine*, *Toronto Life* and *Recipes Only*.

Lucy
Waverman's
SEASONAL
CANADIAN
COOKBOOK

To Bruce, who is always supportive

Contents

Acknowledgements

Many people have been involved in this book — not only my students and family, but the many cookbook authors whose books grace my shelves and whose insights into food have often been a springboard for my own imagination.

My grateful thanks to my recipe tester, Claire Hymas, who could take a concept and turn it into an outstanding recipe, and who made sure all the recipes in this book work; Kim Quigley, who helped with recipe testing and research; my kids — Emma, Katie and Alex — who often ate the first batches of crumbled cake and dry cookies in the interest of palate development; Shelley Tanaka, whose sense of excellence is extraordinary, and who often retested receipes to make sure readers could follow the instructions.

Introduction

Think of a ripe, red beefsteak tomato dripping its sweet juice in August, or the crunch of a crisp, hard apple in the fall. The taste is incomparable. Fresh, seasonal food delivers the taste and texture needed to produce the best results in the kitchen.

No matter how carefully or elaborately a dish is prepared, it will always be better if you use home-grown, tree-ripened produce freshly picked at the height of its flavor. Produce from other countries may be available all year, but it is often picked unripe for shipping and storage, and it seldom has the same flavor or texture as the home-grown variety.

When an ingredient becomes seasonally available, how do you use it to get the best results? This book answers that question — with advice, tips, time-saving techniques and recipes that will show you how to buy, store, prepare and appreciate seasonal food. In addition to produce, I have included seafood and meats, because some of them have their seasons, too.

The recipes are organized by the month. I have used our Canadian seasons as my guide, but occasionally I have included produce that comes from around the world — artichokes may not flourish in Canada, but they do arrive on our shelves in February, bringing a ray of California sunshine into an otherwise gloomy market.

Understanding technique is the key to good cooking, and the techniques in this book are an extension of those described in my first Cooking School cookbook. The techniques also have a seasonal theme — barbecuing in June; how to preserve the summer in August; making marmalade in January when Seville oranges are available. And the holiday celebrations and special entertaining needs that each month brings are reflected in the monthly menus, from a make-ahead cocktail party for pre-Christmas entertaining to a Father's Day barbecue in June.

I have included a combination recipes I use at home, in the Cooking School, from my *Toronto Sun*, *Toronto Life* and *Canadian Living* articles, and some that have been especially developed for this book. Others are tried-and-true recipes from family and friends. Most of the recipes are quick and simple, using easily available ingredients. If the supermarket doesn't have them, the health food store will. Today, with busy work and family schedules, time is of the essence.

For those who want to experiment, there are some recipes that demand more time and attention. I hope you will be encouraged to cook food when it is at its peak, but perhaps you will also be inspired to try something new. How about the joys of a buttery homemade brioche, or the unique flavor of those strange thistle-like artichokes — even boning your own chicken for a spectacular buffet dish.

Whatever you choose to do, I believe this book will help you hone your skills while preparing exciting, enjoyable, seasonal food.

Lucy Waverman
October, 1989

1
January

Dark and gloomy January, the time of New Year's resolutions and diets, but brightened by skiing and diet-sabotaging hearty, meaty casseroles to combat those cold winter nights.

In season
onions
parsnips
potatoes
rutabagas
Seville oranges
turnips

Holidays
New Year's Day
Twelfth Night
Ukrainian Christmas
Robbie Burns Night

Menu
Ski Chalet Dinner for Six

MARMALADE

Marmalade, the typical British spread for toast, comes in all kinds of styles. It can vary from dark to light orange, it can contain chunky peel or thin translucent slivers, and almost endless variations can be made from bitter Seville and sweet oranges, tangerines, lemons, limes and grapefruit. Marmalade can be much more than a spread on toast. It can glaze ham or chicken, flavor poached fruit, flavor cakes, or make a sauce for duck.

The flavor of homemade marmalade is different from commercial. It has more character and is economical to make. About 3 lb (1.5 kg) fruit should yield about 5 to 7 lb (2.5 to 3.5 kg) marmalade. The principles of marmalade-making are similar to other jams, but marmalade is easier because it always sets. But be careful, because if you boil it too long, it can turn to glue.

Seville oranges are full of pectin, which is a natural substance found in the pith, skin and seeds of many fruits. When pectin is combined with sugar and an acid, it forms a jelly. Pectin can also be bought in powdered or liquid form at the supermarket; however, natural pectin has a better flavor because it requires less sugar, and gives the jam a more gentle, lighter texture. Young fruit and acidic fruit usually contain more pectin than older fruit.

Cooking and Storing

• Use fruit as soon as possible after buying. Rinse the oranges well, because the peel is sometimes treated with a wax coating.

• The peel must be tenderized by long slow cooking and to extract all the pectin from the pith and seeds. I find it easier to slowly simmer the whole oranges until they are soft, then cut up the peel. The traditional method is to first slice the oranges, removing the seeds and flesh before simmering everything together.

• Simmer the oranges whole in water for about 2 hours, or until very soft. Cut the oranges in half. Scrape out the flesh and seeds, wrap in cheesecloth and return to the orange water in the pot. Simmer together for 10 more minutes, squeezing the cheesecloth occasionally to remove any further pectin.

• Meanwhile, slice the peel into thin or thick slices, dice it or even puree it in the food processor and return it to the liquid along with the granulated sugar. You will need 5 lb (2.5 kg) sugar for 3 lb (1.5 kg) oranges. Once the sugar has been added, the peel will not become more tender.

• Fast boiling is the secret to a quick set. If the marmalade sets quickly, it will retain the bright color and the fresh flavor. It takes about 15 to 20 minutes to set.

• When you test the marmalade to see if it has set, take the pan off the heat to stop further boiling. Marmalade that boils past the setting point cannot be resurrected.

• Don't spoon the marmalade into jars straight away unless you want all the fruit at the top. It should sit for 20 minutes.

• Sterilize the jars by placing them in a 225°F (108°C) oven for 15 minutes. Place the sealing lids in a bowl and pour boiling water over them.

• If you reuse jars, seal them with new sealing lids or melted paraffin wax.

Setting Tests for Jam and Marmalade

• Use a candy thermometer. Marmalade sets at 220°F (105°C).

• Dip a metal spoon into the marmalade and raise it above the pot. When the liquid running off the spoon becomes a single stream or sheet in the middle of the spoon, the marmalade is set.

• Place a small plate in the freezer for 30 minutes. Remove the plate from the freezer and pour about 1 tsp (5 mL) marmalade onto the plate. Cool at room temperature for 1 minute. Run your finger through the marmalade. If it wrinkles, it is set.

Marmalade comes from the Portuguese word *marmelo*, meaning quince — a hard, acidic, pear-shaped fruit used as a preserve. In Portugal, mashed quince and spices were cooked together until the mixture was thick enough to be sliced as a candy.

To remove foam from marmalade, take a sheet of waxed paper and rub it across the surface; the scum should come off.

Seville Orange Marmalade

Seville oranges originally came from Portugal, but they are now grown all over the world. They first arrive on our supermarket shelves in January, and are in season for about one month.

3 lb	Seville oranges	1.5 kg
10 cups	water	2.5 L
	Juice of 2 lemons	
5 lb	granulated sugar	2.5 kg

1. Place the oranges in a large pot and cover with the water. Cover tightly and simmer on low heat for 1½ to 2 hours, or until the oranges are very soft.

2. Remove the oranges with a slotted spoon. Cool slightly, then cut in half. With a spoon, scape out the pits and flesh and place in a cheesecloth bag. When the oranges are scraped clean, dice or slice the peel into thick or thin slices.

3. Place the cheesecloth bag into the orange liquid and simmer for 10 more minutes to extract any further pectin. Remove the bag and squeeze any extra juice back into the pot.

4. Stir in the sliced orange peel, lemon juice and sugar.

5. Bring to a boil and boil briskly for 15 minutes. Test every 5 minutes until the set is correct. Skim off any froth.

6. Let sit for 20 minutes, then fill the jars.

Makes about ten 8-oz (250 g) jars

Three-Fruit Marmalade

Kim Quigley, a Woodstock cooking teacher, has been making marmalade every January for years. Her current favorite is a tangy three-fruit marmalade made by the traditional method. Use regular oranges, not Seville; they are too bitter for this marmalade.

1	large grapefruit	1
1	large sweet orange	1
1	large lemon	1
7 cups	water	1.75 L
	Granulated sugar	

1. Wash and halve the fruit. Squeeze out the juice and reserve. Scrape out the flesh and place it in a cheesecloth bag along with the seeds. Thinly slice the peel.

2. In a large heavy pot, combine the water, peel and cheesecloth bag. Bring to a boil, then reduce the heat to low and simmer, uncovered, for 2 to 3 hours, or until the peel can be easily squeezed between your fingers. While the mixture is cooking, occasionally squeeze the cheesecloth bag to extract the pectin.

3. Measure the fruit and liquid in a measuring cup and return to the pot. Add an equal amount of sugar.

4. Bring to a boil and boil, uncovered, for 15 to 20 minutes, or until the marmalade is set.

5. Remove from the heat and skim off any foam. Let sit for 20 minutes, then fill and seal the jars.

Makes five 8-oz (250 g) jars

Marmalade Variations
• For the darker-colored Oxford type of marmalade, use 1½ cups (375 mL) brown sugar as part of the sugar quantity.
• Use 2 tbsp (25 mL) molasses to give a slightly different taste and darker color to chunky marmalade made with diced fruit.
• Crush 3 thin slices of ginger root and add to the pan of boiling oranges for a subtle ginger flavor.

ROOT VEGETABLES

Come January, nothing is grown fresh in Canada. However, certain vegetables come through winter storage better than others. They are the vegetables that our great-grandparents left in cool root cellars after the harvest, for eating through the lean months of December, January and February. Versatile, tasty and cheap, these root vegetables are the stars of the winter vegetable counter.

Although any vegetable that grows under the ground is technically a root vegetable, botanically they come from different species. Carrots and parsnips are from the same family, but turnips and rutabagas are a separate breed related to the cabbage. Potatoes are tubers, sweet potatoes come from the morning glory family, while yams are related to lilies.

Turnips and Rutabagas

• Turnips and rutabagas are close relatives but are not the same vegetable. The white-fleshed turnips are smaller than rutabagas and have white bases flowing into purple tops. Their taste is milder and more delicate than rutabagas.

• Rutabagas were originally bred in Sweden, where they were produced from a union of a cabbage and a turnip! In Europe they are known as Swedes. They are yellow fleshed and have a thick brown skin that is waxed when harvested. Today they are more readily available than turnips, but the two names have become interchangeable.

• Look for non-sprouting, hard, round rutabagas and turnips that are firm and feel heavy for their size.

Parsnips and Carrots

• Parsnips look like creamy-colored carrots. When cooked, they have a delicate, sweet, nutty flavor. Look for firm, well-shaped parsnips that are not too large (large parsnips are usually fibrous). Peel them before using.

• Look for small, bright-orange carrots without cracks or limp foliage. If the stem end is black or discolored, the carrot is old and fibrous. For munching raw or making delicate carrot dishes, buy the carrots that are sold with their tops intact; the foliage will indicate freshness and youth. For stocks or stews you can buy the cello-wrapped bags.

Potatoes

• All potatoes are not created equal. Different types have different tastes and textures, and are suitable for different cooking methods. There are three basic types of potato — waxy, floury and all-purpose. Waxy or new potatoes are usually round and white or red. They are best for boiling and potato salads. Floury or baking potatoes are oval-shaped and usually referred to as Idaho or russet potatoes. They are best for baking, mashing and roasting. All-purpose potatoes are white-skinned and round or slightly elongated. They are adequate for all uses, but are never outstanding.

• Look for potatoes that are smooth-skinned and free of cuts or green areas.

• Never store potatoes in the refrigerator — it causes undesirable color and flavor changes, and the damp cold of the refrigerator encourages them to sprout. Instead,

Potatoes have a confusing history. When first brought from America to England by Sir Walter Raleigh as a gift for Queen Elizabeth I, the leaves were eaten and the tubers thrown away! The French thought potatoes were good enough for cattle but not people, and the Scots originally banned potatoes because they were not mentioned in the Bible!

Today, potatoes are beginning to be recognized not only by type but by brand name. Yukon Gold, developed in Ontario, with its yellowish skin and pale-gold, buttery flesh, is one of the most prized of the new varieties; it is excellent for baking, roasting and even boiling. Its distinctive taste is similar to the exceptional European potatoes. Blue Macs, developed in Newfoundland, have a bluish-purple skin and are excellent for boiling and mashing. Although they are quite delicious, they have met consumer resistance because of their color. Ontario is also experimenting with blue-fleshed potatoes.

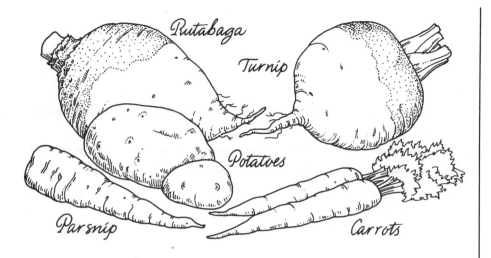

store potatoes in a cool, dark, well-ventilated place to prevent sprouting. They will keep for about one month. (You can eat potatoes that have sprouted, but they will have lost a lot of their nutrients.)

Onions

• Onions are a major ingredient in cooking. How many recipes start with "sauté the onion?" Onions come in a bewildering number of varieties, shapes and colors. Some onions are sweet and mild; some are sharp and pungent. Some are huge and bulbous; others are flattened or tiny.

• **Cooking onions** are usually yellow-skinned and globe-shaped. They are the most popular onion grown in Canada. They do not become very sweet when cooked, but their full flavor enhances many recipes. Do not eat them raw because of their sharp flavor.

• **Spanish onions** are large and yellow-skinned. They are mild in taste and give a delicate sweetness to recipes when cooked. They are good eaten raw.

• **Red onions** are mild onions that look especially attractive when sliced in salads. They can be used for cooking, although they lose some of their color and become pink-hued.

• **Bermuda onions** are large, white- or yellow-skinned onions with a mild flavor.

• **Pearl onions** or **pickling onions** are tiny silver-skinned onions. To avoid the time-consuming task of having to peel so many for one dish, cut off the roots and plunge the onions into boiling water. Boil for 1 minute, drain, and the skins will slip off.

• Bulb-like **shallots** are part of the onion family. The dry, brown skin hides a truly elegant vegetable with a taste that is similar to both garlic and onion.

• **Green onions** are the small, young onion plants that are harvested when immature, before the bulbs have formed. They are mild-tasting and quite perishable. Although **scallions** are often confused with green onions,

The location where onions are grown affects their taste. Red onions grown in Italy are milder than red onions grown in Canada.

The mildest onions come from Georgia and Hawaii. Known as Vidalias or Maui onions, they are so sweet they can practically be eaten as fruits. They make the best onion rings.

Spanish

Red Bermuda

Pearl

Green

Shallots

Quick Creamed Onions
Boil 2 or 3 onions until tender-crisp. Drain, slice and toss with 1 cup (250 mL) sour cream, pepper and salt.

technically they are the immature bulbs of white onions only.
• Look for firm, dry onions that rustle when pressed. They should have a crisp outer skin and show no signs of sprouting. Avoid onions that are flabby or feel damp.
• Store onions in a cool, dark, airy place.
• Onions are low in calories — about 40 per medium-sized onion — and they have a high fiber content.
• To boil vegetables that grow under the ground, place in lots of cold salted water. Cover and bring to boil; boil until tender. This method will cook the firm flesh evenly.

Carrot Straws

An interesting garnish with chicken or beef. Because this doesn't look like a typical carrot dish, confirmed carrot haters may not object.

1 lb	carrots	500 g
¼ cup	butter	50 mL
1 tsp	granulated sugar	5 mL
	Salt and freshly ground pepper to taste	
¼ cup	finely chopped Italian parsley	50 mL

1. Grate the carrots coarsely with a grater or food processor.

2. On medium heat, in a frying pan, heat the butter until sizzling. Stir in the sugar. Toss in the carrots and stir-fry until the carrots soften and brown, about 3 minutes. Season with salt and pepper. Sprinkle with parsley.

Serves 6

Parsnip Cake

Call this a white carrot cake and watch it disappear! Slightly sweet and nutty-tasting parsnips make a fine cake — not unlike carrot but less sweet. The parsnips vanish in the mixture, giving the cake a deep, brown color. My children, who are not parsnip admirers, love the rich, moist texture and taste. For an extra touch, buy some marzipan and make little creamy-colored parsnips to decorate the top.

2 cups less 2 tbsp	all-purpose flour	475 mL
2 tsp	baking powder	10 mL
1 tsp	baking soda	5 mL
1 tsp	salt	5 mL
2 tsp	ground cinnamon	10 mL
1 tbsp	cocoa	15 mL
4	eggs	4
2 tsp	vanilla extract	10 mL
1 cup	granulated sugar	250 mL
1 cup	firmly packed brown sugar	250 mL
1¼ cups	corn oil	300 mL
4 cups	grated parsnips	1 L
1 cup	raisins	250 mL

1. Preheat the oven to 350°F (180°C).

2. Sift together the flour, baking powder, baking soda, salt, cinnamon and cocoa and set aside.

3. In a large bowl, beat the eggs. Add the vanilla, sugars and oil and mix well. Stir the dry ingredients into the wet ingredients. Stir in the parsnips and raisins.

4. Pour into two greased and floured 9-inch (23 cm) round cake pans.

5. Bake for 45 to 50 minutes, or until a cake tester comes out clean. Fill and ice the cakes with Cream Cheese Icing.

Cream Cheese Icing

12 oz	cream cheese	375 g
¼ cup	unsalted butter	50 mL
1 tsp	vanilla extract	5 mL
2 cups	sifted icing sugar	500 mL

1. Cream the cheese and butter with an electric mixer or food processor until soft and smooth. Beat in the vanilla and sugar until incorporated. Spread on top of one cake layer, sandwich with the second layer. Ice the top and sides.

Serves 12

Parsnips and Cream

A rich, heavenly combination that is excellent with roasts. Serve instead of a potato dish.

1	clove garlic, peeled	1
2 lb	parsnips	1 kg
	Salt and freshly ground pepper to taste	
2 cups	light cream, approx.	500 mL

1. Preheat the oven to 375°F (190°C). Butter an 8-cup (2 L) gratin dish. Rub well with garlic.

2. Peel the parsnips and slice about ⅛ inch (3 mm) thick. Layer in the dish, seasoning each layer with salt and pepper. Pour over enough cream to cover the parsnips.

3. Bake for 45 to 60 minutes, or until the top is golden and the parsnips are tender.

Serves 8

Rumblethumps

A mixture of potatoes, cabbage and turnips served as a main course in Ireland or Scotland, but also a fine accompaniment to sausages, hamburgers or chicken dishes. "Rumble" means a mixture, and "thumps" means bashed together! Turnips and rutabagas can both be used.

3	baking potatoes, peeled	3
1/2	small yellow turnip, peeled	1/2
1/4 cup	butter	50 mL
1	onion, chopped	1
1/2	small cabbage, shredded	1/2
	Salt and freshly ground pepper to taste	
2 tsp	cider vinegar	10 mL
1/2 cup	grated Cheddar cheese	125 mL

1. Cut the potatoes and turnip into even-sized chunks. Place in a pot of cold water and bring to the boil. Boil for 10 to 15 minutes, or until the vegetables are tender. Drain well.

2. Place in a large bowl and mash with a potato masher. The mixture should be chunky.

3. Preheat the oven to 400°F (200°C).

4. Heat 2 tbsp (25 mL) butter in a medium frying pan on medium-high heat. Add the onions and sauté until softened, about 2 minutes. Stir in the cabbage and continue to sauté until just tender, about 5 minutes.

5. Scrape the contents of the frying pan into the potato/turnip mixture. Stir together, adding in the remaining 2 tbsp (25 mL) butter. Season well with salt and pepper and stir in the vinegar.

6. Pile into a buttered 8-cup (2 L) gratin dish and sprinkle with the grated cheese.

7. Bake, uncovered, for 20 minutes, or until the top is brown and crusty and contents of dish are hot.

Serves 6

The Irish started to grow potatoes in the sixteenth century, to the exclusion of most other vegetables. When the potato crop failed in 1845, it caused the great potato famine and the beginning of the Irish emigration to Canada and other countries.

Lemon-Scented Potatoes

Excellent with lamb, chicken and pork.

6	baking potatoes, cut in half	6
2 tbsp	olive oil	25 mL
3 tbsp	butter	45 mL
	Grated rind and juice of 1 lemon	
1/4 cup	chopped fresh mint or dill, or 1 tbsp (15 mL) dried	50 mL
	Salt and freshly ground pepper to taste	

1. In a large pot, place the potatoes in cold water to cover. Bring to a boil and boil until just tender, about 8 to 10 minutes. Drain and cool until cool enough to handle. Peel and cut into large dice.

2. Preheat the oven to 400°F (200°C).

3. Melt the oil and butter together in a large baking dish. Stir in the lemon rind and juice and the herbs. Mix in the potatoes and season well.

4. Bake for 30 minutes, uncovered, stirring occasionally, until the potatoes are golden.

Serves 8

Double Baked Potatoes

An interesting potato dish that can be made ahead of time and reheated when needed. I make a lower-calorie version by using low-fat cottage cheese and substituting plain yogurt for the whipping cream.

6	baking potatoes	6
1 cup	cottage cheese	250 mL
4	green onions, chopped	4
1/4 cup	whipping cream	50 mL
1	egg, beaten	1
	Salt and freshly ground pepper to taste	

1. Preheat the oven to 375°F (190°C).

2. Scrub the potatoes, prick with a fork and bake for about 1 hour, or until tender. Cool.

3. In a large bowl, mix together the cottage cheese, green onions, whipping cream and egg. Set aside.

4. Cut off the top quarter of the potatoes. Scoop out the flesh, leaving a little flesh clinging to the skin.

5. With an electric beater or a food mill, mash the potato flesh until smooth. Beat into the cottage cheese mixture. Season to taste with the salt and pepper.

6. Spoon the filling back into the potatoes.

7. Reheat at 375°F (190°C) until warmed through and browned on the top, about 20 minutes.

Serves 6

Potato Latkes

Coarsely shredded potatoes give the latkes lacier edges, while potatoes diced with a steel blade in the food processor result in a denser, smoother texture.

Serve latkes at Hanukkah or with steaks and roasts.

6	baking potatoes, peeled	6
1	onion	1
3	eggs, beaten	3
1 tsp	salt	5 mL
1/4 tsp	freshly ground pepper	1 mL
3 tbsp	all-purpose flour	45 mL
	Vegetable oil for deep-frying	

1. Grate the potatoes and onion by hand or with a food processor. Squeeze out the excess moisture.

2. In a large bowl, combine the potato/onion mixture, eggs, salt, pepper and flour. Let rest for 5 minutes.

3. In a large frying pan, heat 1/4 inch (5 mm) oil over medium heat until it is hot but not smoking.

4. Place about 1/4 cup (50 mL) potato mixture in the hot oil and flatten with a spatula. The latkes will be irregularly shaped.

5. Fry until well browned and crisp around the edges, about 3 minutes per side.

6. Serve hot with applesauce and sour cream.

Makes about 30 latkes

The Ultimate Baked Potato Choose potatoes of the same size, for even cooking. Prick with a fork and bake at 375°F (190°C) for about 1 hour, or until the potatoes are tender when squeezed. *Don't* wrap the potatoes in foil unless you want a steamed potato with soggy skin. Rubbing the potato with butter or salt will also prevent the skin from becoming crisp.

Chicken with Sweet and Sour Onions

My husband Bruce developed this recipe when he was in a creative cooking mood. His unorthodox combination makes an elegant dish suitable for company. Because of the spicing, he served it with couscous, but rice would be suitable, too. I sometimes substitute pork for chicken.

A confit is traditionally a fruit preserved in brandy or vinegar, or a duck or goose slowly cooked in fat and then preserved in it for several months. Today confit is a trendy term for a thick mass of onion or other vegetable served as a garnish.

4	chicken legs with thighs	4
1 tbsp	butter	15 mL
1	large Spanish onion, sliced	1
1 tbsp	ground cumin	15 mL
1 tbsp	ground coriander	15 mL
1 tbsp	ground ginger	15 mL
1/2 cup	raisins	125 mL
1/4 cup	cider vinegar	50 mL
2 cups	chicken stock	500 mL

1. Detach the chicken thighs from the legs.

2. In a heavy pot, heat the butter on medium-low heat. Add the onions, coat with the butter, cover the pan and simmer gently for 10 minutes, or until the onions are soft.

3. Add the cumin, coriander, ginger, raisins and cider vinegar. Bring to a boil, then cook until the liquid has evaporated. Add the chicken stock and bring to a boil. Reserve.

4. In a frying pan on medium-high heat, add the chicken, skin side down. Fry until the skin is browned, about 5 minutes. Turn over and fry the second side.

5. Add the chicken to the onion mixture. Cover the pot and simmer on low heat for 25 minutes, or until the chicken is cooked through.

Serves 4

Egg and Onion Casserole

This casserole makes a terrific brunch dish. Assemble it up to one day in advance, and bake just before serving. The strong onion taste mellows during cooking and won't offend any guests.

By precooking the eggs only very lightly, they will continue to cook and firm up when baked in the oven; otherwise they become dry.

10	eggs	10
1/2 tsp	salt	2 mL
1/2 tsp	freshly ground pepper	2 mL
2 tbsp	butter	25 mL
1	large Spanish onion, sliced	1
1/2 cup	whipping cream	125 mL
pinch	cayenne pepper	pinch
	Salt and freshly ground pepper to taste	
1/2 cup	grated Gruyere cheese	125 mL
1/2 cup	grated Parmesan cheese	125 mL

1. Preheat the oven to 375°F (190°C).

2. In a large bowl, beat 9 eggs lightly with 1/2 tsp (2 mL) salt and 1/2 tsp (2 mL) pepper.

3. Melt 1 tbsp (15 mL) butter in a frying pan on medium-high heat. Sauté the onions until limp, about 5 minutes.

4. Add the cream and bring to a boil. Reduce the cream until thickened, about 4 minutes. Season with the cayenne and salt and pepper to taste. Remove from the pan and reserve. Wipe out the frying pan.

5. On low heat, melt the remaining 1 tbsp (15 mL) butter in the frying pan. Add the 9 beaten eggs and scramble gently, stirring constantly.

As soon as the eggs hold their shape but are still wet, remove from the heat and beat in the remaining egg. Remove from the frying pan and cool.

6. In a buttered 11 × 7-inch (2 L) ovenproof dish, layer the eggs and onions, finishing with the eggs. Top with the cheeses.

7. Bake for 15 minutes, or until the eggs are heated through and the cheese has melted.

Serves 12

Onion Confit

Onion confit is a thick marmalade of onions that is outstanding with roast beef or rack of lamb. I like it with simple fish and chicken dishes, too.

2 tbsp	vegetable oil	25 mL
2	large Spanish onions, thinly sliced	2
1 tsp	granulated sugar	5 mL
1 tbsp	red wine vinegar or balsamic vinegar	15 mL
	Salt and freshly ground pepper to taste	

1. In a heavy pot on medium heat, heat the oil. Add the onions and stir around until they are coated with the oil.

2. Turn the heat to low; add the sugar and vinegar. Cover the pot and let the onions stew gently for 30 minutes, or until soft. Uncover the pot and continue to cook until the liquid has evaporated and the onions are a golden mass. Season with salt and pepper.

Serves 4

CASSEROLES

Comforting casseroles are the backbone of winter cooking. They are hearty, fill the air with delightful aromas, can be made ahead of time and freeze well. And they are usually economical, which is heartening in the debt-ridden days after Christmas.

We tend to think of casseroles as mixtures of meat, vegetables and a starch cooked together to produce a one-dish meal — dishes that are often mush-like concoctions of an overcooked starch combined with undercooked mystery meat. The casseroles that follow are hardly mush-in-a-dish recipes — they'll change your ideas of what a casserole can be.

Technically, a casserole is a heavy cooking pot made from cast-iron enamel, stainless steel or copper, which goes in the oven or on top of the stove, holding contents that are long-cooked and aromatic. Vegetables can be added towards the end of the cooking time, and a starch is usually served with it to mop up the strong gravy.

Onion Quiche
Add 1 1/2 cups (375 mL) light cream and 3 beaten eggs to the onion confit recipe. Pour into a 9-inch (23 cm) mustard-brushed pie shell and bake at 375°F (190°C) for 30 minutes. Serves 6.

Spicy Chicken with Couscous

Couscous is a Middle Eastern chicken or lamb and vegetable stew complemented by couscous grains steamed over the fragrant mixture. My version is an updated, lighter twist on the traditional dish, where the chicken is braised in a tomato-based sauce and the couscous is cooked separately. I use the new packaged quick-cooking couscous, which takes five minutes to prepare.

Preparing Couscous
Traditionally couscous is steamed twice before eating. Sprinkle 2 cups (500 mL) couscous with 2 cups (500 mL) cold water and work the couscous with your fingers to break up any lumps. Pile the couscous into a steamer and steam for 20 minutes. Remove and pour over another 2 cups (500 mL) water. Break up any lumps, return to the steamer and resteam for a further 20 minutes. If you do not have a steamer, improvise with a strainer set inside a large pot. Do not cover couscous when steaming. The first steaming can be done at any time and the second steaming of couscous can be done just before serving.

1	3-lb (1.5 kg) chicken	1
2 tbsp	vegetable oil	25 mL
1	onion, chopped	1
3	cloves garlic, sliced	3
2 tsp	ground ginger	10 mL
1 tsp	turmeric	5 mL
1 tsp	ground cinnamon	5 mL
pinch	cayenne pepper	pinch
1 tsp	freshly ground pepper	5 mL
2	carrots, cut in ¹/₂-inch (1.25 cm) dice	2
2	zucchini, cut in ¹/₂-inch (1.25 cm) dice	2
1	green pepper, cut in ¹/₂-inch (1.25 cm) dice	1
1 cup	chicken stock	250 mL
1¹/₂ cups	drained canned tomatoes, chopped	375 mL
	Salt to taste	
¹/₂ cup	chickpeas	125 mL
¹/₂ cup	raisins, optional	125 mL
¹/₂ cup	finely chopped fresh coriander or parsley	125 mL
2 cups	couscous	500 mL
2 tbsp	butter	25 mL

1. Cut the chicken into eight pieces, removing the backbone. If the breasts are large, cut them in half. Pat dry with paper towels.

2. Heat the oil in a large frying pan over medium heat. Add half the chicken pieces skin side down. Cook until golden, about 5 minutes per side. Remove from the pan and transfer to a large casserole. Cook the remaining pieces and add to the casserole.

3. Add the onion and garlic to the frying pan and sauté until the onion is translucent, about 5 minutes. Stir in the ginger, turmeric, cinnamon, cayenne and black pepper. Sauté for 1 minute.

4. Add the carrots, zucchini and green peppers. Continue to sauté the vegetables until they are coated in oil, about 1 minute. Transfer to the casserole.

5. Pour the stock and tomatoes into the frying pan. Bring to a boil, scraping up any bits. Season to taste with salt. Pour over the chicken pieces. Simmer gently, covered, for about 30 minutes.

6. Stir in the chickpeas and raisins. Continue to cook for 10 more minutes, or until the chicken is cooked through. Sprinkle with the coriander.

7. Prepare the couscous according to the package directions. Stir in the butter.

8. Pile a large spoonful of couscous on a plate or soup bowl. Surround with the chicken pieces, vegetables and sauce. Serve extra sauce and harissa on the side.

Serves 6

Harissa

Harissa is the Middle Eastern version of a hot spicy sauce made with chilies. It can be bought in tubes or bottles at health food stores and Middle Eastern grocery stores. Mix it into the couscous if you want to add spice to the dish.

¼ cup	harissa or hot chili sauce	50 mL
¼ cup	sauce from the chicken	50 mL

1. In a small bowl, stir together the sauce and broth. Serve with the couscous.

Mediterranean Lamb Casserole

This interesting lamb dish is perfect with rice. You can use lamb shanks, lamb stewing meat, or make the casserole with beef. The anchovies disappear in the sauce, leaving a slightly salty background, unidentifiable to anchovy-haters. The best olives are the Greek, Italian or French ones which have lots of taste. The pitted canned olives don't have enough zing for this sauce.

1	lemon	1
2 tbsp	vegetable oil	25 mL
6	lamb shoulder chops	6
1	onion, sliced	1
4	cloves garlic, finely chopped	4
1	14-oz (398 mL) can tomatoes, pureed	1
1 tsp	dried thyme	5 mL
1 tsp	salt	5 mL
½ tsp	freshly ground pepper	2 mL
4	anchovy fillets, chopped	4
¼ cup	finely chopped parsley	50 mL
½ cup	sliced black olives	125 mL

1. Preheat the oven to 325°F (160°C). Slice half the lemon thinly.

2. Heat the oil in a large casserole on high heat. Sear the chops on each side until brown. Remove from the pan.

3. Brown the lemon slices on each side for about 30 seconds, then reserve with the chops.

4. Turn the heat down to medium and add the onions and garlic. Sauté just until limp, about 2 minutes. Stir in the tomato puree, thyme, salt and pepper and boil rapidly for 2 minutes.

5. Return the chops and lemon slices to the casserole. Coat with the tomato sauce. Cover the casserole and bake for 45 minutes, or until the chops are nearly tender.

6. In a small bowl, grate the rest of the lemon rind and combine with the anchovies and parsley. Stir into the casserole along with the olives. Bake for another 15 minutes, or until the lamb is tender.

Serves 6

Stovetop Barbecue

In this recipe, the meat is simmered in a barbecue-type sauce until it is meltingly tender. Serve with cole slaw and potato salad.

5 lb	boneless pork shoulder	2.5 kg
1 cup	chicken stock or water	250 mL
1 cup	tomato sauce	250 mL
1/4 cup	white vinegar	50 mL
1/4 cup	Worcestershire sauce	50 mL
1/4 cup	packed brown sugar	50 mL
1 tbsp	chili powder	15 mL
1/2 tsp	Tabasco	2 mL
2 tbsp	vegetable oil	25 mL
	Salt and freshly ground pepper to taste	

1. Score the surface of the pork fat with a sharp knife.

2. In a bowl, combine the stock, tomato sauce, vinegar, Worcestershire sauce, brown sugar, chili powder and Tabasco.

3. In a heavy pot or Dutch oven, heat the oil on high heat. Add the pork and brown it well on all sides, about 5 minutes. Season with salt and pepper.

4. Pour the sauce mixture over the meat; bring to a boil. Reduce the heat to low and simmer gently, covered, for 2 hours, or until the pork is fork-tender. Baste with the sauce occasionally while cooking.

5. Remove the meat. On high heat, boil the sauce until reduced by one-third. Slice the meat and serve it with the sauce.

Serves 8 to 10

Ski Chalet Dinner for Six

January is the month when people head back onto the ski slopes. Food that can be prepared ahead and either brought up from the city to a chalet or heated up at home after a daily outing, is ideal. No one wants to come off the ski slopes and cook supper. This is a hearty menu that should comfortably feed six ravenous skiers. Everything can be made ahead of time and reheated on the stove or in a 350°F (180°C) oven before serving.

Curried Carrot Bisque

Dill Buttermilk Bread

Beef Shortribs

Potato Bake

Orange and Red Onion Salad

Pecan Pie Squares

Curried Carrot Bisque

Carrots need a flavor injection when they are served in a soup. Curry powder provides that added zing.

2 tbsp	butter	25 mL
1 lb	carrots, peeled and sliced	500 g
3	leeks, washed and sliced	3
2 tbsp	uncooked long-grain rice	25 mL
1 tsp	ground ginger	5 mL
2	cloves garlic, finely chopped	2
1 tsp	curry powder	5 mL
5 cups	chicken stock	1.25 L
1/2 cup	whipping cream	125 mL
	Salt and freshly ground pepper to taste	

Garnish:

1/4 cup	grated carrot	50 mL

1. In a heavy pot, heat the butter over medium heat. Stir in the carrots, leeks, rice, ginger, garlic and curry powder. Sauté for about 5 minutes, or until the leeks soften slightly.

2. Pour in the chicken stock, bring to a boil, lower the heat and simmer for 20 to 25 minutes, or until the vegetables are tender.

3. Puree in a blender or food processor. Return to the heat, add the whipping cream, salt and pepper and simmer for 5 minutes. Garnish with the grated carrot.

Serves 6

Dill Buttermilk Bread

An easy quickbread to eat with the soup and the stew. If you don't have buttermilk, substitute plain yogurt.

3 cups	all-purpose flour	750 mL
4 tsp	baking powder	20 mL
3 tbsp	granulated sugar	45 mL
1/4 cup	finely chopped fresh dill, or 1 tsp (5 mL) dried	50 mL
1 1/2 tsp	baking soda	7 mL
1/2 tsp	salt	2 mL
1/2 tsp	freshly ground pepper	2 mL
1 1/2 cups	buttermilk	375 mL

1. Preheat the oven to 350°F (180°C).

2. In a large bowl, combine the flour, baking powder, sugar, dill, baking soda, salt and pepper.

3. Add the buttermilk a little at a time until a soft dough forms.

4. Turn into a greased 9 × 5-inch (2 L) loaf pan. Bake for 50 minutes, or until the loaf is golden-brown. Serve warm or reheat.

Makes one loaf

Today, the term bisque is used to describe a soup made of pureed vegetables or shellfish, often thickened with rice.

Beef Shortribs

I've never been keen on stewed beef because I usually find it stringy and tasteless, but these shortribs are meaty, tasty, and not at all stringy. They come from the breast section of the animal and are usually sold on the bone, which makes them more succulent. They also cook in less time than stewing beef.

I prefer not to thicken gravies to save calories, but if you wish a thicker gravy, combine 2 tbsp (25 mL) arrowroot or cornstarch with 2 tbsp (25 mL) cold water and stir into the gravy after the cooking is finished. Bring to a boil, stirring, and cook for a few minutes.

6	racks shortribs	6
1/4 cup	all-purpose flour	50 mL
1 tsp	dried thyme	5 mL
1/2 tsp	salt	2 mL
1/2 tsp	freshly ground pepper	2 mL
2 tbsp	vegetable oil	25 mL
1	large onion, chopped	1
2	cloves garlic, finely chopped	2
1/2 cup	dry red wine	125 mL
6	canned tomatoes, chopped	6
3 cups	beef stock	750 mL
1	bay leaf	1
	Salt and freshly ground pepper to taste	
1/4 cup	finely chopped parsley	50 mL

1. Preheat the oven to 325°F (160°C).

2. Remove the fat layer from the top of each shortrib. On a sheet of waxed paper, combine the flour, thyme, salt and pepper. Coat the shortribs with the seasoned flour.

3. Heat the oil in large frying pan. On high heat, brown the ribs on all sides until they are dark-brown. Remove them from the pan and place in large ovenproof casserole.

4. Turn the heat to medium and add the onions and garlic to the frying pan. Sauté until the onions soften slightly, about 2 minutes. Pour in the red wine, bring to a boil and reduce until 1 tbsp (15 mL) remains.

5. Add the tomatoes, stock and bay leaf. Bring to a boil.

6. Pour the liquid over the meat and bake, covered, for 1 1/2 hours, or until the meat is tender. Remove the meat and skim the fat off the gravy. Season to taste. Cut the shortribs into chunks before serving, if desired. Reheat the gravy and the meat together. Sprinkle with parsley before serving.

Serves 6

Potato Bake

Layered potato dishes made with or without cheese are family favorites. The liquid can be stock, milk, or even whipping cream for the richest taste.

2	cloves garlic, finely chopped	2
6	potatoes, peeled and thinly sliced	6
2 cups	grated old Cheddar cheese	500 mL
	Salt and freshly ground pepper to taste	
2 cups	milk	500 mL
1 tsp	dried thyme	5 mL

1. Preheat the oven to 375°F (190°C).

2. Butter an 8-cup (2 L) ovenproof baking dish. Scatter with the garlic.

3. Overlap the potatoes on the bottom of the dish. Sprinkle with the cheese. Repeat the layers, finishing with cheese. Season each potato layer with salt and pepper.

4. Combine milk and thyme and pour over the potatoes.

5. Bake for 1 hour, or until the milk is absorbed and the potatoes are cooked through and golden-brown on top.

Serves 6

Orange and Red Onion Salad

Before using raw onions in salads, sprinkle the onion slices lightly with salt and let sit for 30 minutes, then pat dry with paper towels. The salt will draw out the bitter onion juices so the flavor will not be as strong.

4	navel oranges	4
1	red onion, thinly sliced	1
1 cup	black olives	250 mL
1 tbsp	lemon juice	15 mL
1/2 tsp	Dijon mustard	2 mL
1/3 cup	olive oil	75 mL
2 tbsp	finely chopped parsley	25 mL

1. Over a bowl, remove the skin and white pith from the oranges, reserving any juice. Slice the oranges thinly. Place in a flat dish.

2. Top with the red onion slices and scatter with the olives.

3. In a small bowl, mix together the lemon juice and mustard. Pour in any juice from the oranges. Whisk in the olive oil slowly. Stir in the parsley. Pour over the salad.

4. Chill for 1 hour before serving.

Serves 6

Pecan Pie Squares

A simplified version of pecan pie that takes minutes to put together. Serve with ice cream, if desired.

Base:

1 cup	all-purpose flour	250 mL
1/4 cup	brown sugar	50 mL
1/2 cup	unsalted butter	125 mL

Topping:

2/3 cup	brown sugar	150 mL
1 cup	corn syrup	250 mL
2	eggs	2
1/4 cup	unsalted butter, at room temperature	50 mL
2 tbsp	all-purpose flour	25 mL
1 cup	chopped pecans	250 mL
1/2 tsp	vanilla extract	2 mL
1/4 tsp	salt	1 mL

1. Preheat the oven to 450°F (230°C).

2. To make the base, in a bowl, combine 1 cup (250 mL) flour and 1/4 cup (50 mL) brown sugar. Cut in 1/2 (125 mL) butter. Press firmly into the bottom of an 8-inch (20 cm) square cake pan. Bake for 5 minutes.

3. To prepare the topping, in a small pot, combine 2/3 cup (150 mL) brown sugar with the corn syrup. Simmer for 5 minutes. Cool slightly.

4. In a bowl, beat the eggs, then stir in the sugar mixture. Beat in the 1/4 cup (50 mL) butter, 2 tbsp (25 mL) flour, pecans, vanilla and salt. Spread over the partially baked base. Bake for 10 minutes. Reduce the heat to 350°F (180°C) and bake for 20 minutes. Cool in the pan before cutting.

Makes about 25 squares

Seedless navel oranges are so called because of their belly-button-like flower end. They are seedless and easy to peel and separate into segments.

2
February

*When the cold winds blow and we shall have snow —
nothing is better than being indoors at home snuggled up with
good books, good company and candy.*

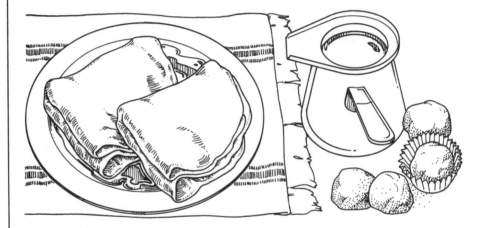

CRÊPES AND PANCAKES

Crêpes and pancakes are both mixtures of eggs, milk and flour, but in different proportions. In fact, *crêpe* is the French word for pancake. Pancakes are thick, usually topped with sweet things and served at breakfast; crêpes are lacy and thin, and are often rolled around savory or sweet mixtures.

Crêpes

• To make successful crêpes, you need a heavy cast-iron, cast-aluminum or non-stick pan about 7 inches (18 cm) in diameter. The pan (unless it is non-stick) should be seasoned by filling it with oil, placing it on medium heat and letting the oil heat up. Remove the pan from the heat and let it sit for 24 hours. The pores of the material open and the oil gives the pan a non-stick surface. Discard the oil after using.

• Crêpe batter must be smooth. The eggs, flour and milk can be combined in a food processor or blender, placed in a bowl and left to sit on the counter for two hours. The grains of starch will swell and the mixture will lighten as well as thicken slightly.

• If you make a crêpe batter by hand, place the flour in a bowl, make a well, add the wet ingredients and slowly incorporate with the dry. Batter made by this method requires less standing time, since the action of combining by hand is gentler than by machine. Let the batter stand for 30 minutes.

• Butter or oil is added to a crêpe batter to help keep the crêpes thin and lacy.

• If the batter thickens too much while standing, slowly incorporate more milk. The consistency should be similar to unwhipped whipping cream.

• For beginners, it is easier to use a batter that is slightly thick, because thin batters break more easily.

• Use medium-high heat for cooking crêpes. High heat will set the batter too quickly, making it difficult to turn.

• Use a scant ¼ cup (50 mL) batter for each crêpe. Cook the underside for about 30 seconds to 1 minute, turn over with a spatula or your fingers and cook the other side for about 30 seconds.

• Although butter is usually recommended for frying crêpes, I prefer a tasteless vegetable oil which will not burn. Brush the pan lightly with the oil only when the pan seems dry.

• The first crêpe is always a mess because the pan isn't hot enough or the batter is too thick. Eat it yourself.

• Turn the crêpes out onto a tea towel, stacking one on top of the other. Fold the tea towel over the crêpes but do not refrigerate them, because this will make the crêpes rubbery.

• To reheat crêpes, butter a baking sheet. Spread the crêpes on it, over-lapping them if necessary. Brush more melted butter over the top of the crêpes to protect them from the air. Bake in a 400°F (200°C) oven for 3 to 4 minutes, or until warmed through.

• If the crêpes are stuffed, place them on a buttered baking sheet, brush them with butter and reheat at 400°F (200°C) for 7 to 10 minutes.

• Crêpes can be frozen, but only for one month. They become brittle and rubbery after that. Lay them on a baking sheet, place in the freezer until frozen, then stack together and store in a freezerproof covered carton. Defrost them as you need them. Stuffed crêpes in a sauce freeze the best. Do not defrost, but reheat them from the frozen state at 350°F (180°C) for 20 minutes, or until the crêpes are heated through and the sauce bubbles.

In Catholic countries, the Tuesday before Lent is a day to eat up all the rich food around the house before succumbing to the rigors of Lent. Pancakes and crêpes use up the rich butter, milk and eggs as well as meat and fish for the fillings. Other countries celebrate Pancake Tuesday or Shrove Tuesday with races and games.

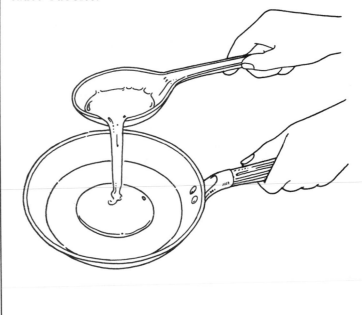

Basic Crêpe Batter

This batter is excellent for all sweet and savory crêpes. You can add 1 tsp (5 mL) sugar for sweet crêpes if desired.

1 cup	all-purpose flour	250 mL
pinch	salt	pinch
3	eggs, beaten	3
1½ cups	milk	375 mL
1 tbsp	melted butter	15 mL
2 tbsp	vegetable oil	25 mL

1. Combine all the ingredients except for the oil in a food processor or blender. Process until smooth. Pour into a bowl, cover and leave on the counter for 2 hours.

2. Place the crêpe pan on medium-high heat. Dip a paper towel into the oil and wipe out the crêpe pan. Take it off the heat and ladle in a scant ¼ cup (50 mL) batter.

3. Tilt and shake the pan so the crêpe mixture coats the bottom evenly. Set the pan back on the heat and cook the batter for about 30 seconds, or until the top is set.

4. With a spatula or your fingers, loosen the crêpe and flip over. Cook for another 30 seconds, or until the bottom is dry. Flip out onto a tea towel.

5. Repeat with the remaining batter, wiping the pan out with oil when it becomes dry.

Makes 18 to 24 crêpes

Crêpe batter can sit for up to 24 hours, refrigerated, before being used.

After using the crêpe pan, wipe it out with salt and an oiled paper towel, but don't wash it.

My favorite crêpe recipe is warm crêpes straight out of the frying pan, dusted with sugar and sprinkled with lemon juice.

Blintzes are really crêpes rolled up envelope style around a sweetened cottage cheese filling, before being refried or baked in the oven. They are often served with sour cream and blueberry or cherry preserves.

Gâteau of Basil Crêpes

Make up the basic crêpe batter but add ¼ cup (50 mL) chopped fresh basil or 1 tbsp (15 mL) dried to the batter mixture. Allison Cumming demonstrated this recipe in one of her cooking classes. She serves it as a spectacular brunch dish, although I like it for the first course of a dinner party.

2 tbsp	butter	25 mL
1	large onion, finely chopped	1
2	cloves garlic, finely chopped	2
4 oz	wild mushrooms, chopped	125 g
8 oz	mushrooms, chopped	250 g
1	egg	1
¼ cup	whipping cream	50 mL
8 oz	goat cheese	250 g
½ tsp	salt	2 mL
¼ tsp	freshly ground pepper	1 mL
pinch	ground nutmeg	pinch
18	basil crêpes	18

1. Heat the butter in a large frying pan on medium-high heat. Sauté the onion and the garlic until the onion is limp, about 2 minutes.

2. Add the mushrooms to the onion mixture, turn the heat down to medium and let the mixture cook for about 15 minutes, or until all the moisture has evaporated.

3. Preheat the oven to 350°F (180°C).

4. Remove the mixture to a large bowl and let cool. Then beat in the egg, cream and goat cheese. Season with the salt, pepper and nutmeg.

5. Butter a 9-inch (23 cm) deep cake pan. Alternately layer the crêpes and the filling, beginning and ending with the crêpes. You can make one high mound or two smaller ones.

6. Cover with foil and bake for 1 hour. Cool, loosen the cake with a spatula and lift onto a serving dish. Serve warm or cold.

Serves 6 to 8

Brandied Crêpes with Orange Sauce

This is the classic crêpe recipe with orange sauce heightened with a touch of lemon to cut the sweetness. I like to serve it when people come for coffee and dessert. The whole dish is made ahead of time and the crêpes sit in the orange sauce in the serving dish. Reheat in a 350°F (180°C) oven or on top of the stove for 5 minutes, or until the crêpes are warmed through.

	Grated rind and juice of 1 orange	
	Juice of 1 lemon	
¼ cup	unsalted butter	50 mL
⅓ cup	granulated sugar	75 mL
2 tbsp	orange liqueur	25 mL
18	crêpes	18
2 tbsp	brandy	25 mL

1. Combine the orange juice and rind, lemon juice, butter and sugar in a heavy frying pan. Bring to a boil on high heat. Boil for 4 minutes, or until the mixture is slightly syrupy. Turn the heat to low and stir in the liqueur.

2. Fold the crêpes into triangles and arrange in the sauce.

3. Heat the brandy until warm, light it and flame the crêpes just before serving.

Serves 6 to 8

Pancakes

• A basic pancake batter consists of egg, milk, flour and baking powder. It can be varied by adding wholewheat flour, nuts, fruits, buttermilk or baking soda, but the final result is still a slightly puffy round disc that is great for breakfast.

• When making pancake batter, don't overmix the wet and dry ingredients; this results in a rubbery pancake.

• Pour the pancake batter into the frying pan with a tablespoon. If you dump the batter in from a height, you will get uneven-sized pancakes.

• When frying pancakes, wait until the edges are bubbly and the bubbles start to burst, then turn them over. The first side takes about 2 minutes; the second side about 1 minute.

• Pancakes don't have to be made and eaten immediately. The batter will stand overnight in the refrigerator and the cooked ones can be reheated successfully by the same method as crêpes.

Blinis are Russian buckwheat pancakes topped with sour cream and caviar. The traditional recipe calls for yeast and separated eggs, but I took a tip from a caterer I know and use a buckwheat pancake mix with a couple of beaten egg whites added to the batter!

Flaming food has two purposes — to boil off the alcohol and for show. If you want to flame crêpes, first heat the liqueur, usually brandy, until it feels warm. Pour over the dish and light the brandy. If there is a lot of fat in the dish it can send flames shooting to the ceiling. In this case, heat the liqueur in a small pot. When it is warm, light it and then pour the flames over the dish.

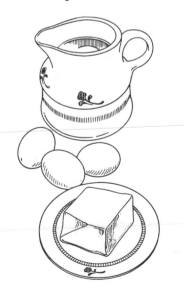

Breakfast Pancakes

This is restaurant critic Cynthia Wine's ulti-mate pancake recipe, which she makes all the time for her four kids. Serve with jam, maple syrup, blueberry preserves and bacon, sausages or ham.

1¹/₂ cups	all-purpose flour	375 mL
¹/₂ tsp	salt	2 mL
1 tbsp	baking powder	15 mL
4	eggs, beaten	4
2 tbsp	melted butter	25 mL
1 cup	milk	250 mL
2 tbsp	vegetable oil	25 mL

1. In a large bowl, mix together the flour, salt and baking powder. Make a well in the center and add the eggs, butter and milk. Stir into the dry ingredients. If the batter is too thick, add a little more milk. The batter should pour off the spoon in a thick stream.

2. Wipe out a frying pan or griddle with oil and heat on medium-high. Pour in 1 tbsp (15 mL) batter for each pancake. Cook for about 1 min-ute on the first side, or until the pan-cakes are bubbling and drying out. Flip over and cook for 30 seconds, or until the bottoms are golden-brown.

Makes about 24 2-inch (5 cm) pancakes

Oven Baked Bacon

To make lots of crispy bacon quickly, place it overlapping slightly on baking sheets. Bake at 450°F (230°C) for 10 minutes, or until crisp. Remove with tongs and drain on paper towels.

Breakfast Pancake Variations

• Add ¹/₂ cup (125 mL) chopped nuts to the dry ingre-dients.
• Add ¹/₄ cup (50 mL) chopped dried fruit to the dry ingredients.
• To make fruit pancakes, add 1 cup (250 mL) chopped apple, pear, peach or blueber-ries to the batter.
• Add crumbled bacon or fried chopped onions to the batter.

Dutch Pancake

A great, easy lunchtime dish, this is a cross between a Yorkshire pudding and a giant popover. Serve it with ham, bacon or sausages and sautéed apples or maple syrup. Ruth Luscenti gave me this recipe after I raved about it at her house in Sault Ste. Marie. "The big puffy pancakes do excit-ing things in the oven," she says. "They bubble, pop and end up in marvelous shapes. It usually impresses everyone, with hardly any work on the cook's part!"

¹/₄ cup	butter	50 mL
6	eggs	6
1¹/₂ cups	milk	375 mL
1¹/₂ cups	all-purpose flour	375 mL
¹/₄ tsp	salt	1 mL

1. Preheat the oven to 425°F (220°C).

2. Place the butter in a 12 × 8-inch (3 L) baking dish. Place in the oven to melt the butter. Watch to make sure it doesn't burn.

3. Meanwhile, in a large bowl, whisk together the eggs, milk, flour and salt until just mixed. Pour the batter into the melted butter and return to the oven.

4. Bake for 20 to 25 minutes, or until puffed and golden. Serve immedi-ately, because the pancake doesn't stay puffed for more than a few minutes.

Serves 6

ARTICHOKES

Life's embarrassing moments! The first time I was served an artichoke in France, I had no idea how to eat it. I had to sit and look at these gorgeous globes until other people ordered and ate theirs. I watched them dip the leaves into the sauce, pull the leaves through their teeth, then savor the heart and the bottom, before I finally attacked mine. It was love at first bite.

Artichokes come from California, and although it is not a Canadian-grown vegetable, it provides a welcome change from all the winter roots and squashes when it first appears in February.

• Most people, and some cookbooks, don't know an artichoke's heart from its bottom. The artichoke bottom is the fleshy area above the stalk; it makes the best eating. The heart is what remains after you have removed the outer leaves. It consists of tender, pale-green leaves, enclosing the bottom and the fuzzy choke. The hearts of small, young artichokes are consumed whole, because they have not had time to develop the thistle-like choke. In older, mature artichokes, the choke has to be removed before you eat the bottom.

• Look for compact, tightly closed heads in the early spring; slightly more conical-shaped heads in the summer and fall.

• The artichoke should be firm and feel heavy for its size. Once the leaves start to separate and the head opens up like a rose, the artichoke is past its prime.

• Bronze-tipped leaves have been "winter kissed" by frost and have a special flavor.

• Artichokes mature in all sizes, from tiny to enormous. Buy equal-sized heads for even cooking. Small artichokes are better for sautéing, braising or marinating; medium-sized ones are best for salads; and the largest artichokes are used for stuffing or as a main dish.

• Store artichokes loose in the vegetable drawer of your refrigerator. They should keep for at least one week.

• When ready to cook, swish the head up and down in cold water to remove any dirt. Cut the stem flush with the base of the leaves to allow the artichoke to sit flat when served.

• The fuzzy choke and spiky, purple-tinged leaves can be removed before cooking, after cooking, or by the person eating it. To remove the choke before cooking, separate the leaves to open up the center; with a serrated-edged knife, cut away the spiky inner leaves and the choke. If you remove the choke after cooking, pull out the central green leaves to expose the choke, then scoop out with a spoon.

• Artichoke leaves are eaten with your fingers, although eating the bottom requires a knife and fork.

A 12-oz (375 g) artichoke contains 25 calories, no fat, 4 grams of dietary fiber, 185 grams of potassium and is low in sodium. It is also a significant source of vitamin C, folic acid, magnesium and phosphorus.

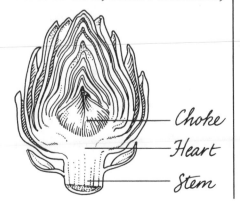

Choke
Heart
Stem

Artichokes Vinaigrette

If you are serving artichokes hot, serve them with melted butter with a squeeze of lemon, or with Hollandaise sauce (page 53). Serve cold artichokes with a vinaigrette, garlic mayonnaise or low-calorie dip.

For this dish, the vinaigrette should be strongly flavored and thick enough to coat the leaves.

Herbed Vinaigrette:

2 tsp	Dijon mustard	10 mL
2	cloves garlic, finely chopped	2
2 tsp	dried basil	10 mL
1 tsp	dried oregano	5 mL
1 tsp	dried thyme	5 mL
1/4 cup	red wine vinegar	50 mL
3/4 cup	olive oil	175 mL

Artichokes:

4	artichokes	4
1	lemon, cut in half	1

1. In a medium bowl, whisk together the mustard, garlic, basil, oregano, thyme and vinegar. Slowly whisk in the olive oil until the mixture thickens.

2. To prepare each artichoke, cut the stem level with the base. Pull off the small outside bottom leaves. With a sharp knife, cut off the top quarter of the artichoke.

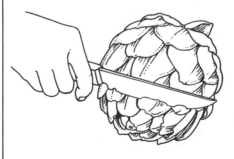

Quick Garlic Mayonnaise
Combine 1/2 cup (125 mL) mayonnaise, 2 tbsp (25 mL) sour cream, 1 clove garlic, finely chopped, 1 tbsp (15 mL) lemon juice, salt and freshly ground pepper to taste and 1 tbsp (15 mL) finely chopped parsley.

Low-Calorie Dip
Combine 1 cup (250 mL) low-fat plain yogurt, 1/4 cup (50 mL) grated cucumber, 1/4 cup (50 mL) grated carrot, salt to taste and 2 tbsp (25 mL) finely chopped fresh dill. Chill.

When cooking a roast chicken or pork, roast small artichokes in the pan beside it.

3. With scissors, snip the pointed tops from the remaining outer leaves. Rub the cut edges with half a lemon to keep them from turning black, or place the artichokes in a bowl of water that has the juice of a lemon in it.

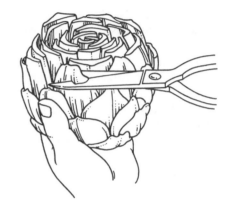

4. Bring a large pot of salted water to a boil. (Do not use an aluminum pot, as it will cause the artichokes to turn black.) Add half a lemon to help the artichokes maintain their color.

5. Immerse the artichokes in the boiling water, pushing them down into the water if they tend to bob up. Turn the heat down to medium and partially cover the pot. Boil for 15 to 40 minutes, depending on the size of the artichokes. To test for doneness, pierce the bottom of an artichoke with a knife; it should be tender. Or pull off a leaf; it should come away easily.

6. Drain the artichokes well, and pour cold water over them to stop the cooking. Turn them upside down on a wire rack to dislodge any water. Serve the vinaigrette in individual small bowls for dipping the artichoke leaves.

Serves 4

Stuffed Artichokes

This is excellent as a first course for a dinner party, or as a light main course.

4	large artichokes	4
1/3 cup	olive oil	75 mL
2	cloves garlic, finely chopped	2
2 cups	fresh breadcrumbs	500 mL
4	anchovy fillets, chopped, optional	4
1/2 cup	grated Parmesan cheese	125 mL
4	tomatoes, peeled, seeded and chopped	4
2 tsp	dried basil	10 mL
1/4 cup	finely chopped parsley	50 mL
	Salt and freshly ground pepper to taste	
1 tbsp	lemon juice	15 mL

1. Cut the artichoke stems level with the bases.

2. In a frying pan on low heat, combine 1/4 cup (50 mL) oil with the garlic. Sauté gently for 1 minute, or until the garlic softens. Stir in the breadcrumbs, anchovies, Parmesan, tomatoes, basil, parsley and salt and pepper. Remove from the heat.

3. Separate the artichoke leaves and stuff the filling between the leaves, working from the outside in, until the leaves are too tightly packed to be separated.

4. Choose a pot just large enough to hold the artichokes and fill it with 1/2 inch (1.25 cm) water. Add the artichokes and pour over the remaining olive oil and the lemon juice.

5. Bring the water to a boil, reduce the heat to low, cover and simmer for 45 to 60 minutes, or until the leaves can be pulled away easily.

Serves 4

CANDY-MAKING

St. Valentine was not the patron saint of candies, but with the amount of goodies sold on Valentine's Day, you'd think he was. Making your own candies is a simple process. Many recipes don't require a candy thermometer, but when you get into the more complicated confections, monitoring the stages of sugar boiling will help to improve the texture of your candy.

• Sugar changes density as it boils. Technically, although water boils at 212°F (100°C), sugar continues to boil at higher and higher temperatures as the syrup becomes more saturated. The higher the sugar temperature, the more water evaporates and the more concentrated the syrup will be. A more concentrated syrup means a harder candy. For example, if the temperature of the sugar reaches 240°F (115°C) on a candy thermometer, the sugar density will be exactly right for fudge; 300°F (150°C) is perfect for hard candy like brittles.

• Allow the sugar to dissolve in the water on low before bringing it to a boil. Stir the sugar occasionally.

• When you use a candy thermometer, make sure it doesn't touch the bottom of the pot — this will give you the temperature of the pot, not the sugar.

• Don't stir the sugar after it starts boiling; this will cause crystallization, and crystallization results in granular candies.

• When you test the sugar, take the pot off the heat to stop the cooking, otherwise the temperature will continue to rise.

Leftover chopped artichokes add pizzazz to salads.

To microwave an artichoke, invert a large artichoke in a deep microwave-safe bowl or measuring cup. Add 2 tbsp (25 mL) cold water. Cover and microwave on High (100%) for about 6 to 8 minutes. Turn the dish halfway through the cooking time. Let stand for 5 minutes.

Artichokes make great inexpensive candlesticks. Cut the stem flush with the base and dig out the choke. Drip some candle wax into the center and push the candle in.

- If sugar sticks to the side of the pot during the boiling process, it will form crystals, giving a poor texture to the candies. To avoid this, brush down the sides of the pot with a pastry brush dipped in hot water.
- A pinch of cream of tartar or 2 tbsp (25 mL) corn syrup will help to prevent the sugar from crystallizing.
- As well as using a candy thermometer, it is possible to estimate the various sugar temperatures by testing the syrup as it cooks.
- 234 to 240°F (112 to 115°C) is the soft ball stage. Drop a spoonful of syrup into cold water and leave for 1 minute. Pick up the ball and roll it between your thumb and forefinger. It should feel like a soft ball.
- 250 to 266°F (121 to 130°C) is the hard ball stage. Test as above, but the syrup should roll into a hard ball that has very little give to it.
- 300 to 310°F (150 to 154°C) is the hard crack stage. Dip a spoon into the syrup and let the syrup drip into cold water. It should form threads that shatter in the water.
- Over 320°F (160°C), the sugar caramelizes; it will start to turn pale-brown and continue to darken as the temperature rises.

Vanilla Fudge

Homemade fudge is a wonderful treat. It can be flavored with chocolate, cocoa or maple, or it can have nuts beaten into it. Tablet is Scottish fudge made with condensed milk instead of whole milk. For a richer fudge, use whipping cream.

2 cups	granulated sugar	500 mL
¹/₂ cup	milk	125 mL
¹/₄ cup	unsalted butter	50 mL
¹/₂ tsp	vanilla extract	2 mL

1. On low heat in a heavy pot, dissolve the sugar in the milk, stirring. Slowly bring to a boil. Raise the heat to medium.

2. Place the candy thermometer in the pot and continue to boil, without stirring, until the sugar mixture reaches the soft ball stage, 240°F (115°C) on the thermometer.

3. Remove from the heat and beat in the butter and vanilla. Pour into a medium bowl. Cool until the mixture is 110°F (42°C) on the candy thermometer. Butter an 8-inch (20 cm) square cake pan.

4. Beat the fudge mixture with a wooden spoon until it begins to lose its glossy look. Spread in the cake pan and cool completely. Cut into 1-inch (2.5 cm) squares.

Makes about 64 squares

Peanut Clusters

Peanuts, raisins and marshmallows held together by chocolate — a decadent candy.

10 oz	chocolate chips	300 g
1 tbsp	unsalted butter	15 mL
1 cup	unsalted peanuts	250 mL
1 cup	raisins	250 mL
1 cup	miniature marshmallows	250 mL

1. In a heavy pot, melt the chocolate chips and butter together. Remove from the heat.

2. Stir in the peanuts, raisins and marshmallows.

3. Using two forks, drop clusters onto waxed paper-lined baking sheets. Refrigerate until set.

Makes about 40 clusters

Almond Brittle

Brittle can be made with peanuts, pecans, walnuts, or any combination, but the nuts should be raw — neither roasted nor salted.

¹/₂ cup	water	125 mL
2 cups	granulated sugar	500 mL
1 cup	corn syrup	250 mL
2 cups	whole blanched almonds	500 mL
2 tbsp	unsalted butter	25 mL
1 tsp	baking soda	5 mL

1. Butter two baking sheets or cover with parchment paper.

2. In a heavy pot, on medium heat, combine the water, sugar, corn syrup and nuts. Bring to a boil, stirring.

3. Boil until a candy thermometer reads 300°F (150°C). Remove from the heat and stir in the butter and baking soda. Pour the brittle onto the baking sheets and quickly spread with a spatula. When the candy has hardened, break into pieces.

Makes about 2 lb (1 kg) brittle

Rum Balls

A favorite confection for many people. They look pretty in little paper cups and will keep at room temperature for two weeks in an airtight container.

1 cup	chopped bittersweet chocolate	250 mL
¹/₂ cup	granulated sugar	125 mL
¹/₃ cup	dark rum	75 mL
3 tbsp	corn syrup	45 mL
2 cups	crushed chocolate wafers	500 mL
1 cup	ground walnuts or almonds	250 mL
	Granulated sugar	

1. In a heavy pot on low heat, melt the chocolate. Remove from heat.

2. Stir in the sugar, rum, corn syrup, chocolate wafers and nuts.

3. Shape into 1-inch (2.5 cm) balls. Refrigerate until firm.

4. Roll in additional sugar. Store in an airtight container.

Makes about 3 dozen balls

Chocolate Truffles

These rich, velvety, sophisticated truffles can be flavored in many ways. Cognac, Cointreau, Grand Marnier, crème de cacao and crème de menthe are some popular choices. For an even more luxurious finish, dip the truffles in melted chocolate instead of cocoa. The truffles are best when eaten within a week. Store in the refrigerator.

8 oz	bittersweet chocolate	250 g
1 oz	unsweetened chocolate	30 g
¹/₄ cup	whipping cream	50 mL
¹/₄ cup	unsalted butter	50 mL
2 tbsp	liqueur	25 mL
¹/₂ cup	cocoa	125 mL

1. Chop the chocolate into even-sized chunks. In a heavy pot on low heat, combine the chocolate, whipping cream and butter.

2. Stir the mixture until melted and smooth, add the liqueur and stir again. Pour into a bowl and cool until the mixture hardens, about 2 hours in the refrigerator.

3. When cool, dip a melon baller into hot water and use to form round truffles from the chocolate mixture. Or dust your hands with cocoa and make free-form balls. Roll in cocoa.

Makes about 2 dozen truffles

Orange Truffles
Add 2 tsp (10 mL) grated orange rind and 2 tbsp (25 mL) orange liqueur to the chocolate mixture.

Champagne Truffles
Add ¹/₄ cup (50 mL) leftover Champagne to the truffle mixture.

Chinese New Year's Dinner for Six

Chinese New Year is celebrated in February. Large paper dragons snake their way through Chinatown, and across Canada, firecrackers pop and people eat special dishes. Each year is designated by a different animal; 1989 is the year of the snake, and 1990 is the year of the horse. Snake people are born leaders; the men are romantic and the women are beautiful! But snakes can strike in different directions, so you have to watch them!

Among the traditional foods at Chinese New Year is a vegetarian dish that includes *fat choi*, a thin, black, hair-like vegetable representing riches. If you can find it, use it in the vegetarian spring rolls.

Spring roll skins are pancake-like coverings made of flour and water. They are tasteless until deep-fried, when they become crisp and flaky. In the Middle East, these pancakes make a kind of sandwich called "brik" — savory mixtures enclosed by the spring roll skin and deep-fried.

Vegetable Spring Rolls

Bean Curd and Greens Soup

Sichuan-style Sweet and Sour Fish

Steamed Rice*

Stir-fried Broccoli with Oyster Sauce

Oranges in Cointreau

Almond Cookies

*See *Lucy Waverman's Cooking School Cookbook*, page 31.

Vegetable Spring Rolls

Crisp crunchy spring rolls are easy to make, and they reheat well on a rack in a 400°F (200°C) oven. Make them ahead for this menu to avoid last-minute frying. You can also substitute different vegetables. Dried Chinese mushrooms give an exotic flavor to the spring rolls, but if they are unavailable, use fresh.

6	dried Chinese mushrooms	6
1	large carrot, finely chopped	1
1	leek, white part only, finely chopped	1
2	small zucchini, finely chopped	2
12	leaves Chinese cabbage, shredded	12
1/2 cup	chicken stock	125 mL
1 tbsp	soy sauce	15 mL
1 tsp	granulated sugar	5 mL
1 tsp	sesame oil	5 mL
1 tbsp	cornstarch	15 mL
1 tbsp	water	15 mL
1 tbsp	vegetable oil	15 mL
1 tbsp	finely chopped fresh ginger	15 mL
	Salt and freshly ground pepper to taste	
1	package spring roll skins	1
3 tbsp	all-purpose flour	45 mL
1/4 cup	water	50 mL
4 cups	vegetable oil for deep-frying	1 L

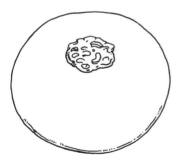

1. Soak the mushrooms in hot water for 20 minutes. Drain, discard the stems and finely chop the heads. Combine the mushrooms with the remaining vegetables. Reserve.

2. To make the final seasoning sauce, in a small bowl, combine the stock, soy sauce, sugar, sesame oil, cornstarch and 1 tbsp (15 mL) water. Reserve.

3. Heat 1 tbsp (15 mL) oil in a wok until very hot. Add the ginger and stir-fry until fragrant. Then add the vegetables and stir-fry until tender-crisp, about 1 to 2 minutes.

4. Pour in the seasoning sauce. Bring to a boil, stirring, until the mixture thickens. Taste for seasoning, adding more soy sauce, sesame oil, salt or pepper as needed. Cool.

5. Separate the spring roll skins by gently pulling them apart. Cover with a cloth. Heap about 2 tbsp (25 mL) vegetable mixture onto the upper third of each spring roll skin. Fold the two sides in to meet the mixture, turn the upper end over the mixture and roll into a cylinder.

6. In a small bowl, combine the flour with ¼ cup (50 mL) water. Brush this mixture on the edges of the spring roll skins to seal them.

7. Heat the 4 cups (1 L) oil in a wok until very hot. Fry three rolls at a time, turning until each side is golden-brown, about 2 minutes. Drain on a rack. Repeat with the remaining spring rolls. Serve with the dipping sauce.

Makes about 18 rolls

Dipping Sauce

⅓ cup	soy sauce	75 mL
¼ cup	rice vinegar	50 mL
1 tsp	finely chopped fresh ginger	5 mL

1. In a small bowl, combine the soy sauce, rice vinegar and ginger together.

Makes about ½ cup (125 mL)

Bean Curd and Greens Soup

Bean curd, or tofu, is available at many supermarkets. Omit it if unavailable.

6 cups	chicken stock	1.5 L
2	⅛-inch (3 mm) slices ginger, smashed	2
2	squares bean curd, diced	2
2 cups	shredded Chinese cabbage or spinach	500 mL
1 tbsp	soy sauce	15 mL
	Salt and freshly ground pepper to taste	
2	green onions, chopped	2

1. In a pot, simmer the stock, ginger, bean curd and cabbage for 10 minutes. Add the soy sauce and salt and pepper.

2. Remove the ginger and garnish the soup with the green onion.

Serves 6

Bean curd, or tofu, is known as "the meat of the fields," because it has such a high protein content. It is rather flat in taste and has the texture of baked custard, but it takes on the taste of the food it is cooked with. It is made from soybeans in the same way that cottage cheese is made from milk.

Sichuan-style Sweet and Sour Fish

Sichuan food, from the west of China, is usually hot and spicy, with chilies everywhere. This sweet and sour sauce is not spicy, but it is not as sweet as Cantonese sauces.

Any fish fillets such as sea bass, pickerel or snapper may be used for this recipe. Shrimp and chicken work well, too. The sweet and sour sauce is not the sticky red variety. It has a clear, tart/sweet taste, and the vegetables give it body. In my cooking classes, this dish is always a winner.

When preparing a batter for deep-fried foods, constarch or flour can be used. Cornstarch makes a light batter that doesn't adhere too efficiently. Flour makes a heavier batter that clings well. Combining the two together results in a light batter that gently coats the food.

3	pickerel fillets, with skin on	3
1/2 tsp	salt	2 mL
1/4 tsp	freshly ground pepper	1 mL
Batter:		
1	egg	1
3 tbsp	all-purpose flour	45 mL
4 tsp	cornstarch	20 mL
3 tbsp	water	45 mL
Sweet and Sour Sauce:		
1 tbsp	soy sauce	15 mL
1 tbsp	dry white wine	15 mL
1/4 cup	granulated sugar	50 mL
1/4 cup	rice vinegar	50 mL
1/4 cup	ketchup	50 mL
1/4 cup	water	50 mL
1 tsp	salt	5 mL
1 tsp	sesame oil	5 mL
1 tbsp	cornstarch	15 mL
1 tbsp	water	15 mL
	Oil for deep frying	
Vegetables:		
1	small onion, diced	1
4	dried Chinese mushrooms, soaked and diced	4
1	tomato, seeded and diced	1
2 tbsp	green peas	25 mL
2 tbsp	raisins	25 mL

1. With the fillets skin side down, slash the fish flesh every inch (2.5 cm) with a diagonal slash. Cut to the skin but not through the skin, so that the flaps of flesh will open up when the fish is picked up by the tail. This will make the fish curl when it is deep-fried. Season with salt and pepper.

2. In a flat dish, mix together all the batter ingredients. Reserve.

3. In a separate bowl, mix together all the ingredients for the sweet and sour sauce. Reserve.

4. At serving time, dip the fish in the batter, opening the slashes so the fish is completely coated.

5. Heat the deep-frying oil in a wok to about 375°F (190°C), or until a cube of bread turns brown in 15 seconds. Hold the fillets by the tail end and slide into the fat. Do not crowd the wok. Fry in two batches if necessary. Fry until golden-brown, ladling the oil over the fish to brown the top. Remove the fish carefully using two spatulas to prevent breakage. Arrange side by side on a serving platter.

6. In the wok or frying pan, heat 3 tbsp (45 mL) oil on high heat. Add the onion, mushrooms, tomato and peas. Toss for a few seconds to soften the onions. Add the raisins and sweet and sour sauce and stir together until boiling. Spoon the sauce over the fish on the platter.

Serves 6

Stir-fried Broccoli with Oyster Sauce

Oyster sauce is a sweet, thick brown sauce that is wonderful with vegetables and noodles. You can make this dish with virtually any vegetable — asparagus, cauliflower, Chinese cabbage or mushrooms.

2 tbsp	vegetable oil	25 mL
1 tbsp	finely chopped fresh ginger	15 mL
1	bunch broccoli, separated into florets	1
3 tbsp	chicken stock	45 mL
1 tbsp	oyster sauce	15 mL
1 tsp	sesame oil	5 mL

1. In a frying pan or wok, heat the oil on high heat. Add the ginger. As soon as it sizzles, stir in the broccoli. Stir-fry until all the broccoli is coated with oil.

2. Pour in the chicken stock. Cover the pan and steam for 2 minutes, or until the broccoli is crisp-tender. Stir in the oyster sauce and sesame oil.

Serves 6

Oranges in Cointreau

Chinese food demands a simple and refreshing dessert. Oranges are often served just peeled. This is a dressed-up version.

4	oranges	4
2 tbsp	Cointreau	25 mL

1. Peel the skin and white pith from the oranges. Cut into thin slices.

2. Marinate in the orange liqueur for 1 hour.

Serves 6

Almond Cookies

These are perfect after a Chinese meal, or with afternoon tea.

1 cup	unsalted butter	250 mL
1 cup	granulated sugar	250 mL
1	egg	1
2 tsp	almond extract	10 mL
2 cups	all-purpose flour	500 mL
1/2 cup	finely ground toasted almonds	125 mL
1/2 tsp	salt	2 mL
36	slivered almonds	36
Glaze:		
1	egg yolk	1
1 tsp	water	5 mL

1. Preheat the oven to 375°F (190°C).

2. In a large bowl, cream together the butter, sugar, egg and almond extract.

3. In a separate bowl, combine the flour, ground almonds and salt. Stir into the creamed mixture.

4. Shape the dough into 1½-inch (3.75 cm) balls and place 2 inches (5 cm) apart on an ungreased cookie sheet. Press a slivered almond into the center of each cookie.

5. To make the glaze, in a small bowl, beat together the egg yolk and water. Brush the glaze on the cookies. Bake for 12 to 15 minutes, or until golden-brown and crisp. Cool on a rack.

Makes 30 to 36 cookies

3
March

At last the darkness of winter is giving way to the slush of spring. New tastes are hitting the grocery shelves, and what seems like a long winter is brightened by the first maple syrup and Easter celebrations.

In season
lamb
maple syrup
rhubarb

Holidays
St. Patrick's Day
Easter

Menu
Ukrainian Easter Feast for Twelve

BEANS AND LEGUMES

Beans have never been fashionable — until now. In the past they were considered cheap peasant food, eaten by those who couldn't afford better. But now we know that beans are a nutritional gold mine, because they are high in fiber, protein and minerals and low in fat, as well as being inexpensive. One of their major benefits is their ability to lower cholesterol and regulate blood sugar. So at a time of the year when most fresh fruit and vegetables are imported, and every-

one is sick of meaty casseroles, try experimenting with beans for new tastes as well as definite health advantages.

Beans are legumes — the family of plants whose seeds grow in pods, including all beans, both dried and fresh, peas and lentils.

Legumes are used in all cultures and in many different forms. They can be made into stews, casseroles, soups, spreads, dips and salads. They can be served whole, pureed and mashed; they can be spicy or subtle. They also blend well with other ingredients and they are the mainstay of vegetarian diets.

Popular Varieties

• **Black beans** or **turtle beans** are prevalent in South America. This vibrant, black-hued bean with a pure-white interior and full-bodied taste has found new popularity in North American cooking. It is used in soups, spreads and even as a pâté. Sour cream sets off its color and taste. It is the basis for the classic Brazilian dish, *feijoada*, a mixture of meats, rice, beans and vegetables. These are not the same as oriental black beans.

• **Black-eyed peas** are actually beans, not peas, and are an important ingredient in Southern cooking. The beans are white with a black outline in the center. They have a smooth texture and a mild taste and, because they don't have a tough skin, do not need presoaking. They are often served mixed with rice.

• **Canellini** is a white variety of kidney bean with a mild, delicate taste. It is used in Italian soups and with pasta.

• **Chickpeas** are also known as garbanzo beans in Spain, and Bengal gram in India. They are popular in Mediterranean countries and the Middle East. They have a vaguely nutty, earthy taste and are sometimes roasted and served as appetizers or made into salads. In India they are ground into a flour used for deep-frying vegetables.

• **Fava beans** are large, brown, wrinkled beans that have an earthy flavor as opposed to the nuttiness of most beans. They require long soaking, because of their tough outer skin. They are mostly served as a puree, are

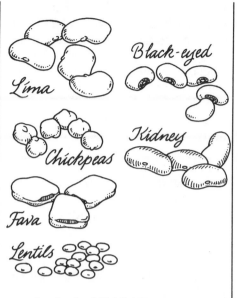

popular in the Middle East and Italy, but are only beginning to appear on North American menus. Fava beans are the first fresh beans of spring and can be bought in the pod mainly at Italian groceries.

• **Kidney beans** are red, kidney-shaped, strongly flavored beans that are used extensively in Mexican and Tex-Mex cooking. They are sometimes called chili beans because of their popularity in chilies.

• **Lentils** are found all over the Middle East and India. There are two major varieties — the Egyptian and the French — plus many sub-varieties. The French lentil is brown or green and is sold whole. It has much more texture and flavor than the Egyptian or red lentil, which does not have an outer seed coat, is more delicate in flavor, and cooks to a puree.

• **Lima beans** are small, pale-green American-bred beans used in succotash, soups or side dishes. Butter beans are a larger variety.

To make beans into a complete protein source, include nuts, seeds, rice, grains or bread. Peanut butter on wholewheat bread, for example, is a complete protein.

Dried beans are high in fiber — $1/2$ cup (125 mL) cooked beans contains 4 grams of dietary fiber. One cup (250 mL) cooked beans supplies about 15 grams of protein — about the same as 2 oz (60 g) meat. Beans are a good source of calcium, magnesium, zinc, niacin, thiamine, riboflavin and iron.

• **Pea beans, navy beans** and **great northern beans** are ivory-colored and are also known as haricots. They are used in the famous Boston baked beans. Navy beans are slightly larger but often packagers do not differentiate between them.

• **Mung beans** are the popular, nutty-flavored Asian beans which are usually sprouted for beansprouts.

• **Peas** are available in two colors — yellow and green. They are sold either whole or split. The split variety does not need soaking before cooking.

• **Pinto beans** are mottled pink beans that turn a reddish-brown when cooked. They are the basis of Mexican refried beans.

• **Pigeon peas** are dark-gray beans used in the Caribbean for dishes like rice and peas and Hoppin' John.

• **Soybeans** are the most nutritious beans, containing all the essential amino acids. They are strongly flavored and can take over a dish. They can be sprouted for beansprouts, made into soybean paste or turned into bean curd. They are also salted and fermented to make oriental black beans.

Buying and Soaking

• Buy dried beans from stores that have a frequent turnover to ensure freshness. Although the beans will keep indefinitely, they cook more quickly when freshly dried. Look for even-sized, smooth-skinned beans.

• Store beans in clear glass jars or plastic containers for easy identification.

• With the exception of lentils, black-eyed peas and split peas, all legumes are soaked before cooking.

To reduce gas, the negative side effect of bean eating, throw out the bean-soaking water and use fresh. Some of the carbohydrate substances that cause gas leach out into the soaking water, and this is the way to eliminate them.

Simmer beans slowly. Cooking them too fast will make the skins break.

Adding acid and salt to beans slows down the cooking process as well as toughening the beans. Add salt, vinegar, tomatoes or citrus juices at the end of the cooking time.

Rinse well before soaking, and discard any shrivelled beans.

Method 1: Cover the beans with three times the volume of cold water to beans and leave to soak overnight or for 12 hours. The beans usually double in size during soaking.

Method 2: Place the beans in twice the amount of water to beans. Bring to a boil and let boil for 2 minutes. Remove from the heat, cover and leave to soak for one hour before cooking.

• To test for proper soaking, cut the bean in half. The inside flesh should be a consistent color and texture.

• After soaking, drain the water and add fresh water to cover the beans. Bring to a boil, partially cover and simmer gently until the beans are tender. Add salt at the end of the cooking time, as salt toughens the beans.

• To determine whether beans are cooked, mash with a fork. If they mash easily, they are cooked.

Chickpea Salad

Chickpea salad is served warm in the Mediterranean. Olive oil added to the warm vegetables gives an extra explosion of flavor.

2	19-oz (540 mL) cans chickpeas	2
1	small Spanish onion, finely chopped	1
1/4 cup	red wine vinegar	50 mL
1 tsp	dry mustard	5 mL
2 tbsp	finely chopped fresh basil leaves, or 2 tsp (10 mL) dried	25 mL
3/4 cup	olive oil	175 mL
	Salt and freshly ground pepper to taste	
1/4 cup	finely chopped parsley	50 mL

1. Preheat the oven to 350°F (180°C).

2. Drain the chickpeas and rinse with water. Place in a medium ovenproof dish that is also suitable for serving. Cover with foil and bake for 10 minutes, or until warm. Remove and gently fold in the onion.

3. To make the dressing, in a bowl, whisk together the vinegar, mustard and basil. Whisk in the oil slowly. Season with salt and pepper.

4. Pour the dressing over the warm chickpeas; sprinkle with the chopped parsley.

Serves 6 to 8

Lima Bean Bake

A vegetarian main dish with a ratatouille-like taste. Serve it with crusty bread or as a vegetable side dish with lamb or chicken.

1 cup	dried lima beans	250 mL
1	bay leaf	1
1	small eggplant, diced	1
1/4 cup	olive oil	50 mL
1	Spanish onion, sliced	1
2	zucchini, sliced	2
2 cups	canned tomatoes, drained and chopped	500 mL
3	cloves garlic, finely chopped	3
	Grated rind of 1 lemon	
1 tsp	dried marjoram	5 mL
1 tsp	dried thyme	5 mL
	Salt and freshly ground pepper to taste	

1. Soak the lima beans overnight in three times their volume of water. Drain the water.

2. In a large pot, cover the beans with water and bring to a boil. Add the bay leaf, turn the heat to low, partially cover and simmer gently for 1 hour, or until the beans are cooked through. Drain the beans, reserving the cooking liquid. Discard the bay leaf.

3. Meanwhile, lightly salt the eggplant and place in colander to drain for 30 minutes. Pat dry.

4. In a large frying pan, heat the oil on high heat. Add the onions and sauté until coated with the oil. Add the zucchini and eggplant and sauté until the vegetables soften slightly, about 5 minutes.

5. Add the tomatoes, garlic, lemon rind, marjoram and thyme. Combine until heated through. Season well with salt and pepper.

6. Preheat the oven to 325°F (160°C).

7. In a large 12 × 8-inch (3 L) greased ovenproof casserole, layer one-third of the beans and moisten with 1/4 cup (50 mL) cooking liquid. Season with salt and pepper. Top with half the vegetable mixture. Repeat the layers, finishing with the beans and remaining cooking liquid.

8. Bake for 1 hour, uncovered, or until the beans are creamy and the vegetables are cooked. If the casserole appears to be drying out, add more bean-cooking liquid.

Serves 6 to 8

Peanuts are not a nut, they are a legume. People who have allergies to peanuts probably should be wary of other members of the legume family, too.

One pound (500 g) dried beans equal 6 cups (1.5 L) cooked beans.

Cassoulet

Essentially cassoulet is a mixture of creamy beans, good meaty pork sausage and preserved duck layered in an earthenware casserole and baked slowly. Making a traditional one takes hours of preparation and cooking time, so I have devised a simpler cassoulet, perfect for a big party. It tastes better the second day and reheats beautifully.

1 lb	dried pea beans or cannellini beans	500 g
1 lb	salt pork, diced	500 g
1	bay leaf	1
1 tbsp	dried thyme	15 mL
1 lb	smoked pork sausage, thickly sliced	500 g
1 lb	spicy pork sausage, thickly sliced	500 g
	Salt and freshly ground pepper to taste	

Garlic Butter:

1 cup	water	250 mL
8	cloves garlic	8
1/4 cup	butter, at room temperature	50 mL
1 tbsp	Dijon mustard	15 mL
1/4 cup	finely chopped parsley	50 mL
1 cup	dry breadcrumbs	250 mL

1. In a large bowl, cover the beans with three times the volume of water and soak overnight. Drain.

2. In a heavy pot, cover the beans with fresh water. Add the salt pork, bay leaf and thyme. Bring to a boil, cover and simmer gently for 1 hour, or until the beans are soft. Check occasionally to make sure all the water has not evaporated. Drain, reserving the salt pork, beans and 1 cup (250 mL) bean-cooking liquid.

3. Preheat the oven to 325°F (160°C).

4. In a 12 × 8-inch (3 L) casserole, layer one-third of the beans, half of the salt pork and half of the sausages. Season well with salt and pepper. Repeat the layers, finishing with the beans. Pour over the cooking liquid. Bake for 30 minutes.

5. While the casserole is baking, make the garlic butter. Bring the water to the boil. Add the garlic cloves and simmer for 10 minutes.

6. Drain the water, remove the garlic from its skin and mash with the butter, mustard and parsley. Stir into the casserole. Sprinkle evenly with the breadcrumbs. Bake for 45 minutes longer, occasionally pushing the breadcrumbs into the beans to form a crust.

Serves 8 to 10

If you run out of dried beans, use canned, but remember to reduce some of the salt in the recipe.

Baked beans originated from the religious restrictions of the Pilgrims, which did not allow them to cook on Sundays. The beans would be started on Saturday night and cooked very slowly on wood stoves to be ready for Sunday night supper. Baked beans was a particularly popular dish in Boston, where stoves were set up in community taverns for the bean-baking.

Mexican Scrambled Eggs

This breakfast or brunch dish can be made with any leftover beans, but the black bean color contrasts beautifully with the creamy eggs. If jalapeño peppers are unavailable, use a pinch of cayenne.

1 cup	cooked black beans	250 mL
¼ cup	bean-cooking liquid or water	50 mL
1 tbsp	lime juice	15 mL
1 tbsp	vegetable oil	15 mL
¼ cup	chopped onion	50 mL
1	tomato, peeled and chopped	1
1 tsp	chili powder	5 mL
1 tsp	finely chopped fresh jalapeño pepper, optional	5 mL
1 tbsp	finely chopped fresh coriander	15 mL
¼ cup	vegetable oil	50 mL
4	flour tortillas	4
1 tbsp	butter	15 mL
8	eggs, beaten	8
¼ cup	sour cream	50 mL

1. In a food processor or by hand, puree the beans, liquid and lime juice.

2. In a frying pan, heat 1 tbsp (15 mL) oil on medium heat. Sauté the onion until softened, about 2 minutes. Add the tomato, chili powder, jalapeño pepper and bean puree.

3. Turn the heat to low and cook the bean mixture for about 10 minutes, stirring occasionally, until the tastes are combined. Stir in the coriander and keep warm.

4. Add ¼ cup (50 mL) oil to another frying pan on high heat. Fry the tortillas until puffed and brown. Keep warm until needed.

5. Turn the heat to medium-low, add the butter and heat until sizzling. Add the eggs and stir until they are creamy, about 5 minutes.

6. Place the tortillas on four serving plates. Top with the scrambled eggs. Top the eggs with the bean sauce and a dab of sour cream.

Serves 4

Hummus

My friend Simmie Clarke lived in the Middle East for a number of years and brought back this dynamite recipe for hummus. Hummus is a chickpea and sesame paste mixture used as a dip with pita bread.

2 cups	canned chickpeas	500 mL
3	cloves garlic, chopped	3
¾ cup	sesame seed paste	175 mL
	Juice of 1 lemon	
¾ cup	cold water	175 mL
	Salt and freshly ground pepper to taste	
¼ tsp	paprika	1 mL
1 tbsp	olive oil	15 mL
2 tbsp	finely chopped parsley	25 mL

1. Drain the chickpeas and rinse with cold water.

2. In a blender or food processor, combine the chickpeas, garlic, sesame seed paste and lemon juice.

3. With the processor running, pour the water through the feed tube until the mixture is smooth and creamy. Season to taste with salt and pepper.

4. Spread on a plate, dust with the paprika, swirl over the olive oil and sprinkle with the parsley. Serve with pita bread cut in wedges.

Serves 6

Sesame seed paste or tahini is available in health food shops and Middle Eastern grocery stores.

Traditionally hummus is served on a flat plate to make it easier to scoop up with the pita. The Egyptians make a similar dip using fava beans.

Spiced Lentil Soup

This soup thickens as it sits. If you make it a day ahead, stir in stock or water before reheating. Add more cayenne for a zestier taste.

2 tbsp	olive oil	25 mL
1	large onion, finely chopped	1
2	cloves garlic, finely chopped	2
1½ cups	red lentils, rinsed	375 mL
1 tbsp	ground cumin	15 mL
1 tbsp	ground coriander	15 mL
6 cups	chicken stock or water	1.5 L
pinch	salt	pinch
1 cup	canned tomatoes, chopped	250 mL
1	bay leaf	1
1 tsp	dried basil	5 mL
1 tsp	dried oregano	5 mL
½ tsp	cayenne pepper	2 mL
2 tbsp	finely chopped parsley	25 mL

1. Heat the oil in heavy pot on medium-high heat. Sauté the onion and garlic until softened. Stir in the lentils, cumin and coriander and coat with the onion/garlic mixture.

2. Add the stock, salt, tomatoes, bay leaf, basil, oregano and cayenne. Bring the soup to a boil, reduce the heat to low, cover the pot and simmer for about 45 minutes, or until the lentils are tender.

3. Taste for seasoning and sprinkle with the parsley before serving.

Serves 8

The Indian meat and lentil dish, *dhansak*, is supposed to combine three to nine different kinds of lentils to achieve the right taste.

A Hindu proverb says, "rice is good but lentils are my life."

MAPLE SYRUP

There is nothing as Canadian as the majestic maple tree, and nothing better than the wonderful maple syrup it produces.

The first running of maple syrup forecast the beginning of spring for the early settlers. As the days grew milder, the sap began to flow back up the trees, and the sugar harvest started. Today we produce about two-thirds of the world's maple syrup, Quebec being the main producer.

To make pure maple syrup, first the trees are tapped and buckets are hung on the spigots. Once the sap is collected, it is boiled for hours until all the water evaporates, and only concentrated maple syrup remains. Maple syrup can be made into maple sugar by further boiling, then allowing the syrup to crystallize.

• Maple syrup is marketed in different colors. The darker the syrup, the stronger the maple flavor. Legislation has been passed making grade and color designations mandatory. If you are a purist, use a lighter syrup for the table and the darker amber one for cooking.

• Store unopened maple syrup in a cupboard, but refrigerate after opening. If you keep it for over six months, freeze it. It does not freeze solid and can be refrozen any number of times.

• If any mold grows, throw out the syrup. The mold can cause bacteria growth which can result in food poisoning.

Parsnip Carrot and Maple Soup

A sweet/tart soothing soup from chef Mark Bussiere at the Metropolis restaurant in Toronto, famous for using Canadian produce exquisitely.

2 tbsp	butter	25 mL
1 lb	carrots, peeled and chopped	500 g
1 lb	parsnips, peeled and chopped	500 g
1	onion, chopped	1
6 cups	chicken stock	1.5 L
1/4 cup	maple syrup	50 mL
1/2 cup	whipping cream	125 mL
1/2 tsp	ground nutmeg	2 mL
2 tbsp	lemon juice	25 mL
	Salt and freshly ground pepper to taste	

Garnish:

1/4 cup	whipping cream	50 mL
1 tbsp	maple syrup	15 mL
1 tbsp	finely chopped fresh mint, or 1 tsp (5 mL) dried	15 mL

1. In a large pot, heat the butter on low heat. Add the vegetables, coat with the butter, cover and cook gently for 10 minutes, or until the vegetables are slightly softened.

2. Pour in the stock, bring to a simmer, cover and simmer gently for 20 minutes, or until the vegetables are very soft. Puree in blender or food processor until smooth.

3. Pour the soup back into the pot, add the 1/4 cup (50 mL) maple syrup, 1/2 cup (125 mL) whipping cream, nutmeg, lemon juice, salt and pepper. Simmer together for 5 minutes to blend the flavors. Taste for seasoning, adding more lemon juice as needed.

4. To prepare the garnish, beat together the whipping cream, maple syrup and mint until the cream holds its shape. Serve the soup garnished with a dollop of the whipped cream.

Serves 8 to 10

Sweet and Sour Pork Chops

This is a fast and easy recipe that kids love. Don't overcook the chops, because dried-out pork can be leathery.

1 tbsp	vegetable oil	15 mL
4	1-inch (2.5 cm) rib pork chops	4
1/2 tsp	salt	2 mL
1/4 tsp	freshly ground pepper	1 mL
3/4 cup	tomato juice	175 mL
1 tbsp	white vinegar	15 mL
1/4 cup	maple syrup	50 mL
1/2 tsp	dry mustard	2 mL

1. Preheat the oven to 350°F (180°C).

2. In a heavy frying pan, heat the oil on high heat. Brown the pork chops on both sides, about 2 minutes per side. Season with the salt and pepper. Place in an ovenproof casserole that holds the chops in one layer.

3. In a small bowl, combine the tomato juice, vinegar, maple syrup and dry mustard. Pour over the chops, cover and bake for 35 minutes. Uncover and bake for 10 minutes longer, or until the pork chops are tender and the sauce thickens slightly.

Serves 4

There is concern that maple trees are suffering from pollution and are not as healthy as they used to be. But the causes are not conclusive. Many factors have affected the trees, and acid rain and pollution are only part of the problem. Defoliation by tent caterpillars and drought have put stress on them, too.

Quick Maple Ideas
• Perk up bottled barbecue sauce with a couple of spoonfuls of maple syrup.
• Add 1/4 cup (50 mL) maple syrup, 1 tsp (5 mL) lemon juice and 2 tbsp (25 mL) butter to cooked carrots.
• Spoon maple syrup over baked squash or sweet potatoes.
• Add 3 tbsp (45 mL) maple syrup to 1 cup (250 mL) whipping cream. Beat as usual and use with pies or as a fruit topping. For fewer calories use 1 cup (250 mL) unsweetened low-fat yogurt and 1 tbsp (25 mL) maple syrup.

French Toast Quebec Style

Try this thick, custardy French toast to wake up your morning tastebuds. It's all prepared the night before. I serve it with blueberry preserves and butter, but you could pour over more maple syrup if you preferred.

3	eggs	3
1/2 cup	maple syrup	125 mL
1/3 cup	milk	75 mL
1/2 tsp	vanilla extract	2 mL
pinch	salt	pinch
6	slices French bread, 1/2 inch (1.25 cm) thick	6
2 tbsp	butter	25 mL

1. In a bowl, beat together the eggs, maple syrup, milk, vanilla and salt.

2. Place the bread slices in a buttered 13 × 9-inch (3.5 L) dish in a single layer. Pour the egg mixture evenly over the bread. Cover and refrigerate for 2 hours or overnight.

3. In a large frying pan on medium heat, melt the butter. Add the bread slices and fry on each side until golden-brown, about 2 minutes per side.

Serves 3

Rhubarb has a medicinal background as well as nutritional. It was once believed that rhubarb cured tired blood.

When cooking the outdoor variety of rhubarb, use more sugar than specified in the recipe.

RHUBARB

Rhubarb's fresh, intense, tart taste makes it a welcome addition to winter eating. It is especially good as a dessert after a heavy meal. Hothouse rhubarb, which is available from late winter, is less stringy, sweeter and better tasting than outdoor rhubarb. Outdoor rhubarb, available in June, is a deeper red color, has fatter stalks and large floppy leaves. Rhubarb mixes well with other fruits such as strawberries, oranges and apples. It tastes so good in pies that it was once called pie plant.

• The stalks should be straight and firm, not wilted and flabby. The leaves should be bright-green.

• Store rhubarb in the refrigerator. It should keep for about one week.

• When cooking rhubarb, trim off the ends. If you are cooking the more mature outdoor variety, you may have to peel the stalks with a vegetable peeler to remove the strings.

Rhubarb Fool

A simple, light dessert. Taste the rhubarb before adding the whipping cream, in case it needs extra sugar.

4 cups	sliced rhubarb	1 L
3/4 cup	brown sugar	175 mL
2 tbsp	water	25 mL
1 tbsp	grated orange rind	15 mL
1 cup	whipping cream	250 mL

1. In a medium pot, combine the rhubarb, sugar, water and grated orange rind. On low heat, cook together until the rhubarb softens, about 10 minutes. Cool and drain the liquid, reserving 1/4 cup (50 mL).

2. Place the rhubarb and reserved juice in a food processor or blender and puree until smooth.

3. Whip the cream until it holds its shape. Fold into the rhubarb puree. Spoon into glass dishes and chill before serving.

Serves 4

Rhubarb Pudding

This dessert is comfort food. It can be made with either apples or rhubarb or a combination. Serve with custard, ice cream or whipping cream.

4 cups	sliced rhubarb	1 L
1 cup	brown sugar	250 mL
1/4 cup	unsalted butter	50 mL
1/2 cup	granulated sugar	125 mL
1	egg	1
1 cup	all-purpose flour	250 mL
1 tsp	baking powder	5 mL
1/4 tsp	salt	1 mL

1. Preheat the oven to 375°F (190°C).

2. Combine the rhubarb and brown sugar and place in a buttered 6-cup (1.5 L) ovenproof dish.

3. In a bowl, cream the butter with the granulated sugar until light and fluffy. Add the egg and mix well.

4. Sift together the flour, baking powder and salt. Stir into the creamed mixture and mix to a soft dropping consistency. If the batter is too stiff, beat in a little milk. Spread on top of the fruit.

5. Bake for 35 minutes, or until the fruit is soft and bubbling and the topping is light-brown.

Serves 6

LAMB

Lamb as traditional Easter fare dates back to the time when spring lamb meant exactly that — lamb born in the spring. It was a great treat to have the delicate taste of roast lamb gracing the Easter table. Today spring lamb is defined as any lamb that is less than a year old.

Canadians have been very resistant to eating lamb, probably because of memories of strong-smelling, strong-tasting mutton. Even today our consumption is less than two pounds per person per year, much lower than in Europe. But consumption is increasing, and New Zealand lamb probably has to be thanked for turning us into lamb eaters. Its mild taste and excellent texture as well as its reasonable price make it an appealing alternative to other meats. The lamb, which is frozen, should be defrosted in the refrigerator overnight or longer to retain all its juices and flavor. However, Canadian lamb is improving in taste and texture and is now a viable fresh alternative to New Zealand lamb.

Lamb Cuts

• Lamb **legs** are tender and delicately flavored. They are best roasted or barbecued. To butterfly a lamb leg for the barbecue, have the butcher remove the bone. Marinate the meat, then lay it flat on the grill. Lamb legs should not be larger than 6 lb (3 kg) for the best texture and flavor.

• Lamb **rib chops** correspond to beef rib steaks. They are tender and can be grilled or sautéed. Look for chops at least 1 inch (2.5 cm) thick for the best texture and flavor.

Children often like to suck rhubarb stalks like candy, but keep the leaves out of their mouths — they're poisonous.

• A lamb **rack** consists of the first eight chops of the rib section, which is sold in one piece. Lamb racks are roasted whole, then sliced into chops for serving. They vary considerably in size, depending on the weight of the lamb.

• A **crown** of lamb is two or more lamb racks tied together to form a crown. It is often stuffed in the center and is always roasted, for a spectacular-looking presentation.

• A **loin chop** from the loin section looks like a tiny porterhouse steak. It is tender and best grilled or sautéed. If the bone is removed and the nugget of meat is tied in a circle, it is called a noisette.

• A **saddle** of lamb, one of the most popular English cuts, is the loin chop section from both sides, unsplit (cut as one piece). It looks like a saddle when it is prepared. It is sometimes stuffed and is usually roasted. To carve a saddle of lamb, the meat is removed in one piece from the bones before being carved into slices. The bones are not served.

• Lamb **shoulder** is fatty but with excellent flavor and texture. For ease of serving, a lamb shoulder should be boned before cooking, otherwise the configuration of the bones makes it very difficult to carve. Shoulders are either braised or roasted. They can also be cut up for stewing lamb.

• Lamb **shanks** from the front legs are exceptionally tasty. They are braised slowly for a long time to break down the connective tissue. Buy one per person.

Dijon Lamb Chops

A fast and easy way to make lamb chops that doesn't involve frying or broiling. The lamb chops come out perfectly every time — as if by magic!

6	rib lamb chops, 1/2 inch (1.25 cm) thick	6
1	lemon, cut in half	1
2	cloves garlic, finely chopped	2
1/4 tsp	salt	1 mL
1/4 tsp	freshly ground pepper	1 mL
2 tbsp	Dijon mustard	25 mL
1/4 cup	finely chopped parsley	50 mL
1 cup	dry breadcrumbs	250 mL

1. Preheat the oven to 500°F (260°C).

2. Rub both sides of the chops with the cut lemon.

3. In a small bowl, combine the garlic, salt, pepper, mustard and parsley. Brush onto the lamb chops, coating them evenly.

4. Dredge the chops with the breadcrumbs. Place the chops on a rack over a baking sheet.

5. Bake for 3 minutes. Turn off the oven but do not open the door for 30 minutes. The chops will be perfectly cooked, slightly pink and succulent. (If you want them better done, bake for 4 minutes before turning off the oven.)

Serves 3 to 4

Farmer's Leg of Lamb

Turnips are often associated with lamb because their earthy flavor balances the richness of the meat. This is an easy, succulent one-dish lamb dinner.

4 lb	lamb leg, fresh or frozen and defrosted	2 kg
1 tbsp	soy sauce	15 mL
1/3 cup	olive oil	75 mL
3 tbsp	finely chopped fresh rosemary, or 1 tbsp (15 mL) dried	45 mL
2	cloves garlic, thinly sliced	2
4	baking potatoes, peeled and cubed	4
1	turnip, peeled and cubed	1
	Salt and freshly ground pepper to taste	

1. Preheat the oven to 400°F (200°C).

2. Remove the thin layer of skin from the lamb. Make slits in the fat all over.

3. In a small bowl, combine the soy sauce and 2 tbsp (25 mL) olive oil. Brush on the lamb. Insert the rosemary and garlic slices into the slits in the fat.

4. Place the potatoes and turnips in a pot of cold salted water. Bring to a boil and boil, uncovered, for 7 minutes, or until crisp-tender. Drain well.

5. Place the lamb on a rack in a roasting pan and roast for 30 minutes. Remove the lamb and the rack.

6. Add the potatoes and the turnips to the roasting pan, basting with any accumulated fat. Pour over the remaining olive oil evenly. Place the lamb on top and season with salt and pepper. Bake for 45 minutes longer, or until the lamb is cooked to taste.

7. Remove the lamb from the oven and let sit for 10 minutes. Slice and serve with the turnip and potatoes.

Serves 6 to 8

Rack of Lamb

This lamb dish was apparently served with mint Hollandaise at Sarah Ferguson's wedding when she married the Duke of York. If you prefer a lighter accompaniment, serve with a simple pan gravy flavored with mint, rather than the Hollandaise sauce.

4	lamb racks	4
2 tbsp	finely chopped fresh mint leaves, or 2 tsp (10 mL) dried	25 mL
1/4 cup	olive oil	50 mL
	Grated rind and juice of 1 lemon	

1. Cut away the fat and meat from last 2 inches (5 cm) of the bones. Trim the remaining fat.

2. In a small bowl, combine the mint, olive oil and lemon. Pour over the racks. Marinate for 1 hour.

3. Preheat the oven to 400°F (200°C).

4. Place the racks on a baking sheet in the oven. Bake for 30 to 45 minutes, or until the juices run pink. Remove from the oven. Let rest for 5 minutes.

5. To serve, cut down between the bones. Serve four chops to each person. Top with mint Hollandaise.

Serves 8

Hollandaise Sauce

In a small heavy pot over low heat, whisk together 3 egg yolks (at room temperature), 1 tbsp (15 mL) lemon juice and 1 tbsp (15 mL) butter. Continue to whisk until the butter melts.

Whisk in 10 tbsp (150 mL) butter 2 tbsp (25 mL) at a time, waiting until the butter is incorporated before adding the next addition. Season with 1 to 2 tbsp (15 to 25 mL) lemon juice, a pinch of salt and a pinch of cayenne pepper. Makes 1 1/4 cups (300 mL).

Mint Hollandaise Sauce

Combine 1/3 cup (75 mL) finely chopped fresh mint, or 2 tbsp (25 mL) dried, with 1/4 cup (50 mL) raspberry vinegar and 1 tsp (5 mL) granulated sugar. Bring to a boil and cook until the vinegar is reduced to 1 tbsp (15 mL). Stir into the Hollandaise.

Creating an Inexpensive
Easter Table Setting
Be creative in your approach.
Look for inexpensive yard
goods, perhaps in yellow, to
use as table linen. Hollow out
yellow apples and use as candle holders. Make a centerpiece out of painted/dyed or
unadorned eggs stacked in a
pyramid shape sitting on some
Spanish moss. Buy foil-
wrapped Easter eggs and scatter over the table.

Ukrainian Easter Feast for Twelve

Easter is an important holiday for Ukrainians. Traditionally they go to a morning church service, then come home and have Easter breakfast — a breakfast in name only — where they serve lavish quantities of salads, eggs, ham, cold meats, roast suckling pig, sausages, pickles and relishes. The highlight of the feast is *pashka*, a wonderful rich Eastern European cheesecake, molded and served with fruit and *kulich*, a special Easter bread. Pashkas can be elaborate or simple, and there are both cooked and uncooked versions. Some call for dried fruit in the mixture, or are garnished with fresh fruit.

Fresh Pickerel with Lemon and Dill

Perogies

Baked Ham

Pickled Beets and Relishes

Cole Slaw*

Pashka

Fresh Pickerel with Lemon and Dill

Pickerel is a freshwater fish. Simply baked, it makes a stunning appetizer. This recipe is from restaurant critic and native Winnipegger, Cynthia Wine.

1/3 cup	butter	75 mL
12	pickerel fillets	12
	Juice of 2 lemons	
1/4 cup	finely chopped fresh dill	50 mL
	Salt and freshly ground pepper to taste	
Garnish:		
12	lemon slices	12
	Fresh dill sprigs	

1. In a large frying pan, melt the butter on medium-high until it foams. Add the fillets one at time until the pan is full but the fillets do not overlap.

2. Sauté the fillets on one side for 10 minutes, turn over and sauté on the other side until white juices appear, about another 3 minutes.

3. Season with the lemon juice, dill, salt and pepper and keep warm.

4. Continue with the remaining fillets. Garnish the fish with the lemon slices and dill sprigs.

Serves 12

*See *Lucy Waverman's Cooking School Cookbook*, page 146.

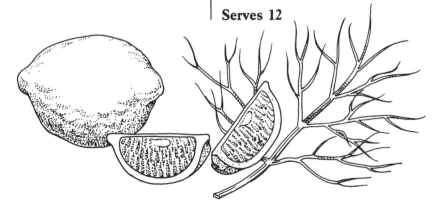

Perogies

Perogies are little pouches of dough filled with savory fillings such as cheese and potato, or cabbage. Although they can be bought, they are far better homemade. Make a double patch and freeze them. They can be fried or boiled, served in soups, as an appetizer smothered with sour cream and onions, or as a side dish. This recipe is from Judy Comfort, an ex-Winnipegger who now lives in Nova Scotia and makes the definitive light perogy.

1/4 cup	melted butter	50 mL
2 cups	all-purpose flour	500 mL
1 tsp	salt	5 mL
1	egg	1
2/3 cup	cold water	150 mL
Filling:		
1 cup	creamed cottage cheese	250 mL
2 cups	cooked mashed potatoes	500 mL
1	green onion, finely chopped	1
1 tsp	finely chopped fresh dill	5 mL
	Salt and freshly ground pepper to taste	

1. Grease a 13 × 9-inch (3.5 L) baking dish with the melted butter. Set aside.

2. Sift the flour and the salt into a bowl.

3. Whisk the egg and water together in a small bowl, then stir into the flour. With your hands, knead the dough until smooth and shiny. Form into two balls. Cover with a damp tea towel and set aside.

4. To make the filling, place the cottage cheese in a sieve and run under cold water until the curds separate. Tap the sieve to drain off any excess water and allow the curds to sit for 10 minutes, or until dry.

5. Mix the cottage cheese with the remaining filling ingredients.

6. On a lightly floured board, roll out the dough one ball at a time until 1/8 inch (3 mm) thick and 14 inches (35 cm) square. Do not overwork the dough.

7. Cut into 3-inch (7.5 cm) squares. With your hand, stretch each square slightly without making holes. Place 1 tbsp (15 mL) filling in the center of each square. Fold the edges over to form a triangle, pinching the edges. Use a little flour to help seal the edges if the dough becomes too moist from the filling.

8. Bring a large pot of water to a simmer. Toss in the perogies and simmer for a few minutes, or until the perogies rise to the surface. Don't crowd the pan.

9. Drain the perogies in a colander and place them in the buttered baking dish, coating them on all sides with the butter.

10. Preheat the oven to 350°F (180°C). Bake the perogies, uncovered, for 10 to 15 minutes, or until plumped and slightly crisp underneath. Serve with fried onions and sour cream.

Makes 30 perogies

Cheese pashka shaped in a pyramid or block is a traditional Ukrainian and Russian Easter dessert. There are special molds you can buy, but an ordinary clean plastic flower pot with a hole in the bottom works beautifully. Line the pot with dampened cheesecloth, pour the mixture in, weight down and leave for 24 hours.

Baked Ham

Pineapple was originally used with ham because its acidic juices tenderized the tough tissues. Today hams are tender to begin with, but the tradition of serving ham and pineapple remains. Ham or suckling pig is the traditional centerpiece at an Eastern European Easter feast.

1	6-lb (3 kg) ham	1
1	19-oz (540 mL) can sliced pineapple rings	1
20	cloves, approx.	20
Glaze:		
1/2 cup	brown sugar	125 mL
1/2 cup	pineapple juice	125 mL
1/2 cup	sherry	125 mL
2 tbsp	dry mustard	25 mL

1. Soak the ham in cold water overnight to remove the salt.

2. Preheat the oven to 350°F (180°C).

3. Wrap the ham in aluminum foil. Place in a baking pan and bake for 2 to 2½ hours, or until tender.

4. Remove the foil and cut off the outer skin of the ham. Drain the pineapple rings, reserving ½ cup (125 mL) juice. Decorate the ham by placing pineapple rings over the surface. Stud each ring with a clove.

5. To make the glaze, in a small pot, combine the brown sugar, pineapple juice, sherry and mustard. Bring to a boil. Brush over the ham and pineapple.

6. Bake the ham for 30 to 40 minutes, basting frequently, until it is nicely glazed. If any glaze remains, boil it down until it is syrupy. Brush the glaze over the ham 5 minutes before it leaves the oven.

Serves 12

Pashka

This easy, uncooked version of pashka comes from Julia Antonoff. The dessert must be started two days before you need it, because the cheese has to drain.

3 lb	cream cheese	1.5 kg
12	hard-cooked egg yolks	12
1 cup	unsalted butter	250 mL
2¼ cups	granulated sugar	550 mL
1 tbsp	vanilla extract	15 mL
1¼ cups	ground almonds	300 mL
	Slivered almonds and raisins for garnish	

1. Place the cream cheese in a colander lined with cheesecloth. Fold the ends of the cheesecloth over the cheese. Place a small plate on top and weigh down with several tin cans for about 24 hours.

2. Press the egg yolks through a sieve and reserve.

3. With an electric mixer, beat together the butter and the sugar until light and fluffy. Add the vanilla. With the mixer at low speed, blend in the cream cheese.

4. When the cream cheese is thoroughly incorporated, beat in the egg yolks and almonds. Continue to beat until smooth and creamy.

5. Line a clean medium-sized flower pot with cheesecloth. Spoon the mixture into it. Fold the cheesecloth over the top. Place a weight on top and let it stand on a rack over a plate overnight in a cool place.

6. The next day, turn the pashka out onto a serving platter and decorate with the slivered almonds and raisins. Serve with fresh fruit.

Serves 12

4
April

The first crocuses are bursting through the earth, and our first fresh wild vegetable, fiddleheads, are beginning to peek out of the ground. Spring is a new beginning.

In season
asparagus
fiddleheads
mushrooms

Holidays
Passover

Menu
Passover Dinner for Twelve

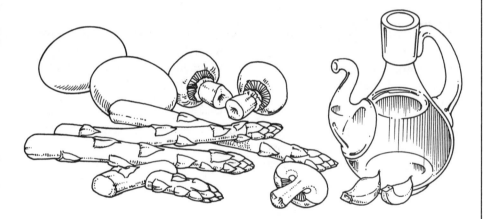

BRIOCHE

Whenever I holiday in France, I have a love affair with the bread — the crisp long French sticks and the buttery, flaky croissants. But it is the brioche that I've always loved the best.

Brioche is a light, round, batter-type bread full of butter and eggs, usually baked in a round, fluted mold. It is delicious with butter and jam, and the individual ones make wonderful hors d'oeuvres when hollowed out and filled with savory mixtures.

Brioche is actually very simple to make. Using my easy, foolproof method, the ingredients are combined in the food processor and, although the dough has to rise three times, it takes no more than ten minutes to mix, knead and shape. The result is a bread that is more full flavored and buttery.

The dough itself can be flavored with herbs, spices, cheese or vegetables, or it can be wrapped around fillings such as sausages or cheese. It can also be used as a pastry base for sweet and savory tarts.

To test brioche for doneness, push a straw or knife through the center. The brioche is baked when the knife comes out clean.

• Fluted brioche molds have slanted sides. They are available in large and small sizes. You can also use large or small muffin tins, a loaf pan or ring mold, Pyrex bowl or cake pan. Oven-proof coffee cups make pretty individual molds.

• Brioche can be made by hand, but because of the amount of butter used, it is much easier to make with either an electric mixer or a food processor.

• Traditional rich brioche mixtures have a ratio of one part butter to three parts flour.

• Traditionally brioche was made by incorporating a ball of already risen yeast dough with a ball of egg and flour dough. They were beaten together by being thrown on a board, left to rise, then shaped and allowed to rise again. The method I use is much easier. I make a yeast dough with eggs and let it rise three times. The end result is the same.

• Because traditional brioche needs three risings, make it leisurely over two days. A less buttery brioche can be made with two risings.

• In a traditional rich brioche, the second rising should occur in the refrigerator. The slow rising in the refrigerator prevents the butter from melting, which would make the dough too soft to shape.

• To form brioche in the traditional shape, slice off about one-sixth of the dough. With floured hands, shape the remainder into a plump ball by easing the edges of the dough under. Place the dough in the mold. Make a depression in the top of the brioche with your thumb. Roll the remaining dough into a ball and place it in the depression to form a topknot.

• Never glaze the topknot where it joins the main part of the brioche, otherwise the topknot won't rise.

• After being placed in the molds, brioche must rise until doubled in bulk, otherwise the bread will be dense in texture instead of light.

• For the best texture, brioche should always be baked in a hot oven.

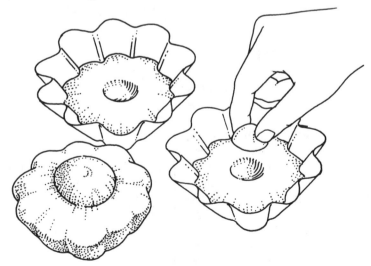

Rich Brioche

This is the traditional high butter brioche which rises three times. It has the lightest, fluffiest texture and is used mainly as a bread.

4	eggs	4
1 tbsp	dry active yeast	15 mL
3 tbsp	warm water	45 mL
1 tsp	granulated sugar	5 mL
2 cups	all-purpose flour	500 mL
pinch	salt	pinch
2 tsp	granulated sugar	10 mL
¾ cup	cold unsalted butter, diced	175 mL
1 tsp	water	5 mL

1. In a small bowl, blend 3 eggs with a fork and set aside.

2. In another small bowl, mix the yeast with the 3 tbsp (45 mL) warm water. Add the 1 tsp (5 mL) sugar and let the yeast dissolve completely.

3. Add the flour, salt, 2 tsp (10 mL) sugar, liquid yeast mixture and beaten eggs to the food processor. Pulse until well mixed. The dough will look like little pellets.

4. Add the butter 2 tbsp (25 mL) at a time. Process until well mixed. Remove from the processor and place on a floured board.

5. Knead the dough until it is soft and elastic, sprinkling the board with more flour, if needed.

6. Place the dough in a large bowl and allow it to rise until doubled in bulk, about 3 hours.

7. Remove the dough from the bowl and spread it out on a lightly floured board, to form a rectangle. Press lightly on the dough to release the air. Fold the dough in three and replace in the bowl. Allow it to rise for another 2 hours or overnight in the refrigerator.

8. Punch the dough down after the second rising and form the brioche in the mold. Let it rise again in a warm place until doubled in bulk, about 45 minutes, before baking.

9. Preheat the oven to 400°F (200°C). Mix together the remaining egg and 1 tsp (5 mL) water. Brush the glaze on the brioche, making sure it does not drip onto the mold.

10. Bake for 20 minutes, lower the heat to 350°F (180°C) and bake for a further 25 minutes, or until the brioche starts to shrink slightly from the sides of the mold.

Makes eight 3-inch (7.5 cm) brioche or one large one

Savarins, rum babas and Austrian kugelhofs are all sweet butter/yeast concoctions similar to the brioche.

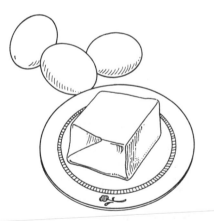

Simple Brioche

This is a recipe for a less rich brioche dough. The method of combining the ingredients is the same, but much less butter is incorporated. There are only two risings, and the second can take place after the dough has been formed around filling ingredients.

4	eggs	4
1 tbsp	dry active yeast	15 mL
3 tbsp	warm water	45 mL
1 tsp	granulated sugar	5 mL
2 cups	all-purpose flour	500 mL
pinch	salt	pinch
2 tsp	granulated sugar	10 mL
1/4 cup	cold unsalted butter, diced	50 mL
1 tsp	water	5 mL

1. In a small bowl, blend 3 eggs with a fork and set aside.

2. In another small bowl, mix the yeast with the 3 tbsp (45 mL) warm water. Add the 1 tsp (5 mL) sugar and let the yeast dissolve completely.

3. Add the flour, salt, 2 tsp (10 mL) sugar, liquid yeast mixture and beaten eggs to the food processor. Pulse until well mixed. The dough will look like little pellets.

4. Add the butter in two lots. Process until well mixed. Remove from the processor and place on a floured board.

5. Knead until the dough is soft and elastic, sprinkling the board with more flour, if needed.

6. Place the dough in a large bowl and to allow it to rise until doubled in bulk, about 3 hours.

7. Punch the dough down and form the brioche in the mold. Let rise again in a warm place until doubled in bulk, about 45 minutes, before baking.

8. Preheat the oven to 400°F (200°C). Mix together the remaining egg and 1 tsp (5 mL) water. Brush the glaze on the brioche, making sure it does not drip onto the mold.

9. Bake for 20 minutes, lower the heat to 350°F (180°C) and bake for a further 25 minutes, or until the brioche starts to shrink slightly from the sides of the mold.

Makes eight 3-inch (7.5 cm) brioche or one large one

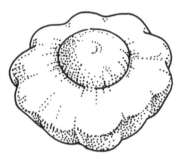

Herbed Brioche

Add 1 tbsp (15 mL) chopped fresh tarragon or 1 tsp (5 mL) dried, 1 tbsp (15 mL) chopped fresh thyme or 1 tsp (5 mL) dried and 1 tbsp (15 mL) chopped parsley to the flour before adding the wet ingredients to the food processor.

Spinach Mozzarella Brioche

Serve this as an hors d'oeuvre or as a bread with a vegetable soup or any veal or chicken dish. You can use thick smoked sausages instead of the spinach and mozzarella. Roll out the dough into a 9 × 5-inch (23 × 12 cm) rectangle. Place the sausage along the long edge and roll up the dough over the sausage. Place in a loaf pan and bake.

1	recipe Simple Brioche dough	1
2 cups	cooked spinach	500 mL
1 cup	grated mozzarella cheese	250 mL
	Salt and freshly ground pepper to taste	
1	egg	1
1 tsp	water	5 mL

1. Once the dough has finished its first rising, roll it in a 10 × 15 (25 cm × 37 cm) rectangle.

2. In a bowl, combine the spinach, cheese, salt and pepper. Place the filling along the long edge of the rectangle. Roll up into a loose cylinder.

3. Pull the two ends of the cylinder together to make a doughnut shape. Seal with some beaten egg, if needed.

4. Place on a baking sheet and leave to rise for 40 minutes, or until doubled in bulk.

5. Preheat the oven to 400°F (200°C).

6. Beat together the egg and water. Brush over the brioche.

7. Bake for 20 minutes, lower the heat to 350°F (180°C) and bake for a further 20 minutes, or until the dough is puffed and golden-brown.

Serves 8 to 10

Brie in Brioche

I serve this as a spectacular party piece on a dessert buffet, and it's always the first to go. I have used frozen puff pastry instead of brioche in my lazy days. Make the recipe ahead of time and reheat at 300°F (150°C) for 30 minutes when needed. After baking, the dish needs to sit for 45 minutes to allow the cheese to cool down slightly, otherwise it will run everywhere when the bread is cut.

2	recipes Simple Brioche dough	2
1	10-inch (25 cm) round Brie, chilled	1
1 cup	chopped pecans	250 mL
1/2 cup	packed brown sugar	125 mL
1	egg, beaten	1

1. Preheat the oven to 400°F (200°C).

2. Once the dough has finished its first rising, roll out one recipe to a circle that is 2 inches (5 cm) bigger than the cheese. Place it on a baking sheet and place the cheese on top. Sprinkle the nuts and brown sugar over the cheese.

3. Roll out the second recipe of brioche and cover the cheese with it. Seal the edges with the beaten egg and make a fluted edge. Decorate with any leftover dough. Brush the brioche with the beaten egg.

4. Bake for 40 minutes, or until the dough is golden-brown.

Serves 20

Scottish Bread Pudding

Substitute one loaf of egg bread or an Italian loaf if brioche isn't available. Serve the pudding with caramel whisky sauce or ice cream.

1	large brioche	1
2 cups	milk	500 mL
4	eggs	4
1 cup	granulated sugar	250 mL
2 cups	light cream	500 mL
1/2 cup	golden raisins	125 mL
2 tsp	vanilla extract	10 mL
1/2 tsp	ground nutmeg	2 mL
1/2 tsp	ground cinnamon	2 mL

1. Cut the brioche into large cubes and place in a large bowl. Pour over the milk and let soak until the bread has absorbed the milk, about 10 minutes.

2. Preheat the oven to 325°F (160°C). Butter a 12 × 8-inch (3 L) baking dish.

3. In a large bowl, beat together the eggs and granulated sugar until thick and glossy. Beat in the light cream, raisins, vanilla, nutmeg and cinnamon. Pour over the bread mixture and combine. Transfer to the baking dish.

4. Place the baking dish in a larger pan and add boiling water to the large pan until it comes halfway up the sides of the baking pan. Bake for 1 hour, or until a knife inserted in the center comes out clean. Serve with caramel whisky sauce.

Serves 8

Caramel Whisky Sauce
Combine 1/2 cup (125 mL) unsalted butter, 1 cup (250 mL) brown sugar and 1/2 cup (125 mL) whipping cream in a pot. Bring to a boil, stirring constantly. Boil for 2 minutes, cool slightly and stir in 1/2 cup (125 mL) Scotch, rye, bourbon, Irish whisky or dark rum. Makes about 2 cups (500 mL).

ASPARAGUS

Asparagus is one of the first signs of spring. Its faintly nutty taste and vivid green color help it to enhance both the palate and plate. By late spring, asparagus from California has been on the market for some time, but our first homegrown asparagus hits the shelves in late April or early May, depending on weather conditions.

Buying and Cooking

• Look for bright-green stalks with tightly closed, compact tips. Avoid limp, wilted stalks. If the tips are feathery or beginning to open, the asparagus is past its prime.

• Store asparagus in the refrigerator, but if you are keeping it for more than a day, wrap the stalks in a damp paper towel to keep them fresh.

• Asparagus stalks can be gritty. Rinse them in cool water before using. Snap off the stem end to remove the inedible woody part of the stalk. (Snapping it instead of cutting detaches only the woody part and not any of the edible stalk.)

• Thicker stalks of asparagus need peeling before cooking. The outer skin is tough and woody. When it is removed, the asparagus takes less time to cook and the texture is more luscious. With a vegetable peeler, peel each stalk up to the furled head.

• Choose stalks of similar size for even cooking.

• Ideally, asparagus should be cooked in a tall narrow pot filled with about 2 inches (5 cm) water, so the stalks boil in the water while the heads steam. A metal coffee can will work for this.

• Other cooking methods for asparagus include filling a frying pan half full with water, bringing it to a boil and laying in the asparagus stalks. Boil until tender-crisp — a matter of minutes. Stir-frying is a popular method as well. Cut stalks into 1-inch (2.5 cm) lengths. Toss in hot oil over high heat until cooked.

• Once cooked, asparagus should be drained well and refreshed with cold water to set its color. As asparagus can retain water, place it on a tea towel for a minute to absorb excess moisture.

Asparagus Vinaigrette

This dish makes a great appetizer, or it can be part of a brunch or buffet menu. Add 2 tbsp (25 cm) grated orange rind to the dressing for a flavor change, or use lemon juice instead of vinegar.

1 lb	asparagus, cooked until crisp-tender	500 g
1 tsp	Dijon mustard	5 mL
2 tbsp	white wine vinegar	25 mL
1/3 cup	olive oil	75 mL
	Salt and freshly ground pepper to taste	

1. Place the cooked asparagus on a platter.

2. In a small bowl, combine the mustard and vinegar. Whisk in the olive oil. Season with the salt and pepper. Pour over the asparagus stalks.

Serves 4

The Perfect Asparagus Dish

Asparagus is at its best when served simply and unadorned. Serve this as a first course.

1 lb	asparagus	500 g
1/3 cup	melted butter	75 mL
1 tbsp	lemon juice	15 mL
	Salt and freshly ground pepper to taste	

1. Peel the asparagus if the stalks are thick. Boil the asparagus in a tall pot on high heat until crisp-tender. Drain well, refresh with cold water and drain again. Lay on a platter.

2. Combine the butter, lemon juice, salt and pepper. Pour over the asparagus.

Serves 2

Asparagus Italian Style

I first tasted asparagus like this in Rome in the spring. Serve as a first course.

2 lb	thick asparagus, cooked until crisp-tender	1 kg
	Salt and freshly ground pepper to taste	
1/3 cup	melted butter	75 mL
1/2 cup	grated Parmesan cheese	125 mL

1. Preheat the oven to 350°F (180°C).

2. Lay the asparagus in an ovenproof dish in two layers. Season with salt and pepper. Pour over the butter and sprinkle on the Parmesan.

3. Bake for 10 minutes, or until the cheese is crusty and golden.

Serves 4

Asparagus was once considered a medicinal plant. It cured heart troubles, toothaches and even bee stings. Today it is a known diuretic. It has high quantities of vitamins C and A and is low in calories and sodium.

Thick asparagus stalks (about the size of your thumb) are the most succulent, but thin stalks are wonderful for stir-fries.

Stir-fried Asparagus

To turn this into a complete meal, add about 8 oz (250 g) slivered chicken, flank steak or pork to the wok for 2 minutes before adding the asparagus. Use thin asparagus, if available, to avoid peeling. If you do not have sesame oil, sprinkle with sesame seeds.

2 lb	asparagus	1 kg
2 tbsp	vegetable oil	25 mL
1 tbsp	finely chopped fresh ginger	15 mL
1/4 cup	chicken stock or water	50 mL
1 tbsp	soy sauce	15 mL
1 tsp	sesame oil	5 mL

1. Slice the asparagus into 1-inch (2.5 cm) lengths.

2. Heat the oil in a frying pan or wok on high heat. Add the ginger and stir-fry for 30 seconds.

3. Add the asparagus and stir-fry for 1 minute. Pour in the chicken stock, cover the pan and let the asparagus steam for 2 minutes, or until crisp-tender.

4. Sprinkle with the soy sauce and sesame oil before serving.

Serves 4

The Europeans grow white asparagus, which has to be grown under mounds of earth so the sun doesn't turn it green. They think the green is superior, whereas we tend to prefer the white! Personally, I find the white more beautiful but less tasty.

If you don't like to eat asparagus, use it as an attractive floral centerpiece for an elegant dinner party. Stick a few daisies between the stalks.

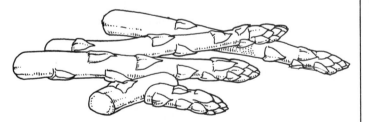

FIDDLEHEADS

Fiddleheads are the young edible tips of the ostrich fern; they look like the graceful spiral tip on the tuning end of a violin. They are handpicked in the woods, usually near streams, and have become a gourmet's delight, partly because their season is so short. Fiddleheads are fresh for only a couple of weeks, and are usually available at farmers' markets. Although they are similar to asparagus, they have a more earthy taste.

If you decide you want to pick your own fiddleheads, you have to be able to recognize the right variety. There are lots of ferns growing near streams; most of them taste awful and some can make you sick. Look for ferns growing together in clumps and covered with a brown, paper-like substance.

• Look for fiddleheads that are no more than 2 inches (5 cm) wide, because they get tough and bitter as they grow bigger.

• Wash fiddleheads in at least four changes of water to help get rid off the brown papery substance surrounding them as well as the dirt that can be engrained in the fronds. Swish them around in the water to help release the dirt.

• Cut off the tough brown part at the base of the fern.

• Fiddleheads freeze well, so they can be available all year. Preserve your own by blanching in hot water for 1 minute. Freeze in single layers on baking sheets, then store in freezer bags.

Sautéed Fiddleheads

¹/₄ cup	butter	50 mL
8 oz	fiddleheads, washed	250 g
	Salt and freshly ground pepper to taste	

1. In a large frying pan, over medium-high heat, melt the better. Add the fiddleheads and sauté for 3 minutes, or until they begin to soften.

2. Cover the pan, lower the heat to medium and steam for 3 minutes longer, or until crisp-tender. Season with salt and pepper.

Serves 4

Fiddlehead Shrimp Salad

8 oz	cooked fiddleheads	250 g
8 oz	cooked baby shrimp	250 g
1	red onion, chopped	1
1 tsp	Dijon mustard	5 mL
2 tbsp	lime juice	25 mL
1 tbsp	soy sauce	15 mL
¹/₃ cup	vegetable oil	75 mL
1 tsp	sesame oil	5 mL
	Salt and freshly ground pepper to taste	
1	head red leaf lettuce	1

1. Combine the fiddleheads, shrimp and onion in a bowl.

2. In a small bowl, beat together the mustard, lime juice and soy sauce. Slowly whisk in the vegetable and sesame oils. Season with salt and pepper. Pour over the fiddlehead mixture.

3. Arrange the leaf lettuce on a platter and top with the fiddlehead/shrimp.

Serves 4 to 6

Fiddlehead Soup

A bright spring soup which can be made with frozen fiddleheads if fresh ones are not available.

3 tbsp	butter	45 mL
3	leeks, white part only, sliced	3
1 lb	fiddleheads, washed	500 g
5 cups	chicken stock	1.25 L
¹/₂ cup	whipping cream	125 mL
	Salt and freshly ground pepper to taste	
1 tsp	grated lemon rind	5 mL

1. In a large pot, melt the butter on medium heat until it sizzles. Add the leeks and fiddleheads and sauté for 2 to 3 minutes, or until coated with the butter.

2. Cover the pot and steam the vegetables for 5 minutes. Add the stock, bring to a boil, lower the heat and simmer, covered, for 20 to 25 minutes, or until the fiddleheads are soft.

3. In a food processor or blender, puree the soup until smooth. Press the soup through a sieve to remove any fibers. Return it to the pot, add the cream and simmer for 5 minutes. Season well with the salt, pepper and lemon rind. If the soup is too thick, add stock to thin it down.

Serves 6 to 8

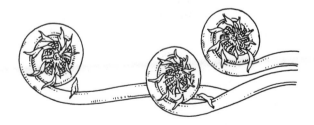

Stir-fried Beef with Fiddleheads

A quick main course served with rice. Substitute asparagus for fiddleheads, if desired.

8 oz	flank steak, thinly sliced	250 g
2 tbsp	soy sauce	25 mL
2 tbsp	vegetable oil	25 mL
2 cups	fiddleheads, washed	500 mL
1/2 cup	chicken stock or water	125 mL
1 tbsp	finely chopped fresh ginger	15 mL
1 tbsp	finely chopped garlic	15 mL
1 tsp	sesame oil	5 mL
2	green onions, finely chopped	2

1. Marinate the flank steak in 1 tbsp (15 mL) soy sauce.

2. In a wok or frying pan, heat 1 tbsp (15 mL) oil on high heat. Stir in the fiddleheads and stir-fry for 1 minute.

3. Pour in the stock, cover the wok and steam the fiddleheads until crisp-tender, about 5 minutes. Reserve the fiddleheads and any liquid.

4. Dry the wok and add the remaining oil. Stir in the ginger and garlic, stir-fry for 30 seconds, then toss in the meat. Continue to stir-fry until the meat is seared on the outside and pink within, about 2 minutes.

5. Return the fiddleheads and liquid to the wok, add the remaining soy sauce and sesame oil. Stir everything together to combine the flavors, then sprinkle on the green onions.

Serves 2

Mushrooms are not plants, since they have no root systems and no chlorophyll; they are a fungus.

MUSHROOMS

They have magical powers, they were created by a bolt of lightning, they are the food of the chosen and they are available on our supermarket shelves. These magical mystery objects are the edible fungus — mushrooms.

Cultivated mushrooms are available all year; they are grown in sheds in controlled-temperature environments in beds of specially treated synthetic compost. They need high humidity and complete darkness to grow properly, but it is the heat from the light that inhibits growth, not the light itself. They are harvested by pickers wearing miners' lamps!

Buying and Storing

• Choose mushrooms that are clean, plump and firm. The caps should be unblemished and uniform in color — either white, cream or brown, depending on the variety. Reject mushrooms that are soft, misshapen or dirty.

• Generally the caps should be completely closed over the stem. Once the gills (the dark fluted underside) are exposed, the mushroom is past its prime. However, the brown, flat European variety is more flavorful when the gills are open.

• Buy short-stemmed mushrooms, because the cap is more tender than the stem.

• Mushrooms need to breathe when stored. Do not keep them in plastic containers or plastic bags. Mushrooms expel moisture and become slimy if the moisture is trapped. Store in paper bags or in a bowl covered by a tea towel.

• Use mushrooms within a few days

of buying. They deteriorate quickly.
• Do not wash mushrooms, because they absorb water. Brush off any soil with a brush or a damp kitchen towel. As they grow in sterile soil, there is no need to peel, soak or wash them.
• If the stem is dry at the tip, cut it off.
• As mushrooms are low in calories — only 19 calories in 1 cup (250 mL) — have no cholesterol and supply small amounts of protein and trace minerals, they are a practically perfect fungus.
• Mushrooms are available in different sizes. Button mushrooms are good for pickling, or when you want the look of a whole mushroom in a dish. Medium-sized mushrooms are all-purpose, and the large ones are best for stuffing and grilling.
• If you are using dried mushrooms, soak them in warm water for 30 minutes before using, to rehydrate them.

Wild Mushrooms

• **Chanterelles** are grown in Nova Scotia as well as other parts of Canada. They have a yellowish head inverted like a cup, with a frilled edge and thick gills. They are delicious sautéed on their own or used in sauces.
• **Cèpes** (the French name) or **porcini** (the Italian name) are thick, meaty, earthy-tasting mushrooms with an affinity for garlic and butter. Mainly found in France and Italy, they are available dried in Canada.
• **Enoki** are Japanese mushrooms with long feathery stalks and a tiny cap at the end. They don't have much taste, but they make attractive decorations on plates.
• **Oyster** mushrooms are being cultivated in several provinces. They are fleshy with shell-shaped caps and have a mild flavor when cooked.
• **Shiitake** mushrooms are the most flavorful. They are of Japanese origin with a rich, meaty taste and texture. Try them in pasta dishes or sauces.

Many species of mushrooms are poisonous. Do not go foraging for wild mushrooms unless you know what you are doing.

Mushrooms double in size every 24 hours once they push through the soil.

Cèpe

Oyster

Enoki

Chanterelle

White

Shiitake

Mushroom and Onion Soup

A delicate soup with both the flavor of the green onions and barely cooked mushrooms coming through. You will need approximately twenty-five green onions for the best flavor.

1/4 cup	butter	50 mL
5	bunches green onions, green stalks and white bulbs, chopped	5
4 cups	chicken stock	1 L
8 oz	mushrooms, thinly sliced	250 g
1/2 cup	whipping cream	125 mL
	Salt and freshly ground pepper to taste	
Garnish:		
6	mushrooms, thinly sliced	6
1/4 cup	sour cream	50 mL
pinch	cayenne pepper	pinch

1. In a heavy pot, melt the butter on medium heat. Add the green onions and simmer slowly for 10 minutes, covered.

2. Add the chicken stock and bring to a boil, stirring constantly. Simmer for 15 minutes, uncovered. Add the mushrooms to the soup and simmer for a further minute.

3. Process the soup in a blender or food processor. Return the soup to the pot and add the whipping cream and salt and pepper to taste. Bring to a boil and simmer for 5 minutes. Check for seasoning, adding salt and pepper as needed.

4. Ladle the soup into bowls. Garnish with the raw mushrooms, sour cream and a sprinkle of cayenne.

Serves 6

To keep tempura batter cold, add an ice cube after it is mixed.

Mushroom Tempura

Try this with thickly sliced shiitake mushrooms for an authentic Japanese taste. Or use other vegetables such as green pepper, cauliflower, spinach and zucchini for a mixed vegetable tempura. This batter is great with shrimp, too. Make sure the water is ice-cold for the lightest batter. You can fry the tempura early in the day and reheat in a 400°F (200°C) oven for 5 minutes. It loses some of its crispness, but it frees you from last-minute deep-frying.

3/4 cup	cornstarch	175 mL
1/4 cup	all-purpose flour	50 mL
1 tsp	baking powder	5 mL
1/2 tsp	salt	2 mL
1/4 tsp	freshly ground pepper	1 mL
1/2 cup	cold water	125 mL
1	egg, beaten	1
	Vegetable oil for frying	
8 oz	small mushrooms	250 g

1. In a medium bowl, combine the cornstarch, flour, baking powder, salt and pepper.

2. In a small bowl, combine the water and egg. Stir into the dry ingredients.

3. In a wok or frying pan, heat 1/2 inch (1.25 cm) oil on high heat.

4. Dip the mushrooms into the batter and fry until golden-brown on all sides, about 1 minute. Drain on paper towels and serve at once.

Serves 4

Mushroom and Watercress Salad

Serve as a first course or as a side salad with fish or chicken. Use oyster or shiitake mushrooms instead of cultivated, or use a combination of all three.

2 tsp	Dijon mustard	10 mL
¼ cup	white wine vinegar	50 mL
1	clove garlic, finely chopped	1
¾ cup	olive oil	175 mL
	Salt and freshly ground pepper to taste	
8 oz	mushrooms, thinly sliced	250 g
1	red onion, thinly sliced	1
2	bunches watercress, stems removed	2
2 tbsp	finely chopped parsley	25 mL

1. In a small bowl, combine the mustard, vinegar and garlic. Whisk in the olive oil. Season with the salt and pepper.

2. Place the mushrooms in a salad bowl and pour over half the dressing. Leave to marinate for 1 hour.

3. Sprinkle the red onion and watercress over the mushrooms. Toss everything together with the remaining dressing. Sprinkle with the parsley.

Serves 6

Passover Dinner for Twelve

Passover is the Jewish holiday that celebrates the exodus of the Jewish slaves from Egypt. Led by Moses, they fled so quickly that they had no time to let their bread rise, so they baked it unleavened. Today this is symbolized by eating matzo or unleavened bread for the eight days of Passover, as well as eliminating yeast, flour and, depending on where you are from, legumes and any ingredient that may have come in contact with a grain.

The first and second nights of Passover, when the Haggadah (the story of the Jewish exodus) is read, are the seder nights. There are no special laws governing the seder meal except that lamb may not be eaten. What you eat is generally determined by your family's tradition.

During Passover, cooking presents a whole new challenge, as you try to devise interesting dishes without ingredients you use daily. In this menu all the dishes can be made ahead of time and reheated when needed.

Chopped Chicken Liver

Chicken Soup with Matzo Balls

Stuffed Veal Breast

Sauté of Two Potatoes

Grated Zucchini

Passover Lemon Chiffon Cake

To keep watercress fresh after buying, stick it head down in water, because it breathes through its leaves. The watercress should stay crisp for one week in the refrigerator.

Chopped Chicken Liver

My friend Mona Kornberg makes wonderful chopped liver. She uses mayonnaise instead of chicken fat or margarine, which results in a light, creamy mixture.

2 lb	chicken livers	1 kg
1/3 cup	vegetable oil	75 mL
2	onions, chopped	2
3	cloves garlic, finely chopped	3
4	hard-boiled eggs, peeled	4
1 tbsp	sherry	15 mL
1 1/2 tsp	salt	7 mL
	Freshly ground pepper to taste	
1/3 cup	mayonnaise	75 mL

1. Cut the chicken livers in half and remove any green spots.

2. Heat the oil in a frying pan on medium heat. Add the onions, garlic and chicken livers and sauté until the chicken livers are cooked through and the onions are golden, about 8 minutes.

3. Place the mixture in a food processor with the hard-boiled eggs and blend until smooth (do not overblend).

4. Place the mixture in a bowl and stir in sherry, salt, pepper and mayonnaise. Taste and adjust the seasonings.

5. To serve, spoon on top of lettuce leaves and garnish with a sprig of parsley.

Serves 12

Chicken Soup with Matzo Balls

Matzo balls are a kind of dumpling traditionally served at Passover with chicken soup. The test of a good Jewish housewife is her ability to create the perfect matzo ball — not the kind that sit like bullets in your stomach for days, but light, airy ones. The secret ingredient in these matzo balls is soda water. The recipe is from my sister-in-law, Florence Geneen. Chicken soup is made in the same manner as chicken stock; use an old hen for maximum flavor.

1 cup	matzo meal	250 mL
1/4 cup	melted shortening or vegetable oil	50 mL
4	eggs	4
1/4 cup	water	50 mL
1/4 cup	soda water	50 mL
1/2 tsp	salt	2 mL
1/4 tsp	freshly ground pepper	1 mL
12 cups	chicken soup, hot*	3 L

1. In a large bowl, mix together all the ingredients except the soup. Let sit for 30 minutes.

2. Bring a large pot of water to a boil. With wet hands, form the matzo mixture into twelve 2-inch (5 cm) balls and drop into the boiling water. Turn the heat to medium-low and simmer for 25 minutes, or until the balls double in size and are cooked through.

3. Ladle the soup into bowls and serve one ball in each bowl.

Serves 12

*See *Lucy Waverman's Cooking School Cookbook*, page 41.

Stuffed Veal Breast

Veal breast is an underrated meat. It is inexpensive, juicy, lean and easy to stuff. It can be made ahead, carved and reheated in the sauce. Veal breast can be bought on or off the bone. (I buy it on the bone, ask the butcher to cut it off and then use the bones for spareribs.) Ask the butcher to cut a pocket for stuffing.

1/2 cup	dry white wine	125 mL
10	dried apricots, chopped	10
10	pitted prunes, chopped	10
2 tbsp	vegetable oil	25 mL
1	small onion, finely chopped	1
1	clove garlic, finely chopped	1
1 tbsp	grated orange rind	15 mL
2 tsp	dried tarragon	10 mL
1/2 cup	matzo meal	125 mL
1	egg	1
1/4 cup	finely chopped parsley	50 mL
1/2 cup	chicken stock or water, approx.	125 mL
	Salt and freshly ground pepper to taste	
4 lb	boneless veal breast	2 kg
1 tsp	dried thyme	5 mL
1 tsp	dried rosemary	5 mL
1	orange	1
6	cloves garlic, peeled	6
1	bay leaf	1
2 cups	chicken or veal stock	500 mL

1. To prepare the stuffing, bring the wine to boil and pour over the apricots and prunes. Soak for 30 minutes. Drain, reserving any soaking liquid.

2. Heat 1 tbsp (15 mL) oil in a frying pan on medium heat. Sauté the onion and chopped garlic until the onion is softened, about 2 minutes. Remove from the heat.

3. In a large bowl, combine the grated orange rind, tarragon, matzo and egg with the onion/garlic mixture, apricots and prunes. Add enough stock to make a moist stuffing. Season well with salt and pepper.

4. Cut a pocket in the veal breast and loosely fill with the stuffing. Sew or skewer the pocket closed.

5. Sprinkle the veal with the thyme, rosemary, salt and pepper.

6. Heat the remaining 1 tbsp (15 mL) oil on medium heat in a large ovenproof casserole. Brown the veal on all sides slowly, about 10 minutes.

7. Preheat the oven to 325°F (160°C).

8. Remove the rind and white pith from the orange. Cut the orange into thin slices. Scatter the whole garlic cloves, bay leaf and orange slices over the veal. Pour over the reserved prune-soaking liquid and 2 cups (500 mL) stock. Cover and bake for 2 hours, or until the veal is tender.

9. Remove the veal from the casserole. Skim any fat from the liquid. Puree the contents of the pan in a food processor or blender until smooth. Return to the pan.

10. Bring the sauce to a boil and boil for 1 minute to combine the flavors. Return the veal to the sauce and reheat when needed.

11. Carve the veal into slices and serve the veal and sauce together.

Serves 12

Traditionally a seder is a multi-course feast including eggs with salt water (to symbolize the Jewish tears on leaving their homes); gefilte fish (a type of kosher quenelle); chopped liver; chicken soup with matzo balls; chicken, veal or beef; and special cakes made without flour or leavening.

Sauté of Two Potatoes

8	baking potatoes, peeled and diced	8
2	sweet potatoes, peeled and diced	2
1/2 cup	olive oil	125 mL
	Salt and freshly ground pepper to taste	
1/4 cup	finely chopped fresh dill	50 mL

1. Bring a pot of water to a boil on high heat. Add the baking potatoes. Boil for 5 minutes. Add the sweet potatoes and boil for a further 5 minutes, or until the potatoes are tender but firm. Drain well.

2. Heat the oil in a large frying pan on medium-high heat. Sauté the potatoes until browned, about 7 to 10 minutes. Season well with salt, pepper and dill.

Serves 12

Grated Zucchini

2 lb	zucchini	1 kg
2 tbsp	olive oil	25 mL
2	cloves garlic, finely chopped	2
2 tsp	dried basil	10 mL
1 tsp	lemon juice	5 mL
	Salt and freshly ground pepper to taste	

1. In a food processor or by hand, grate the zucchini.

2. In a frying pan, heat the oil on high heat. Stir in the garlic and zucchini. Sauté until the zucchini is limp, about 2 minutes. Sprinkle in the basil and lemon juice and season with salt and pepper. Serve immediately.

Serves 12

Passover Lemon Chiffon Cake

Passover jelly rolls are made with cake meal, a finely ground matzo meal. The lemon filling is also good on its own served with Passover macaroons. Potato starch gives a lighter texture than cornstarch. To make this during the rest of the year, you can substitute the more readily available cornstarch for the potato starch.

7	eggs, separated	7
1 1/4 cups	granulated sugar	300 mL
	Grated rind and juice of 3 lemons	
3 tbsp	potato starch	45 mL
2 cups	cold water	500 mL
1	Passover jelly roll	1

1. In a medium bowl or an electric mixer, beat the egg yolks until light in color. Beat in 1 cup (250 mL) sugar until the mixture is light and fluffy. Beat in the lemon rind and juice.

2. Transfer the mixture to a heavy pot. Dissolve the potato starch in 1/2 cup (125 mL) cold water. Stir into the lemon mixture along with the remaining cold water. Cook on medium heat, stirring occasionally, until thick, about 7 minutes.

3. In an electric mixer, whisk the egg whites until they hold their shape. Beat in the remaining 1/4 cup (50 mL) sugar until the mixture is thick and glossy. Stir one large spoonful of the egg whites into the lemon mixture to lighten it. Fold in the remaining whites.

4. Oil a 10-inch (25 cm) springform pan and line the sides with slices of the jelly roll. Pour in the lemon mixture and chill overnight.

Serves 12

5
May

In May the days are warmer and longer, and we can finally plant our summer gardens. The perennial herbs are beginning to poke through, and some of the early spring vegetables — spinach and sorrel — are on the market.

In season
asparagus
chives
fiddleheads
sorrel
spinach

Holidays
Mother's Day
Victoria Day

Menu
Afternoon Tea for Sixteen

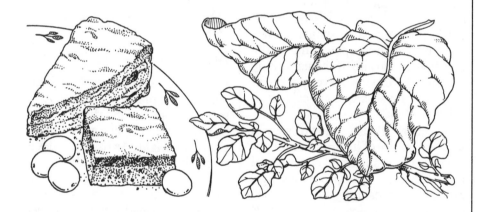

SALMON

Today salmon is a luxury fish that retails at more than twelve dollars a pound, but this was not always the case. In colonial America, salmon was so plentiful and cheap that some servants had clauses in their contracts stipulating that it could only be served a certain number of times a week!

Times have changed, and now salmon is an extravagant item on the grocery list. There are two main reasons for this — pollution and over-fishing. Salmon is basically a saltwater fish that spends most of its time in the sea, but returns to the freshwater rivers in which it was born in order to spawn. Increasing pollution is killing our lakes and rivers, leaving the salmon fewer clean, clear waters in which to breed.

The second problem is overfishing. Salmon tastes best when it starts its journey to the spawning grounds. Gourmets prize the fat, firm flesh, so most salmon is fished at this time. The next best fishing period is when the salmon are in the ocean, where they feed on plankton and crustaceans. At both times the fish are caught before spawning, which means there are fewer salmon each year. To combat this, the government has enforced stricter salmon-fishing laws, and efforts have been made to restock fishing grounds.

In Canada, we are fortunate to have both Pacific and Atlantic salmon to feast on. There are several different species, and each one has a specific flavor and texture.

Pacific Salmon

• The **chinook** salmon spends up to eight years in the ocean before spawning. It is the largest and tastiest of all the Pacific salmon. It swims the farthest upstream to spawn and is the best fighter, earning it the name king salmon. A chinook leaves its birthplace for the seas a few weeks after it is born.

• **Sockeye** is also known as **red** salmon because of its bright-red flesh. Because it has a high oil content and retains its color after processing, it is excellent for canning. It also barbecues and smokes well. Sockeye spend up to two years in fresh water before going to the ocean.

• **Coho** is also known as **silver** salmon because of its silver skin. It has a flabbier texture than sockeye and remains in the freshwater rivers for the first year of its life.

• **Humpback** or **pink** salmon go to sea soon after their birth. The males develop a hump in their backs during the spawning season. The humpback has less taste than the other varieties and is used extensively for canning.

• **Chum** or **dog** salmon is sold smoked. It has pale-pink, coarse flesh.

Atlantic Salmon

Atlantic salmon is less abundant than Pacific salmon, so it is more expensive and more difficult to find. Atlantic salmon is preferred by many gourmets because it has a high fat content, making it very moist when it is cooked or smoked. It has a delicate taste and texture and is similar to trout or Arctic char, but oilier. Our Atlantic salmon is the same fish that is caught in Scotland and Norway. The salmon live in the ocean, but when it is time to spawn, some come to Canadian rivers; others to Scottish or Norwegian ones.

Buying and Cooking

• Look for salmon that has a small head and a plump underbelly. The scales will glisten and the skin should be a silvery color. The eyes should be clear and bright. As fish becomes less fresh the eyes turn cloudy.

• Press the salmon; it should be firm to the touch, not spongy. Salmon should also smell fresh and delicate and not have a fishy odor.

• Store salmon in the refrigerator covered with a tea towel. Do not store it in a plastic bag or cover with plastic wrap. The enclosed moisture will cause the fish to deteriorate much more quickly.

• Fresh salmon should be poached, broiled, baked or barbecued, since these cooking methods best preserve the fish's flavor and texture.

• Special fish poachers are available. They are long oval-shaped containers with a rack inside for the fish to sit on and a tight cover to contain the

If you want to remove the skin from salmon, it is easier to do when the fish is warm.

steam. They usually have to be stretched over two burners. A covered roasting pan with a rack inside makes a good substitute.

• Before cooking a whole salmon, wash the fish and scrape the skin with the back of a knife to remove any scales.

• Poaching liquid for salmon may be a flavored liquid (court bouillon), fish stock or water.

• For poaching whole fish, leave the bones in and the head and tail on. This will help the salmon to retain its juices and flavor. It is easy to remove the bones once the fish is cooked.

• Wrapping the fish in cheesecloth helps to keep it from breaking apart when it is lifted out of the poacher.

• Place the salmon in the fish poacher in the cold court bouillon or other poaching liquid, making sure the poaching liquid covers the salmon. On high heat, bring the liquid to a boil, turn the heat to low, cover and poach for 10 minutes per inch (2.5 cm), once the liquid is barely shivering. Placing the salmon in cold liquid rather than boiling liquid prevents the outside from being cooked before the inside is ready. Serve at once or allow to cool in the broth. Skin the top layer before serving.

• Salmon can be oven-poached, wrapped in a double thickness of foil after being sprinkled with wine and herbs. Fold up the foil and bake at 450°F (230°C) for 10 minutes per inch (2.5 cm).

• When poaching salmon steaks, the steaks are first "seared" in boiling liquid to seal in the juices; then the heat is turned down and they continue to poach, uncovered, in simmering liquid.

Court Bouillon

A court bouillon is a flavored liquid used for poaching fish. It is seasoned with herbs and spices, acidulated with wine, vinegar or lemon, and flavored with vegetables. This liquid will add flavor to the fish.

Use this for salmon or other large fish. After using, court bouillon can be strained and frozen for up to six months. Add water to top it up.

12 cups	water	3 L
1 cup	dry white wine	250 mL
1/2 cup	white wine vinegar	125 mL
2	onions, sliced	2
2	carrots, sliced	2
2	bay leaves	2
6	stalks parsley	6
1 tsp	dried thyme	5 mL
1 tbsp	whole peppercorns	15 mL

1. In a large pot on high heat, bring all the ingredients to a boil. Simmer for 20 minutes.

Makes about 12 cups (3 L)

Canadian Cooking Method
The following method for cooking whole fish or fish steaks is known as the Canadian Cooking Method because it was first promoted by the Canadian Fisheries Department and then by American food writer, James Beard. Measure the fish at its thickest vertical point, usually in front of the dorsal fin. Bake at 450°F (230°C) for 10 minutes per inch (2.5 cm). The fish should be cooked perfectly. The same method also works for poaching fish.

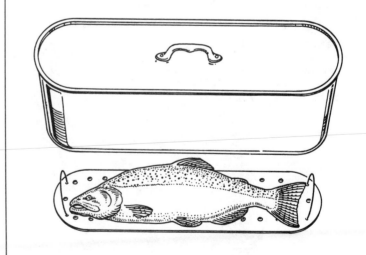

Poached Salmon

This is one of the most delightful ways to eat salmon, especially in the spring. It feeds a large group of people and is perfect for festive lunches or buffet dinners.

12 cups	court bouillon, approx.	3 L
1	5-lb (2.5 kg) salmon, head and tail on	1

1. Place the court bouillon in a fish poacher or roasting pan. Wrap the fish in cheesecloth and add to the pan. Cover and bring to a boil on a high heat.

2. As soon as the liquid boils, turn the heat to low and poach the fish for 10 minutes per inch (2.5 cm).

3. If serving hot, remove the fish from the poacher, unwrap the fish and place it on a serving platter. Remove the top layer of skin and serve immediately. If serving cold, let the fish cool in the broth for maximum flavor and juiciness.

Serves 12 to 16

To serve whole poached salmon hot, unwrap the cheesecloth and place the fish on a serving platter. Strip off the top layer of the skin. Serve from the skinned side first and lift the salmon off the bone, which can then be pulled out easily; continue to serve the second side.

To serve a poached salmon cold, cool the fish in the broth. Remove when cold, set on a board and remove the top skin. With a sharp knife, starting at the head end, cut between the flesh and the bone. Gently ease the flesh off and onto a platter. Pull up the bones and discard. Turn the second side over and lay on top of the first side. Remove the skin. The salmon is now boned and ready for serving. Decorate with overlapping cucumber slices to represent scales.

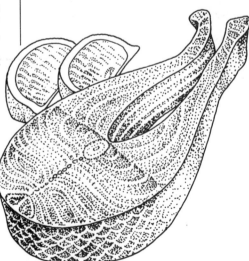

Oven-poached Salmon

Using this method, you can poach two salmons at the same time, which is helpful if you are having a large party.

1	5-lb (2.5 kg) salmon, head and tail on	1
¼ cup	butter or vegetable oil	50 mL
1	lemon, thinly sliced	1
⅓ cup	dry white wine	75 mL
¼ cup	dill sprigs or other fresh herbs	50 mL
	Salt and freshly ground pepper to taste	

1. Preheat the oven to 450°F (230°C).

2. Wash the salmon. Butter a large sheet of aluminum foil large enough to enclose the salmon and lay the fish on it. Place the lemon slices in the cavity and pour over the white wine. Sprinkle with the herbs, salt and pepper.

3. Double wrap the foil around the salmon, making sure there are no holes.

4. Bake for 10 minutes per inch (2.5 cm). Remove from the oven to a serving platter.

5. Unwrap the foil, sliding the salmon onto the platter. Remove the top skin, then slice down to the bone. Turn the fish over when the first side is finished.

6. Serve with Hollandaise sauce (see page 53), dill sauce or lemon butter.

Serves 12 to 16

Poached Salmon Steaks

2 cups	court bouillon	500 mL
6	salmon steaks, 1 inch (2.5 cm) thick	6

1. Half fill a large frying pan with court bouillon. Bring to a boil.

2. Plunge in the salmon steaks, lower the heat to a gentle simmer, cover and poach for 10 minutes, or until white juices rise up. Remove from the poaching liquid.

3. Serve with Hollandaise sauce (see page 53) or lemon butter.

Serves 6

Broiled Salmon

If you are broiling salmon fillets, broil them skin side up for 2 minutes; turn the fish over, then broil skin side down for 4 minutes, or until the white juices rise up. Broiling the fish skin side down for a longer time should prevent the fish from breaking apart.

¼ cup	olive oil	50 mL
2 tsp	dried tarragon, basil or fennel	10 mL
6	salmon steaks	6

1. Preheat the broiler. In a small bowl, combine the olive oil and herbs. Place the salmon steaks on a baking sheet and pour the oil mixture over them.

2. Grill the steaks about 4 inches (10 cm) from the heat for about 4 minutes per side, or until the white juices rise up.

Serves 6

Salmon Linguine

Serve as a first course or as a main course with a green salad. This dish is rich but worth every bite. If you have some leftover salmon, add it to the sauce at the last minute.

8 oz	filleted fresh salmon or gravlax	250 g
¼ cup	dry white wine	50 mL
½ cup	butter	125 mL
1 cup	whipping cream	250 mL
½ tsp	fennel seeds	2 mL
2 tbsp	chopped fresh chives or green onion tops	25 mL
	Salt and freshly ground pepper to taste	
1 lb	fresh linguine	500 g
¼ cup	grated Parmesan cheese	50 mL

1. Cut the salmon into thin slices and reserve.

2. In a pot on high heat, boil the wine until 1 tbsp (15 mL) remains.

3. Add the butter, turn the heat to medium, and stir until melted. Add the whipping cream, fennel seeds and chives. Bring to a boil, add the salmon and simmer for 2 minutes, or until the salmon is cooked through. Season with salt and pepper.

4. Meanwhile, bring a large pot of salted water to a boil on high heat. Add the linguine and cook until just tender, about 3 minutes. Drain well.

5. Stir the Parmesan into the salmon sauce and pour over the linguine.

Serves 4

To glaze a whole poached salmon, boil down 3 cups (750 mL) court bouillon to 2 cups (500 mL). Stir together 1 tbsp (15 mL) gelatin with ¼ cup (50 mL) hot bouillon. When it is liquid, stir into the remaining hot court bouillon, bring to a boil, stirring, then cool. Brush the glaze on the cold salmon when the liquid becomes syrupy, to give the fish a nice, glossy finish.

If you are planning to serve a whole poached salmon cold, cook it for ten minutes less than the suggested cooking time and let the fish cool in the foil or liquid.

Salmon with Orange Pepper Salsa

Although frying salmon steaks is not my favorite way of serving them (I find the texture is not as good), try this method with frozen salmon steaks which may have lost some flavor and texture in the freezing process.

1	large orange, peeled	1
1/2 tsp	freshly ground pepper	2 mL
4	salmon steaks, defrosted, about 1 inch (2.5 cm) thick	4
1/4 cup	butter	50 mL
1	small onion, chopped	1
1 cup	diced green pepper	250 mL
1/4 cup	orange juice	50 mL
1/2 cup	whipping cream	125 mL
1 tsp	dried basil	5 mL
2 tbsp	finely chopped parsley	25 mL
	Salt to taste	

1. Remove all the white pith from the orange and slice the orange in rounds. Cut each round in four.

2. Sprinkle the pepper over the steaks. Melt the butter in a large frying pan on medium-high heat. Add the steaks and sauté for about 4 minutes per side, or until white juices start to rise. Remove from the pan and keep warm.

3. Add the onions and peppers to the frying pan and sauté until softened, about 2 minutes. Pour in the orange juice and reduce by half. Pour in the whipping cream and any juices from the salmon. Bring to a boil and reduce until slightly thickened.

4. Add the basil, parsley, orange segments and salt. Simmer together until heated through. Serve over the steaks.

Serves 4

Salmon Scallops with Ginger Lime Butter

Salmon scallops are thin slices of salmon cut on the diagonal from a salmon fillet. Because the scallops are thin, they do not need turning when broiled. If scallops are unavailable, use salmon steaks and broil for 4 to 5 minutes on each side. Serve with spiced spinach (see page 82) and rice.

1/4 cup	butter	50 mL
1 tsp	finely chopped fresh ginger	5 mL
	Grated rind and juice of 1/2 lime	
1 1/2 lb	salmon fillet	750 mL
1 tbsp	olive oil	15 mL
	Freshly ground pepper and salt to taste	

1. In a food processor or by hand, cream the butter, ginger, lime rind and juice. Wrap in a cylinder shape and refrigerate until needed.

2. With a sharp knife angled almost parallel to the skin, slice the salmon into slices 1/2 inch (1.25 cm) thick starting at the tail end.

3. Line a baking sheet with parchment paper or foil. Place the salmon on top. Brush with the oil and season with pepper.

4. Preheat the broiler. Broil the salmon 6 inches (15 cm) from the heat for 3 minutes, or until white juices dot the surface.

5. Sprinkle with the salt. Slice the butter into four rounds and place on top of the salmon or, if the butter is still soft, place about 1 tbsp (15 mL) on top of each scallop.

Serves 4

Gravlax with Mustard Sauce

Gravlax is salmon that has been "cooked" in a marinade for three days. Originally a Scandinavian dish, it is a good substitute for smoked salmon and costs less when you make it yourself. Its subtle, sensuous taste is perfect for appetizers and hors d'oeuvres as well as an excellent first course served with mustard sauce. Use a mixture of black and white peppercorns if available. Once the herbs are scraped off the salmon, it should keep in the marinade, refrigerated, for 10 days.

1	5-lb (2.5 kg) salmon	1
2 tbsp	coarsely crushed peppercorns	25 mL
1 tbsp	coarsely crushed coriander seeds	15 mL
1	large bunch fresh dill, chopped	1
1 tsp	dry mustard	5 mL
3 tbsp	coarse salt	45 mL
¼ cup	granulated sugar	50 mL
¼ cup	brandy	50 mL
¼ cup	dry white wine	50 mL

1. Have the salmon filleted by the fishmonger; discard the head and tail but leave the skin on.

2. In a small bowl, combine the peppercorns, coriander seeds, dill, mustard, salt and sugar. Press evenly onto the flesh side of the salmon fillets.

3. Combine the brandy and wine and pour into a dish large enough to hold the salmon. Immerse one salmon fillet skin side down. Place the second side on top so that the flesh sides meet.

4. Cover with plastic wrap, place a tray on top of the fillets, then weight down with three tin cans or other heavy weights.

5. Refrigerate for 3 to 4 days, turning every 12 hours.

6. To serve, remove from the marinade and scrape away the dill and seasonings. Slice thinly and serve with the mustard sauce.

Serves 24 to 30 as an appetizer

Mustard Sauce

If you want a sauce with less bite to it, beat in ¼ cup (50 mL) whipping cream. This recipe will make enough to accompany eight servings of gravlax.

⅓ cup	Dijon mustard	75 mL
¼ tsp	Tabasco	1 mL
3 tbsp	granulated sugar	45 mL
2 tbsp	white vinegar	25 mL
⅓ cup	vegetable oil	75 mL
3 tbsp	finely chopped fresh dill	45 mL

1. In a small bowl, mix together the mustard, Tabasco, sugar and vinegar to form a paste.

2. With a wire whisk, slowly beat in the oil until a mayonnaise-like mixture is formed. Stir in the dill.

3. Refrigerate until needed. The sauce should keep for one month in the refrigerator.

Makes about 1 cup (250 mL)

Dill Sauce
To make a dill sauce for cold salmon, mix together ¼ cup (50 mL) mayonnaise, ¼ cup (50 mL) sour cream, 1 tbsp (15 mL) lemon juice, 2 tbsp (25 mL) finely chopped fresh dill and ½ cup (125 mL) finely chopped cucumber.

Salmon Cheesecake

A savory cheesecake with a cracker crust. Although it looks spectacular baked in a springform pan and cut like a cheesecake, you can also bake it in a 13 × 9-inch (3.5 L) baking dish and cut it into squares. If you bake the cheesecake in the rectangular pan, reduce the baking time by 15 minutes. Use cheese crackers or plain crackers for the crust. The cheesecake can be made with fresh salmon, smoked salmon or gravlax.

Sorrel is a perennial herb that grows like a weed. It has a distinct lemony taste and is exceptionally good with fatty foods. Like spinach, the fresh leaves look like a large quantity in a pot but reduce down to practically nothing when cooked. Spoonfuls of cooked, pureed sorrel are often added to sauces for fish, sweetbreads and even goose to enhance the flavor and give the dish color. Sorrel, potatoes and leeks combined with chicken stock and cream make a wonderful soup.

Crust:

¹/₂ cup	melted butter	125 mL
1¹/₂ cups	crushed crackers	375 mL
2 tsp	Dijon mustard	10 mL
1 tbsp	finely chopped fresh dill	15 mL

Filling:

¹/₄ cup	butter	50 mL
1	onion, chopped	1
2 lb	cream cheese	1 kg
4	eggs	4
¹/₂ cup	light cream	125 mL
8 oz	smoked salmon, finely chopped	250 g
2 tbsp	finely chopped fresh dill	25 mL

1. Preheat the oven to 325°F (160°C). Grease a 10-inch (25 cm) springform pan with 1 tbsp (15 mL) melted butter.

2. To make the crust, in a bowl, combine the remaining melted butter, cracker crumbs, Dijon mustard and 1 tbsp (15 mL) dill. Mix well and spread in the bottom of the prepared pan. Pat down gently. Chill.

3. To make the filling, heat ¹/₄ cup (50 mL) butter in a small frying pan on medium-high heat. Sauté the onion until softened but not brown, about 2 minutes. Reserve.

4. Beat the cream cheese in a food processor or mixer until smooth. Blend in the eggs and cream and continue beating until smooth. Add the onion, salmon and 2 tbsp (25 mL) dill and mix just until blended.

5. Pour the filling into the prepared pan. Bake for 1 hour and 15 minutes, or until the cheesecake is firm to the touch.

6. Turn the oven off and leave the cheesecake in the oven for another hour with the door ajar. Remove from the oven and cool to room temperature. Cut into wedges and serve with a cucumber salad as a first course, or cut in squares for an hors d'oeuvre.

Serves 12 as appetizer; 15 as an hors d'oeuvre

Salmon Tartare

Salmon tartare is raw salmon that is "cooked" in lemon juice like a Mexican seviche. It is chopped and served like beef tartare. Serve as an appetizer on crackers or melba toast, or as a first course garnished with sliced smoked salmon.

8 oz	boned salmon	250 g
2	shallots or green onions, finely chopped	2
2 tbsp	capers, chopped	25 mL
	Juice of 1 lemon	
1 tsp	white vinegar	5 mL
2 tbsp	chopped fresh dill	25 mL
1 tbsp	olive oil	15 mL
	Salt and freshly ground pepper to taste	

1. Chop the salmon finely. Mix with the shallots and capers.

2. Stir in the lemon juice, vinegar, dill, olive oil, salt and pepper. Cover and marinate for 2 hours or overnight.

Serves 4

SPINACH

Spinach likes cool growing conditions and is at its best in the spring. Its dark-green leaves have an abundance of nutrients including iron, vitamin A and folic acid. Unfortunately its reputation has suffered from parents forcing their children to eat over-cooked and watery spinach to make them strong and healthy. And it's a shame, because when cooked properly, spinach has a luxurious taste and silky texture.

There are two types of spinach — smooth-leafed, and crinkly or curly-leafed. Most of the cello-packaged spinach is crinkly-leafed.

Buying and Cooking

• Buy crisp-looking bunches with dark-green leaves. Avoid any yellowing or limp bunches. If buying cello-packed spinach, make sure there is no sign of dampness. It can turn the whole package slimy in no time.
• Cello-packed spinach is spinach packed in plastic to ensure freshness. It is usually washed before being packaged, and the stems are trimmed, which makes it easy to use.
• Store spinach in the refrigerator in a covered bowl or plastic bag for up to three days for maximum freshness.
• Spinach can conceal grit and dirt in its leaves and, if not properly washed, can turn anyone into a spinach-hater. To clean spinach, remove the stems and discard. Rinse the leaves in warm water to remove any grit. If the spinach is very gritty, fill a sink with warm water and let the spinach soak in it for a few minutes. Shake the leaves and rinse in cold water before cooking.

• To cook spinach, place in a pot with the water that clings to its leaves after washing. Cover the pot and steam the spinach on medium heat for 5 to 7 minutes, or until it has collapsed.
• Rinse the spinach with cold water, cool for a few minutes until cool enough to handle, then squeeze all the excess water out of the leaves. (When you think you have squeezed out all the moisture, squeeze again to make sure.)
• One pound (500 g) raw spinach makes approximately 1 cup (250 mL) when cooked.

Creamed Spinach

When you feel the need to splurge, try spinach simmered in whipping cream. It is decadent. For a less rich dish, stir in ½ cup (125 mL) sour cream instead of whipping cream, but do not bring to a boil.

2	bunches spinach	2
1 tbsp	butter	15 mL
1 cup	whipping cream	250 mL
	Salt and freshly ground pepper to taste	
pinch	ground nutmeg	pinch

1. Wash the spinach, place in a large pot on medium heat, cover and steam for 5 to 7 minutes, or until limp. Rinse with cold water, then squeeze dry.

2. Heat the butter in a frying pan on medium-high heat. Add the spinach and sauté until heated through. Pour in the whipping cream and boil until the spinach absorbs the cream, about 6 to 8 minutes. Season with salt, pepper and nutmeg.

Serves 4

Florentine in a recipe title means spinach is included in the dish. In Indian cooking, the word "sag" denotes spinach in the dish. The Greeks use spinach in their classic triangle, spanakopita. In Provence in the southwest of France, spinach is used in a dessert tart with raisins and sugar.

New Zealand spinach, which is beginning to come on the market in Canada, is not really spinach but a cousin, with thick leaves and a stronger flavor. It is cooked in the same manner as spinach.

¹/₂ cup (125 mL) cooked spinach contains 28 calories and one-fifth the amount of iron an adult needs daily.

Italian Spinach Pie

This pie is similar to a quiche, but with an Italian feeling. Ricotta is an Italian-style cream cheese with a rich, smooth texture. Use cottage cheese, if ricotta is unavailable.

2 cups	cooked spinach	500 mL
1 cup	ricotta cheese	250 mL
2	eggs	2
1/2 cup	sun-dried tomatoes, chopped, optional	125 mL
1/4 cup	shredded fresh basil leaves, or 1 tbsp (15 mL) dried	50 mL
1 tbsp	olive oil	15 mL
	Salt and freshly ground pepper to taste	
1	partially baked 9-inch (23 cm) shortcrust pie shell*	1

1. Preheat the oven to 375°F (190°C).

2. Roughly chop the spinach and mix with the ricotta cheese, eggs, sun-dried tomatoes, basil, olive oil, salt and pepper.

3. Add the mixture to the pie shell and bake in the lower third of the oven for 30 minutes, or until the mixture sets.

Serves 6

There is an old recipe for spinach that calls for 2 lb (1 kg) spinach and 1 lb (500 g) butter. You cook the spinach, and each day you stir in 4 oz (125 g) butter. After four days you eat it!

To ensure a baked bottom pastry crust, place a baking tray in the oven while the oven is preheating. When the oven is hot, place the pie pan on the tray. This will cause the pastry to start to bake on contact with the hot tray.

*See *Lucy Waverman's Cooking School Cookbook*, page 94.

Spiced Spinach

The slightly tangy taste and dark-green color of the spinach enhance salmon steaks or chicken.

1	bunch spinach	1
1 tbsp	butter	15 mL
2	green onions, finely chopped	2
2	cloves garlic, finely chopped	2
1 tsp	Dijon mustard	5 mL
1 tsp	ground cumin	5 mL
pinch	cayenne pepper	pinch
1/4 cup	plain yogurt	50 mL
	Salt and freshly ground pepper to taste	

1. Remove the stems from the spinach and wash in warm water to remove the dirt.

2. Place the spinach in a heavy pot with the water that clings to its leaves. Steam on medium heat until the leaves wilt, about 5 minutes. Drain and rinse with cold water to cool. Squeeze the spinach dry.

3. In a frying pan, heat the butter on medium heat until sizzling. Add the green onions and garlic and sauté until the green onions have softened.

4. Stir in the spinach, mustard, cumin and cayenne. Sauté until the spinach is hot.

5. Stir in the yogurt and cook together on low heat for 5 minutes. Season with salt and pepper.

Serves 4

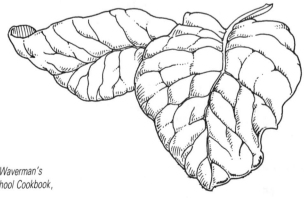

Spinach Avocado Salad

Spinach makes a great salad. This one has oriental overtones and makes an elegant first course for a dinner party. Sesame oil has a pungent flavor, so mix it with other oils when using it in a dressing. The salad and dressing can be tossed in a large bowl instead of being presented as in this recipe.

¹/₂ cup	sliced almonds	125 mL
1	large bunch or 10-oz (284 g) package fresh spinach	1
1	avocado, peeled and quartered	1
8	mushrooms, sliced	8
4	green onions, chopped	4
1 tbsp	soy sauce	15 mL
2 tbsp	vegetable oil	25 mL
¹/₄ cup	lime juice	50 mL
1 tbsp	brown sugar	15 mL
1 tsp	sesame oil	5 mL

1. Preheat the oven to 350°F (180°C). Spread the almonds on a baking sheet and bake for 10 minutes, or until browned.

2. Wash and dry the spinach and trim off the tough stems. Tear into bite-sized pieces. Divide the leaves among four plates. Cut each avocado quarter into four slices and arrange in a pinwheel shape on the spinach bed.

3. Place the mushroom slices over the avocado slices. Sprinkle with the green onions. Scatter the almonds over the salad.

4. In small bowl, whisk together the soy sauce, vegetable oil, lime juice, brown sugar and sesame oil. Pour the dressing over the salad.

Serves 4

Afternoon Tea for Sixteen

Afternoon tea is not the same thing as high tea; high tea is served between five and seven and is really a light supper with salads, sausage rolls and heavier foods. On the other hand, afternoon tea is a custom that is making a big comeback. It's a pleasant, civilized way to entertain, and it isn't centered around alcohol.

The tradition of afternoon tea started in early Victorian times, when the custom was to serve huge breakfasts and extravagant dinners in the homes of the nobles. In between, aristocratic British ladies who were a bit peckish in the afternoon had bread and butter and cakes served with their afternoon tea.

Traditionally, little sandwiches without crusts are served first, followed by scones with jam and cream, then a selection of cakes — usually a plain one and a fancier one — and a few cookies.

Tea itself is as complex and adventurous a subject as wine. If you taste a number of different teas, you will discover that the aroma, color, flavor and aftertaste change from tea to tea as they do from wine to wine.

Cucumber Watercress Sandwiches

Egg Rollups

Smoked Salmon Pinwheels

Scottish Scones

Orange Peel Cake

Brown Sugar Shortbread

Walnut Toffee Shortbread Squares

Down-Home Gingerbread

There are three categories of tea — unfermented, semi-fermented and black. Fermentation is the process of oxidizing the tea leaves so they develop heat and turn a coppery brown color. Unfermented tea is green tea, while semi-fermented teas are oxidized until the leaves are tinged with brown around the edges. Black tea leaves are fully oxidized.

Cucumber Watercress Sandwiches

Use either homemade* or store-bought mayonnaise. English cucumbers are seedless and crisper than regular ones; use them if they are available.

1 cup	mayonnaise	250 mL
¹/₂ cup	watercress leaves	125 mL
1 tbsp	lemon juice	15 mL
16	thin slices white bread	16
1	cucumber, peeled and thinly sliced	1

1. In a food processor or blender, puree the mayonnaise, watercress leaves and lemon juice.

2. Spread the mayonnaise on eight slices of bread. Cover with the cucumber slices. Place the second slice of bread on top. Trim off the crusts and cut each sandwich into four triangles.

Makes 32 triangles

If you want thin slices of bread, freeze the loaf for 30 minutes before slicing. If the bread is still too thick, roll the slices with a rolling pin.

Cut off the crusts after making party sandwiches, for a neater appearance.

Egg Rollups

The traditional egg sandwiches with the green gherkin centers. The carrot adds a pretty color to the eggs. If you combine the ingredients while the eggs are still warm, the mayonnaise is better absorbed. The eggs can be chopped and mixed in the food processor.

1	loaf white or brown bread, sliced horizontally	1
¹/₂ cup	butter, at room temperature	125 mL
12	hard-boiled eggs, grated	12
³/₄ cup	mayonnaise	175 mL
1 tbsp	Dijon mustard	15 mL
¹/₄ cup	finely grated carrot	50 mL
	Salt and freshly ground pepper to taste	
10	sweet gherkins	10

1. Cut the crusts from the bread. Spread each slice with a light coating of soft butter.

2. In a medium bowl, combine the grated egg, mayonnaise, mustard and carrot. Season with salt and pepper. Spread the filling evenly on the bread. Place the gherkins across one long end of the bread. Roll up into cylinders.

3. Wrap each roll tightly in plastic wrap. Refrigerate for at least 8 hours. Slice each roll into six sandwiches.

Makes about 30 sandwiches

*See *Lucy Waverman's Cooking School Cookbook*, page 55.

Smoked Salmon Pinwheels

Always use thinly sliced bread for these sandwiches, and make sure your butter is slightly softened so it will spread more easily. Bakeries will slice bread horizontally for you.

8 oz	cream cheese	250 g
¹/₂ cup	butter, at room temperature	125 mL
¹/₂ cup	finely chopped fresh dill	125 mL
1	loaf white or brown bread, sliced horizontally	1
1 lb	thinly sliced smoked salmon	500 g
	Freshly ground pepper	
¹/₄ cup	capers, optional	50 mL
1	red onion, finely chopped	1

1. In a small bowl, beat together the cream cheese and butter until smooth. Blend in the dill.

2. Trim the crusts from the bread. If necessary, roll with a rolling pin to make the slices thinner.

3. Spread each long slice with the cream cheese mixture.

4. Lay the smoked salmon on top, leaving ³/₄ inch (1.75 cm) clear at one long end of the bread. Sprinkle the salmon with the pepper, capers and onion.

5. Roll the bread up tightly, finishing with the end that is clear of smoked salmon.

6. Repeat with the remaining slices of bread. Wrap each roll tightly in plastic wrap. Chill overnight. Cut into ¹/₂-inch (1.25 cm) slices before serving.

Makes about 30 pinwheels

Scottish Scones

A flaky, moist scone that reheats well. Serve with whipped cream and strawberry jam. The recipe can also be made in a food processor. Combine the butter with the dry ingredients, then add the liquid ingredients through the feed tube.

2 cups	all-purpose flour	500 mL
¹/₂ tsp	salt	2 mL
1 tbsp	baking powder	15 mL
2 tsp	granulated sugar, optional	10 mL
¹/₄ cup	butter	50 mL
³/₄ cup	milk	175 mL
3	eggs	3

1. Preheat the oven to 450°F (230°C). In a bowl, sift together the flour, salt, baking powder and sugar. With a knife, cut the butter into small pieces and add to the flour mixture. With your fingers, rub the butter into the flour mixture.

2. In a separate bowl, combine the milk and 2 eggs.

3. Make a well in the center of the flour mixture and add the milk/egg mixture. With a wooden spoon, stir in the milk and eggs. With your fingertips, gather the dough together in a ball and knead lightly on a floured board. The mixture should be soft and elastic.

4. Pat out by hand or roll out to 1-inch (2.5 cm) thickness. Cut into 2-inch (5 cm) rounds. Place on a floured baking sheet.

5. Beat the remaining egg. Brush on the scones. Bake for 10 to 15 minutes, or until pale gold.

Makes 12 to 16 scones

Party sandwiches are deceptive; people can eat more than you think. Plan on four to six triangles per person. Each triangle, square or circle should be small enough to be devoured in two or three bites.

Party sandwiches can be made the day before, wrapped in a damp tea towels and refrigerated until cut.

Orange Peel Cake

This heavy, moist, English-style cake is at its best after resting for 24 hours. You can substitute chocolate chips for the raisins.

	Rind of 2 oranges	
1 cup	raisins	250 mL
1 cup	granulated sugar	250 mL
¹/₂ cup	unsalted butter	125 mL
2	eggs	2
1 cup	plain yogurt	250 mL
2 cups	all-purpose flour	500 mL
1 tsp	salt	5 mL
1 tsp	baking soda	5 mL
Orange Syrup:		
¹/₂ cup	orange juice	125 mL
¹/₄ cup	granulated sugar	50 mL
1 tbsp	brandy, optional	15 mL

1. Preheat the oven to 325°F (160°C).

2. Grind the orange rind, raisins and 2 tbsp (25 mL) sugar in a food processor until chopped. Reserve.

3. In a large bowl or electric mixer, cream the remaining sugar and butter until light and fluffy. Add the eggs and yogurt and beat together.

4. In a separate bowl, sift together the flour, salt and baking soda and stir into the batter. Mix in the orange rind/raisin mixture.

5. Cut a round of parchment paper or oiled waxed paper to fit the base of a well-greased and floured 10-inch (3 L) springform pan. Pour in the batter.

6. Bake for 1 hour, or until a skewer inserted comes out clean.

7. Remove the sides from the pan and replace the sides again while the cake is still hot. This is to make sure the cake is loosened from the sides so the syrup can drip down.

8. In a small pan, heat the orange juice, ¹/₄ cup (50 mL) sugar and brandy, stirring until the sugar is dissolved.

9. Using the point of a skewer, make holes over the top of the cake. Pour on the syrup. Let sit for 24 hours before removing the sides of the pan.

Makes one 10-inch (25 cm) cake

Brown Sugar Shortbread

2¹/₂ cups	cake and pastry flour, sifted	625 mL
²/₃ cup	packed dark brown sugar	150 mL
1 cup	unsalted butter	250 mL
¹/₄ cup	granulated sugar	50 mL
1 tsp	ground cinnamon	5 mL

1. Preheat the oven to 350°F (180°C).

2. In a large bowl, combine the flour and brown sugar. Cut in ³/₄ cup (175 mL) butter until the mixture resembles coarse crumbs.

3. Melt the remaining butter and work into the flour mixture. Transfer to an unfloured board and knead for just 2 to 3 minutes, until a very soft dough is formed.

4. Cut the dough into two sections and shape each into a 7-inch (17 cm) round. Place on a baking sheet.

5. Bake for 1 hour, until lightly browned. Sprinkle with the granulated sugar and cinnamon.

Makes two 7-inch (17 cm) rounds

How to Make a Good Cup of Tea

Use cold water in the kettle for maximum oxygen. Bring it to a boil and pour a little into the tea pot (I prefer a china tea pot) to warm it. Add 1 tsp (5 mL) tea per person and an extra teaspoon for the pot. If you are using tea bags, use one per two people. Pour in the boiling water and let the pot sit for 5 minutes to brew the tea properly. Remove the tea bags before serving. If you are using loose tea, you need a strainer to pour the tea through.

Serve milk, not cream, with tea and, in the true British manner, the milk goes into the cup first for a better mix.

Walnut Toffee Shortbread Squares

A rich, nutty square, quickly made and consumed. Substitute almonds for walnuts, if desired.

Base:

1 cup	all-purpose flour	250 mL
1/4 cup	firmly packed brown sugar	50 mL
1/2 cup	unsalted butter	125 mL

Topping:

2	eggs	2
3/4 cup	firmly packed brown sugar	175 mL
1/2 tsp	baking powder	2 mL
pinch	salt	pinch
2/3 cup	grated coconut	150 mL
1 cup	chopped walnuts	250 mL
1/2 tsp	vanilla extract	2 mL
2 tsp	ground cinnamon	10 mL

1. Preheat the oven to 350°F (180°C).

2. To make the base, in a bowl, combine the flour and 1/4 cup (50 mL) brown sugar. Cut in the butter until crumbs are formed. Press into a lightly greased 8-inch (2 L) square baking dish.

3. Bake for 15 minutes.

4. To make the topping, in a bowl, combine the remaining ingredients together. Spread on top of the pastry as soon as it comes out of oven. Return to the oven and bake for an additional 20 minutes. Cool in the pan and cut into 1 1/2-inch (3.75 cm) squares.

Makes 24 squares

Down-Home Gingerbread

This gingerbread is moist and tasty, but store it for at least a day before serving. Serve sliced and buttered, if desired.

1/2 cup	unsalted butter	125 mL
1/2 cup	brown sugar	125 mL
1/4 cup	molasses	50 mL
1 1/2 cups	all-purpose flour	375 mL
1 tsp	baking soda	5 mL
1 tbsp	ground ginger	15 mL
2 tsp	ground cinnamon	10 mL
1	egg	1
2/3 cup	milk, scalded	150 mL

1. Preheat the oven to 325°F (160°C).

2. In a small pot on medium heat, melt together the butter, sugar and molasses. Leave to cool.

3. In a bowl, sift together the flour, baking soda, ginger and cinnamon. Stir in the cooled butter mixture, then beat in the egg and milk. Pour the mixture into a greased 9 × 5-inch (2 L) loaf pan.

4. Bake for 1 hour, or until the cake feels springy to the touch. Cool in the pan.

Makes one loaf

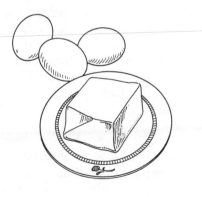

Earl Grey tea is named after Earl Grey, who saved the life of a mandarin in China. He was sent a gift of the delicately scented tea, together with its recipe. Today the tea — a mixture of Chinese and Indian teas — is a popular blend, with a slightly smoky but distinctive taste.

Orange pekoe refers to the size of the tea leaf, not the type of tea.

6
June

June is "busting out all over," with fresh strawberries and the pleasures of the first summer barbecues (and eating outside before the bugs get you!).

In season
asparagus
lettuce
peas
rhubarb
strawberries

Holidays
Father's Day

Menu
Father's Day Barbecue for
Eight

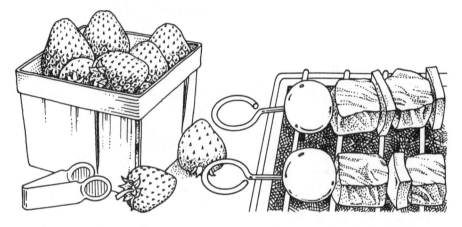

BARBECUING/ GRILLING

Grilling is today's hot cooking technique. Restaurants are featuring everything from grilled garlic to grilled goat cheese, as more and more people discover that grilled food is full of flavor, looks fresh and attractive, and is not masked by rich sauces.

Although the terms barbecuing and grilling are now used interchangeably, technically, grilling means to cook food quickly on high heat, directly over the heat source. Barbecuing is the traditional mid-western method of cooking larger cuts of meat; chicken or ribs are placed on a rack over a drip pan beside the coals, not over them. This method cooks food slowly, at a low temperature. There is no open flame in this kind of barbecuing — just a consistent low temperature of about 225°F (108°C) over a prolonged period of time. The meat is usually finished by being coated with barbecue sauce, and the food remains very moist.

Virtually anything can be cooked on a grill. Try thinking of different foods to barbecue. Don't limit yourself to hamburgers and steaks; think fish, seafood and vegetables.

Gas Barbecues

For many people, a gas barbecue is the choice today, because it is easy to use. But there are still some tips that will take the worry out of using it.
• To check the gas level in the tank, pour boiling water over the tank. Where the tank feels hot, gas has evaporated; where the tank feels cold, gas remains.
• When you have finished barbecuing, turn the barbecue off at the tank so no gas is left in the gas lines, then turn off the taps. This is a safety precaution to prevent gas from escaping and causing an explosion the next time you light the barbecue.
• When lighting the barbecue, turn the gas on at the main tank, then at the tap. Don't lean over the barbecue when lighting.
• To check for gas leaks, mix 2 tbsp (25 mL) dishwashing detergent with 2 tbsp (25 mL) water. Open the valves, wet the fittings and turn on the gas. If bubbles form, gas is leaking. Take the tank in for repair.
• Preheat the grill for 10 minutes before cooking.

Charcoal Barbecues

There are many who believe that using charcoal is the superior way to barbecue. We did a taste test at the cooking school with meat barbecued on both charcoal and gas. Ten percent of the class recognized the charcoal taste; the remainder couldn't tell the difference. If you are part of the ten percent, the rules for lighting charcoal are as stringent as for gas.

• Although briquets last longer than charcoal, they contain artificial fillers and binders. Pure lump charcoal starts more quickly and burns hotter.
• Use an electric fire starter. Starter fluids and cubes can flavor the food.
• If you don't have an electric starter, the fire will burn merrily if you use scrunched-up newspapers and kindling in the base of the barbecue. Set them alight, then add the charcoal.
• Charcoal fires take about 45 minutes to heat properly. Do not begin to barbecue until the coals are white.
• If the barbecue is too hot, push the food to the sides of the grill, where it is cooler. Raising or lowering the grill also affects cooking temperatures. If the barbecue has vents, opening the vents increases the temperature; closing them lowers it.

General Barbecue Tips

• Buy special barbecue equipment. Invest in long wood-handled tongs for turning meat, a long metal spatula for turning fish, a basting brush for brushing sauce on meat, and a plant sprayer for putting out flareups. If you like to barbecue fish, buy a hinged basket to prevent breakage.
• Brush the grill with oil before barbecuing, to prevent meat from sticking.
• Don't pierce barbecued meat with a fork; this will cause the juices to leak out. Use tongs.
• If your barbecue has a lid, close it if you are cooking large or thick pieces of meat. This will turn the barbecue into an oven, raising the temperature so the food will cook more quickly.

Barbecuing dates back to the time of the Spanish explorers, who would use a rack set over a fire (called a *barbacoa*) to smoke and cook meat to preserve it.

To judge the heat of the barbecue coals, hold your hand about 6 inches (15 cm) from the coals. If you can hold your hand there comfortably for 2 seconds, the coals are hot — about 400°F (200°C). If you can hold your hand over the coals for 4 seconds, the heat is medium — about 300°F (150°C). At 6 seconds, the heat is low — about 200°F (90°C).

To prevent food from sticking to the rack, clean the barbecue grill right after using, while the rack is still hot. Use a stiff brush or crumpled aluminum foil.

Most marinades will keep indefinitely in the refrigerator, so make a large quantity and have it on hand. Use ¹/₂ cup (125 mL) marinade for each pound (500 g) of meat.

- To prevent flareups, trim meat of any excess fat and keep the coals and the grill clean.
- Douse flareups with a spray bottle of water.
- Sugar caramelizes on the grill, so do not use it in marinades. Instead, brush sugar- or tomato-based glazes on the meat during the last 10 minutes of barbecuing.
- Barbecued steaks and chops should be 1¹/₂ inches (3.75 cm) thick for the best flavor and texture.
- If you prefer to leave the fat on meat, slash through it before barbecuing, to prevent the meat from curling.
- Use high heat unless otherwise specified; with a charcoal barbecue, this means cooking food directly over the hottest part of the coals.
- Turn steaks or chops when small bubbles appear on the top.
- Let roasts and whole chickens rest for 10 minutes before carving to let the juices retract.

Barbecuing Chicken and Fish

Chicken and fish are the two most difficult foods to barbecue. Chicken skin scorches, and often the inside flesh is raw while the outside is singed. Fish, on the other hand, falls apart easily, leaving flakes on the grill or on the coals.

- If you are cooking chicken with the skin on, grill on medium heat. This will prevent the worst flareups and should help to cook the flesh evenly.
- Whole chickens should be cut through on either side of the backbone. Remove the backbone and flatten out the bird; it will grill more evenly and quickly when spread-eagled.

- When using boneless, skinless chicken breasts, flatten them slightly with a mallet so they are all the same thickness. Because they have no skin and no fat, grill them on high heat and oil well to prevent sticking.
- To check for doneness, press the thickest part of the flesh; it should feel firm.
- Fish steaks, such as tuna, swordfish or salmon, should be about 1 inch (2.5 cm) thick.
- When barbecuing fish fillets with the skin on, first grill flesh side down for 2 to 3 minutes, then place skin side down for the remaining cooking time. This prevents breakage and makes the fish much easier to remove from the barbecue.
- Always grill fish over high heat, otherwise it will become mushy and wet and will be more likely to fall apart.
- Cook whole large fish in a hinged grill, to make them easier to turn.

Marinades

Marinate all cuts of meat, poultry and fish for extra flavor and tenderness. Marinate meat at room temperature unless a marinating period of more than four hours is called for, because refrigeration retards marination. If meat is marinated in the refrigerator, remove it one hour before needed to allow it to come to room temperature. Room temperature meat cooks more evenly.

Use a stainless-steel or china bowl for marinating. Other metals can impart a taste to the meat.

- Marinades consist of an acid and oil. The acid cuts through the meat fibers to tenderize them, while the oil prevents sticking.

- Use acids such as vinegar, lemon juice, wine, fruit juice or yogurt.
- Use vegetable, olive, sesame or peanut oil.
- Add herbs, spices, mustards and seasoning sauces to the marinade for extra flavor.
- Never reuse a marinade; the juices from the raw meat will taint the marinade mixture.

Barbecue Sauces

Barbecue sauces are usually brushed on steaks, chicken wings or spareribs during the last 15 to 20 minutes of cooking time, to add zest and spiciness. They can also be served as a dip with the barbecued meat.

Multi-purpose Marinade

This marinade is good for almost everything that goes on the grill. Use tarragon, thyme, basil or your favorite herb combination. Add mustard, soy sauce and Tabasco for more flavor.

³/₄ cup	vegetable or olive oil	175 mL
¹/₄ cup	wine vinegar or lemon juice	50 mL
2	cloves garlic, finely chopped	2
3 tbsp	chopped fresh herbs, or 1 tbsp (15 mL) dried	45 mL
	Freshly ground pepper	

1. In a medium bowl, whisk together all the ingredients. Refrigerate.

Makes 1 cup (250 mL)

Italian-style Marinade

This marinade is suitable for veal, beef and sausages.

¹/₂ cup	olive oil	125 mL
¹/₄ cup	dry red wine or red wine vinegar	50 mL
1 tbsp	dried oregano	15 mL
1 tbsp	dried basil	15 mL
1	clove garlic, finely chopped	1
1	bay leaf	1

1. In a small bowl, mix everything together.

Makes ³/₄ cup (175 mL)

Chinese-style Marinade

Use this marinade on fish, boneless chicken breasts and pork tenderloin.

2 tbsp	soy sauce	25 mL
1	clove garlic, finely chopped	1
1 tsp	finely chopped ginger	5 mL
¹/₄ cup	vegetable oil	50 mL
1 tsp	sesame oil	5 mL
1 tbsp	lemon juice	15 mL

1. In a small bowl, whisk together all the ingredients.

Makes ¹/₂ cup (125 mL)

Don't use acids in fish marinades unless the fish is thick or oily, like mackerel or kingfish. The acid will start to "cook" a finer-grained specimen.

Indonesian-style Marinade

Use this on shrimp, beef, chicken and pork.

1	onion, chopped	1
1	clove garlic, finely chopped	1
1/2 tsp	curry powder	2 mL
1/2 tsp	ground coriander	2 mL
1/2 tsp	ground turmeric	2 mL
1/2 tsp	chili powder	2 mL
	Juice of 1 lime	
1/4 cup	peanut butter	50 mL
1/4 cup	vegetable oil	50 mL
1/4 cup	water	50 mL

1. In a medium bowl, mix all the ingredients together.

Makes about 1 cup (250 mL)

Best Barbecue Sauce

This is the ultimate barbecue sauce. My family has been using it for years, but each year I adapt it slightly to make it even better. This is the current version. Increase the chilies for a hot sauce. The sauce keeps indefinitely in the refrigerator.

2 cups	pureed tomatoes	500 mL
1	small onion, finely chopped	1
4	cloves garlic, finely chopped	4
1/4 cup	cider vinegar	50 mL
1/4 cup	dry red wine	50 mL
2 tbsp	Worcestershire sauce	25 mL
1/4 cup	brown sugar	50 mL
2 tbsp	chili powder	25 mL
1 tsp	ground cumin	5 mL
1 tsp	ground coriander	5 mL
2 tsp	dry mustard	10 mL
1	dried whole chili	1

1. In a large pot, bring all the ingredients to a boil. Simmer for 30 minutes, or until thickened.

Makes 2 cups (500 mL)

Grilled Salad

Serve this salad straight off the grill or cold. If you do not have balsamic vinegar, use wine vinegar. Radicchio is the red, slightly bitter Italian lettuce. Because it has lots of texture, it grills well. When you cut the vegetables, leave the roots attached to prevent them falling apart on the grill.

1/2 cup	olive oil	125 mL
1 tsp	dried thyme	5 mL
1 tsp	paprika	5 mL
2	heads radicchio, quartered	2
4	Belgian endive, halved	4
8	green onions	8
4	small zucchini, quartered	4
Dressing:		
1/2 cup	olive oil	125 mL
2 tbsp	balsamic vinegar	25 mL
	Salt and freshly ground pepper to taste	

1. In a small bowl, combine the olive oil, thyme and paprika.

2. Brush the vegetables with seasoned oil.

3. On high heat, grill the vegetables, brushing them occasionally with more seasoned oil. Turn the vegetables once. The vegetables are cooked when they have grill marks and start to become limp.

4. To make the dressing, in a small bowl, whisk the oil and vinegar together. Season with salt and pepper. Pour over the vegetables just before serving.

Serves 8

Spicy Beer Barbecue Sauce
This sauce is excellent with beef, lamb, hamburgers or sausages. It keeps in the refrigerator indefinitely, and is a good way to use leftover flat beer.

Combine 1/3 cup (75 mL) chili sauce or spicy barbecue sauce with 1/4 cup (50 mL) beer, 2 tsp (10 mL) horseradish, 1/2 tsp (2 mL) granulated sugar and 1 tsp (5 mL) Dijon mustard. Blend well and refrigerate until needed. Makes 3/4 cup (175 mL).

Sweet and Sour Glaze
Glazes will produce a crisp outer coating on vegetables, chicken wings and spareribs. Glazes have a high sugar content, which means they are lightly brushed on during the final 5 minutes of cooking. Longer cooking will cause the sugar to burn.

For a quick glaze, in a medium bowl, combine 1/4 cup (50 mL) vinegar, 1/4 cup (50 mL) granulated sugar, 1/4 cup (50 mL) ketchup and 1 tsp (5 mL) soy sauce. Makes 3/4 cup (175 mL).

Chili New Potatoes

Choose potatoes of equal size for even cooking. Serve with spareribs or hamburgers.

¹/₄ cup	vegetable oil	50 mL
2 tsp	chili powder	10 mL
2 lb	mini new potatoes	1 kg
	Salt and freshly ground pepper to taste	

1. Combine the oil and chili powder. Roll the potatoes in the chili mixture and season with salt and pepper. Wrap in a double thickness of foil.

2. Grill on high heat for 20 minutes, or until the potatoes are tender. Turn the package twice during cooking.

Serves 6

Grilled Halibut

Barbecued halibut has lots of flavor and texture; but any firm-fleshed fish such as grouper, swordfish or tuna can be substituted.

	Freshly ground black pepper	
¹/₄ cup	olive oil	50 mL
2 tbsp	finely chopped fresh rosemary, or 2 tsp (10 mL) dried	25 mL
4	6-oz (180 g) halibut steaks or fillets	4

1. In a medium bowl, mix together the pepper, olive oil and rosemary. Pour over the fish and marinate for 1 hour.

2. Grill the steaks on high heat for 4 minutes on each side. The fish is done when little white bubbles appear on the flesh.

Serves 4

Caribbean Grilled Chicken

Serve with steamed rice and a salad for a quick summer meal. Use chicken legs with the thighs attached.

2 tbsp	dark rum	25 mL
1 tbsp	soy sauce	15 mL
2	cloves garlic, finely chopped	2
	Grated rind and juice of 2 limes	
1 tsp	brown sugar	5 mL
¹/₄ cup	vegetable oil	50 mL
¹/₄ tsp	cayenne pepper	1 mL
	Salt and freshly ground pepper to taste	
6	chicken legs, thighs attached	6

1. In a bowl, combine the rum, soy sauce, garlic, lime rind and juice, sugar, oil, cayenne, salt and pepper.

2. Place the chicken legs in a large dish and pour over the marinade. Marinate for 2 hours, turning occasionally.

3. Grill the chicken on medium heat for 10 minutes per side, basting occasionally with the marinade, until the juices run clear.

Serves 6

Swordfish with Basil Chili Sabayon

Swordfish is a firm, oily fish with a taste similar to chicken. It needs to be basted frequently to prevent it from drying out. Because the steaks vary in size, you may only need three to serve six.

2 tbsp	finely chopped fresh basil, or 2 tsp (5 mL) dried	25 mL
1	dried red chili pepper, chopped	1
2 tbsp	dry white wine	25 mL
1 tbsp	white wine vinegar	15 mL
4	egg yolks	4
2 cups	hot chicken or fish stock	500 mL
2 tbsp	butter	25 mL
	Salt, freshly ground pepper and lemon juice to taste	
6	swordfish steaks, 1 inch (2.5 cm) thick	6
1/2 cup	melted butter or olive oil	125 mL

1. In a pot, heat the basil, chili pepper, wine and vinegar on high heat. Reduce until no liquid remains, but the basil is still moist. Cool.

2. On low heat, beat in the egg yolks. Whisk until the yolks begin to thicken. Whisk in the stock and cook until the sauce thickens slightly.

3. Beat in the butter. Add salt, pepper and a little lemon juice if needed.

4. Salt and pepper the steaks, then dip them in the melted butter.

5. Grill the steaks on high heat for 5 minutes on each side, or until white juices start to appear. Brush frequently with more butter. Serve with the sauce.

Serves 6

Seafood Satays

These satays are spicy, succulent and superb. The sauce (which can be made ahead of time and reheated) will keep well for one week in the refrigerator. If Chinese chili paste is unavailable, use any hot Mexican or Caribbean chili sauce. Use regular milk if you cannot find coconut milk. You can also serve this sauce on top of hamburgers made with lean ground pork.

1 tbsp	finely chopped fresh ginger	15 mL
2	cloves garlic, finely chopped	2
1/4 cup	vegetable oil	50 mL
1 tsp	Chinese chili paste	5 mL
2 tbsp	finely chopped green onion	25 mL
	Grated rind and juice of 1 lime	
12 oz	scallops	375 g
12 oz	shelled shrimp	375 g
Peanut Coconut Sauce:		
1 tbsp	vegetable oil	15 mL
1	small onion, diced	1
1	clove garlic, finely chopped	1
1 tsp	Chinese chili paste	5 mL
1 tsp	finely chopped fresh ginger	5 mL
1 cup	crunchy or smooth peanut butter	250 mL
1 tbsp	soy sauce	15 mL
2 tbsp	lime juice	25 mL
1/2 cup	coconut milk or milk	125 mL
1 tsp	sesame oil	5 mL

1. In a small bowl, mix together the ginger, garlic, oil, chili paste, green onion, lime rind and juice. Pour over the scallops and shrimp. Marinate for 4 hours at room temperature, or overnight in the refrigerator.

2. Soak the bamboo skewers for 30 minutes. Thread the shrimp and scal-

Grilled Green Onions

Serve these on top of hamburgers or with chicken breasts. Discard the top 2 inches (5 cm) of green from twelve clean green onions. Brush the onions with about 2 tbsp (25 mL) vegetable or olive oil. Grill, turning occasionally, for about 5 minutes, or until the onions are browned. Serves 6.

Bamboo skewers should be soaked in water for 30 minutes to prevent them from burning on the barbecue.

Grilled Mushrooms

Serve these with hamburgers or steak. Cut the stems off 16 large mushrooms, so the mushrooms will sit flat on the barbecue. In a medium bowl, combine 1/2 cup (125 mL) olive oil, 1 finely chopped clove garlic, 1 tsp (5 mL) dried thyme, and salt and pepper to taste. Grill the mushrooms, turning them occasionally and brushing with the seasoned oil. Cook for about 5 minutes, or until the mushroom juices come to the surface. Serves 4.

lops alternately on the skewers. Grill on high heat for 3 to 4 minutes, turning twice during the cooking time.

3. To make the sauce, heat the oil in a frying pan. Sauté the onion, garlic and chili paste until softened. Add the ginger, peanut butter, soy sauce and lime juice. Stir over medium heat for about 1 minute. Slowly mix in the coconut milk and sesame oil, stirring until the sauce is evenly mixed. Brush onto the satays before removing from the grill. Serve the remaining sauce separately.

Serves 8

Zippy Chicken

Try this chicken in chicken salad recipes or on a croissant with chutney.

4	whole chicken breasts, boned and skinned	4
1/2 cup	plain yogurt	125 mL
1/2 tsp	curry powder	2 mL
1/4 tsp	salt	1 mL
1/4 tsp	freshly ground pepper	1 mL

1. Place the chicken breasts between two pieces of waxed paper and flatten with a mallet until they are of an even thickness.

2. In a large bowl, mix together the yogurt, curry powder, salt and pepper. Stir in the chicken breasts and marinate for 1 hour.

3. Grill the breasts on high heat until seared, about 1 minute. Turn over and sear the other side. Turn again and cook for 1 minute more, or until the juices run clear.

Serves 4

Grilled Veal Chops

The marinade in this recipe gives a tangy taste and depth of flavor to the veal, which can be a rather bland meat. For the best results, use veal rib or loin chops cut 1 inch (2.5 cm) thick. Coarse-grained mustard has visible mustard seeds in it. Serve these chops with the marinade sauce or with Parsley Watercress Pesto Butter.

2 tsp	coarse-grain French mustard	10 mL
2 tsp	Dijon mustard	10 mL
2 tbsp	white wine vinegar	25 mL
1/4 cup	olive oil	50 mL
1 tsp	freshly ground pepper	5 mL
1 cup	finely chopped green onion	250 mL
1	clove garlic, finely chopped	1
4	veal chops	4
1/4 cup	dry white wine	50 mL
1 cup	whipping cream	250 mL

1. In a medium bowl, combine the mustards, vinegar, olive oil, pepper, green onion and garlic. Brush this marinade on the veal chops and marinate the meat at room temperature for 2 to 3 hours. Reserve 1/2 cup (125 mL) marinade for the sauce.

2. Grill the veal on high heat for 5 to 7 minutes per side, brushing the meat occasionally with the marinade.

3. Meanwhile, in a pot, combine the reserved marinade with the wine and whipping cream. Bring to a boil and boil for a few minutes, or until the sauce thickens slightly. Serve the sauce with the chops.

Serves 4

Parsley Watercress Pesto Butter
In a food processor, combine 2 chopped cloves garlic with 1/2 cup (125 mL) chopped fresh parsley, 1/2 cup (125 mL) chopped watercress and 1 tbsp (15 mL) pine nuts. Puree, then blend in 1/2 cup (125 mL) butter. Roll into a log shape. Wrap in plastic wrap, refrigerate and cut off rounds when needed. Makes about 1 cup (250 mL).

Butterflied Leg of Lamb

A boned lamb leg is usually easily available. Use only a lamb leg, as other cuts are too fatty for barbecuing and will cause flareups.

¹/₂ cup	olive oil	125 mL
¹/₃ cup	lemon juice	75 mL
2 tbsp	Dijon mustard	25 mL
2	cloves garlic, finely chopped	2
1	onion, finely chopped	1
1 tbsp	dried rosemary	15 mL
1 tbsp	dried marjoram	15 mL
1	bay leaf	1
1 tsp	cayenne pepper	5 mL
1	3- to 4-lb (1.5 to 2 kg) leg of lamb, boned and butterflied	1

1. In a medium bowl, combine all the ingredients except the lamb. Pour the marinade over the lamb, rubbing the liquid into the crevices in the meat. Marinate for 12 hours, refrigerated.

2. Place the meat on the grill, fat side down. Close the barbecue lid and cook over medium-high heat for 30 to 40 minutes, basting frequently and turning the meat every 10 minutes. When the juices bubble to the surface, the meat is ready. Carve across the grain into thin slices. Because a lamb leg is not of an even thickness, this should provide well-done as well as rare meat.

Serves 6

Beef shortribs are cut from the plate and rib section. They are shortrib bones with layers of fat and lean meat. They are sold either in thick or thin strips.

Pork sideribs are the least expensive ribs. They have a lot of bone in relation to meat but the meat is flavorful. Pork backribs are meatier than sideribs. Country-style pork ribs are cut from the loin and are meatier and more fatty than backribs.

Barbecued Korean Ribs

Shortribs are meaty and full flavored, and the long marinating time tenderizes the meat. Serve medium-rare for the best flavor and texture. Use any hot sauce if you do not have Chinese chili paste.

4 lb	beef shortribs, 1 inch (2.5 cm) thick	2 kg
1	small onion, finely chopped	1
4	cloves garlic, finely chopped	4
¹/₂ cup	soy sauce	125 mL
¹/₄ cup	honey	50 mL
¹/₂ cup	beer	125 mL
2 tbsp	sesame oil	25 mL
1 tsp	finely chopped fresh ginger	5 mL
1 tsp	Chinese chili paste	5 mL

1. Score the fat side of the ribs, opposite the bone, ¹/₂ inch (1.25 cm) apart and ¹/₂ inch (1.25 cm) deep. Place the ribs in a large shallow bowl.

2. Combine all the remaining ingredients in a medium bowl. Pour over the ribs. Marinate in the refrigerator for 24 hours, turning the ribs occasionally. Reserve the marinade.

3. Place the ribs on the grill. Close the lid and barbecue on medium-high heat for 15 to 18 minutes, basting with the reserved marinade and turning every 5 minutes, until brown and crisp.

Serves 4

Crunchy Barbecued Spareribs

Simmer the spareribs first to remove some of the fat and to tenderize them.

1	onion, sliced	1
2	cloves	2
1	bay leaf	1
1 tsp	dried thyme	5 mL
6	whole peppercorns	6
	Water to cover ribs	
4 lb	spareribs	2 kg
2 cups	Best Barbecue Sauce (see page 92)	500 mL

1. In a large pot on high heat, bring all the ingredients except the spareribs and the barbecue sauce to boil. Immerse the spareribs. They should be covered by the water. Simmer for 30 minutes. Drain.

2. Brush the ribs with the barbecue sauce. Grill on medium heat, basting and turning frequently, for 15 to 20 minutes, or until the ribs are crisp and brown. Serve the remaining sauce separately.

Serves 4 to 5

Hamburgers with Roquefort

Add a French twist to the classic hamburger. When you bite into the burger, you'll find a nugget of Roquefort. Serve on a croissant and top with Dijon mustard.

1 lb	lean ground beef	500 g
1/2 tsp	salt	2 mL
1/4 tsp	freshly ground pepper	1 mL
1/4 cup	Roquefort cheese	50 mL
	Vegetable oil for brushing	

1. Combine the meat with the salt and pepper. Divide into three portions.

2. Divide the Roquefort into three balls. Form each hamburger around a piece of Roquefort and flatten slightly.

3. Brush the burgers with the oil and grill on high heat for 4 minutes per side for rare; 5 minutes for medium.

Serves 3

Barbecued Cheese

Use cheese with a rind, such as Brie or Camembert, to prevent it from leaking all over the grill. Or you can use goat cheese, which will get warm but won't melt. Serve with fruit and crackers as a dessert.

1	1-lb (500 g) round of Brie	1
1/2 cup	olive oil	125 mL
1 tbsp	finely chopped fresh rosemary, or 1 tsp (5 mL) dried	15 mL
1 tbsp	finely chopped fresh thyme, or 1 tsp (5 mL) dried	15 mL
1	bay leaf	1
1/2 tsp	freshly ground pepper	2 mL

1. Scrape the rind off the top of the cheese.

2. In a small bowl, mix together the oil, rosemary, thyme, bay leaf and pepper. Pour over the cheese and marinate for 30 minutes.

3. Place the cheese, rind side down, directly on the grill. Close the lid and grill for 5 minutes, or until the cheese is melted.

Serves 4

When barbecuing hamburgers, use ground beef that has about 20 percent fat. It produces a juicier hamburger. Ground chuck works very well. Handle the patties lightly; overhandling results in dry, crumbly burgers.

To season hamburger meat, spread the meat on a board so that the seasoning penetrates all the hamburger. (If this is done in a bowl, it is hit and miss effort.)

Use 6 ounces (180 g) meat for each adult hamburger; 4 ounces (125 g) for kids. The burgers should be about 1 inch (2.5 cm) thick for even cooking.

Hamburgers can be served on Italian pada buns, pita, Chinese steamed buns, French sticks, Portuguese cornbread, bagels, seven-grain buns or flour tortillas.

PEAS

Fresh sweet garden peas are a real treat for the short time they are in season. However, these little green peas are not the only pods around — look for snow peas and sugar snaps as well.
• Buy green, plump, unblemished pods that feel velvety to the touch. The peas inside should be shiny and green. Don't buy pea pods that are bursting at their seams; these pods are overmature, and the peas will be mealy.
• Refrigerate the pods for up to two to three days. After this they will lose their flavor.
• Shell the peas just before using.
• Cook the shelled peas in as little water as possible to preserve their flavor. Try steaming them or cooking in ½ cup (125 mL) water for each 1 lb (500 g) peas.
• Snow peas are available year round, but they have more flavor in the spring and summer. Choose firm, smooth, bright-green pods that do not have little peas inside. Remove the strings before cooking by pinching the string at the stem end and pulling toward the stalk. Sauté, or boil in lots of water until crisp-tender.
• Sugar snaps have fatter pods than snow peas and are eaten whole. However, the strings should be removed before cooking. They have a crisp, juicy texture and are cooked the same way as snow peas.
• When buying peas, rub two pea pods together. If they squeak, the peas are fresh.

One pound (500 g) peas, shelled, will feed two people.

There are about 71 calories in ½ cup (125 mL) cooked peas.

One pound (500 g) unshelled peas will yield about 1 cup (250 mL) shelled peas.

Peas French Style

This recipe is especially good for slightly more mature peas. The juices can be thickened with a little cornstarch, if desired.

1	head Boston lettuce, shredded	1
6	green onions, chopped	6
3 tbsp	butter	45 mL
2 lb	peas, shelled	1 kg
pinch	granulated sugar	pinch
1 tbsp	finely chopped parsley	15 mL
¼ cup	chicken stock or water	50 mL
	Salt and freshly ground pepper to taste	

1. Place the lettuce in the bottom of a heavy pot. Layer the onions on top and dot with the butter.

2. Add the peas, sugar, parsley and chicken stock. Cover the pot tightly and bring to a boil on a high heat.

3. As soon as the liquid boils, turn the heat to low and simmer for 5 minutes, or until the peas are cooked. Season well with salt and pepper.

Serves 4 to 6

Sweet Sugar Snaps

Sugar snaps have so much flavor, they are best left unadorned. Serve with chicken, roasts and steaks.

1 lb	sugar snaps	500 g
1 tbsp	butter	15 mL
	Salt and freshly ground pepper to taste	

1. Remove the strings from the sugar snaps. Bring a large pot of water to the boil, add the sugar snaps and boil for 4 minutes, or until crisp-tender.

2. Drain, refresh with cold water and

return to the pot. Add the butter and season with salt and pepper. Serve at once.

Serves 6

Snow Pea and Carrot Sauté

The snow peas and the carrots should be the same size for even cooking. Sesame oil is made from sesame seeds; it is used lavishly in Oriental cooking. It is not used for frying because the taste is very strong — a few drops is enough to flavor a dish.

1 lb	snow peas or green beans	500 g
1 lb	carrots	500 g
¼ cup	vegetable oil	50 mL
	Salt and freshly ground pepper	
1 tsp	sesame oil, optional	5 mL

1. Remove the strings from the snow peas. Peel the carrots, then cut them on the diagonal so the slices are about the same thickness and shape as the snow peas.

2. Bring a large pot of water to a boil on high heat. Add the carrots. Bring the water to a boil again, and boil the carrots for 3 minutes.

3. Add the snow peas to the boiling water, then drain immediately. Pour cold water over the vegetables until they are cold. Shake dry.

4. In a frying pan, heat the vegetable oil. Quickly sauté the snow peas and carrots together until hot. Season with the salt, pepper and sesame oil.

Serves 8 to 10

STRAWBERRIES

Did you know that during the two weeks of the Wimbledon tennis tournament, the spectators eat enough strawberries to fill two tennis courts? Strawberries are one of the world's favorite fruits.

• Choose firm, red, ripe berries (strawberries don't ripen after picking). The size of the strawberry has no bearing on its taste. In fact, often the small ones are sweeter and less watery than the larger berries.

• Make sure the hulls are attached; the hulls should be bright-green.

• Don't buy boxes that are stained; it means some berries are overripe.

• Don't soak berries in water; they will absorb the water and become soggy. Instead, rinse the berries right before eating.

• Don't hull the berries before rinsing. The hull acts as protection; strawberries deteriorate more quickly with the hulls removed.

• To store strawberries, place them in a carton in a single layer, removing the overripe ones. Refrigerate. They should last for three days.

• To freeze strawberries without sugar, wash, then hull the berries. Freeze flat on baking sheets. When frozen, pack the berries in freezer containers or plastic freezer bags.

• To freeze strawberries with sugar, add ½ cup (125 mL) granulated sugar per 4 cups (1 L) whole or sliced berries. Stir together, then freeze in freezer containers. These berries are excellent for pies and muffins, but remember to subtract some of the sugar from the recipe.

One cup (250 mL) strawberries has about 58 calories. Strawberries are also an excellent source of vitamin C and fiber.

Use damaged strawberries to make ices, milkshakes, mousses or a face mask. Try using them as a freckle remover, too.

Freezing strawberries removes some of the flavor and changes the texture, but the strawberries can be used in mousses, pies and ice creams.

Strawberry and Orange Soup

Take this refreshing cold soup iced to a picnic, or serve before a barbecue in frosted mugs.

2 cups	sliced strawberries	500 mL
	Juice of 1 orange	
1 tsp	icing sugar	5 mL
3 tbsp	honey	45 mL
1 cup	plain yogurt	250 mL
1/2 cup	milk	125 mL
1	5 1/2-oz (156 mL) can apricot nectar	1
1 tbsp	peach schnapps, optional	15 mL

1. In a food processor or blender, combine 1 1/2 cups (375 mL) strawberries with the orange juice and icing sugar. Puree until smooth.

2. Add the honey, yogurt, milk, apricot nectar and liqueur. Combine together.

3. Transfer to a large bowl and garnish with the remaining strawberries.

Serves 6

Quick Strawberry Ideas

• Serve unadorned strawberries with a bowl of brown sugar and sour cream.
• Puree strawberries, flavor with icing sugar and spoon over whole strawberries.
• Spread a croissant with cream cheese and top with sliced strawberries.
• Garnish chicken salad with sliced strawberries.
• Melt bittersweet chocolate. Using a toothpick, dip clean, dry, unhulled strawberries into the chocolate. Dry on waxed paper and serve as a dessert sprinkled with icing sugar.

Strawberry Brûlée

An easy, light version of the classic crème brûlée.

4 cups	strawberries, hulled	1 L
2 cups	whipping cream	500 mL
2 tbsp	lemon juice	25 mL
1/4 cup	sherry	50 mL
1/4 cup	granulated sugar	50 mL
1/2 cup	brown sugar	125 mL

1. Slice the strawberries thickly and arrange on the bottom of an 8-cup (2 L) gratin dish.

2. In a large bowl, beat the cream until it holds it shape. Beat in the lemon juice, sherry and granulated sugar. Continue beating until thick and light.

3. Spoon the mixture on top of the berries and chill for 1 hour or overnight.

4. Just before serving, sprinkle the brown sugar over the cream. Broil until the sugar melts and caramelizes. Serve at once.

Serves 4 to 6

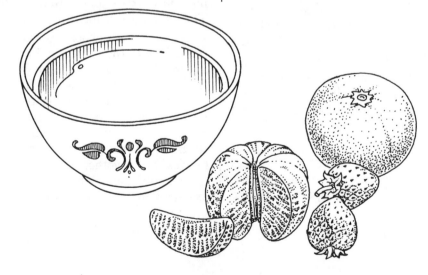

Father's Day Barbecue for Eight

An eclectic menu that uses the barbecue for every course except dessert. The menu has lots of strong, interesting flavors — perfect for a father whose tastes are a little adventurous. The slow barbecued brisket can be made ahead of time and reheated.

Grilled Shrimp

Barbecued Corn

Texas Beef Brisket

Grilled Red Onion Slices

Grilled Zucchini

Strawberry Shortcake

Grilled Shrimp

These shrimp are messy to eat but terrific. Splitting the shrimps down the back means the marinade penetrates the flesh; leaving the shell on seals in the juices and makes the barbecuing easier.

1 cup	olive oil	250 mL
	Grated rind and juice of 2 lemons	
1 tsp	salt	5 mL
1 tbsp	dried thyme	15 mL
1/4 cup	finely chopped parsley	50 mL
3	cloves garlic, finely chopped	3
1	dried red chili pepper, chopped, optional	1
2 tsp	chili powder	10 mL
2 lb	large shrimp, shell on	1 kg

1. In a large bowl, combine all the ingredients except the shrimp.

2. Split the shrimp down the back, leaving the tails attached and shells on. Toss the shrimp in the marinade and marinate overnight in the refrigerator.

3. Grill the shrimp on high heat, turning occasionally, for 5 minutes, or until pink and slightly curled. Serve with the shell on.

Serves 8 as an appetizer; 4 as a main course

Barbecued Corn

Soaking the corn in ice water ensures that the husks don't burn on the barbecue.

8	cobs corn, with husks	8
1/2 cup	butter, at room temperature	125 mL
	Salt and freshly ground pepper to taste	

1. Pull back the husks of the corn and remove the silk.

2. Spread the kernels with butter, salt and pepper.

3. Pull the husks back up, and tie them with string. Soak the corn in ice water for 30 minutes.

4. On medium heat, grill the corn for 15 to 20 minutes, or until tender, turning occasionally.

Serves 8

To cook by indirect heat, place a drip pan in the bottom of the barbecue. Bank charcoal beside the pan on either side or, if you are using a gas barbecue, turn off one side of the barbecue and place the drip pan on the lava rocks on that side. Place the meat over the drip pan.

Barbecue Woods
Barbecuing over woods gives a different, smoky taste to the meat but should not overwhelm it. Soak a handful of wood chips in water for 30 minutes. Toss the chips onto the heat source or wrap them in foil, puncture the foil in a few places and place the package on the heat source. You can also use soaked herb stalks or vine cuttings.

Mesquite, the current trendy wood, gives a light, woody flavor to food. It's best with beef, lamb or pork. Hickory is very smoky and good for ribs. Apple and cherry wood give a fruity flavor to fish, chicken and pork. Alder is often used today to flavor barbecued salmon.

Texas Beef Brisket

In the Old West, cowhands were fed by cooking a whole cow over a pit for the entire day. Mesquite would be sprinkled on the coals, and over the long cooking time, the flavored smoke would permeate the meat.

This smaller version is cooked for six hours, and part of this can be in the oven. The dish reheats beautifully. For the best flavor and texture, use a fatty brisket.

2 tsp	salt	10 mL
1 tsp	freshly ground pepper	5 mL
1 tsp	cayenne pepper	5 mL
2 tsp	dried thyme	10 mL
4 lb	beef brisket, untrimmed	2 kg
4 cups	Best Barbecue Sauce (see page 92)	1 L

1. In a small bowl, mix together the salt, pepper, cayenne and thyme. Rub this seasoning mixture over the entire brisket.

2. Preheat the barbecue and add a handful of soaked mesquite chips to the heat source. Sear the brisket on high heat for 5 minutes per side.

3. Move the brisket to the side of the grill, so that the meat cooks by indirect heat. Cover the barbecue and cook the meat slowly for 2 hours, turning occasionally. Add more mesquite after 1 hour. Remove the brisket from the barbecue.

4. Preheat the oven to 225°F (108°C). Place the brisket in a heavy pot and bake for 4 hours, or until tender. (You can also leave the brisket on the barbecue for this remaining cooking time.)

5. Slice the meat across the grain and serve with the barbecue sauce.

Serves 8

Grilled Red Onion Slices

These can be grilled early, then reheated on a platter in the oven.

8	red onions	8
1/2 cup	olive oil	125 mL
1 tbsp	dried basil	15 mL
	Salt and freshly ground pepper to taste	
2 tsp	granulated sugar	10 mL

1. Peel the onions and slice into rounds 1 inch (2.5 cm) thick.

2. In a medium bowl, whisk together the olive oil, basil, salt, pepper and sugar. Pour over the onions and marinate for 15 minutes.

3. Grill the onions on high heat for 3 minutes per side, brushing occasionally with more marinade, until limp and browned.

Serves 8

Grilled Zucchini

One of the best vegetables on the barbecue, zucchini retains its taste and juiciness when grilled.

6	zucchini	6
	Salt	
	Olive oil	

1. Slice the zucchini lengthwise into 1/4 inch (5 mm) slices. Sprinkle the slices with salt and let stand for 45 minutes. Brush the slices with oil.

2. Grill the zucchini slices for 3 minutes. Brush with more oil, then turn and barbecue for 1 or 2 minutes, or until the slices are brown.

Serves 8

Strawberry Shortcake

The classic shortcake. You can fill it with raspberries or blueberries, if desired.

4 cups	strawberries, hulled	1 L
5 tbsp	granulated sugar	75 mL
2 cups	all-purpose flour	500 mL
1 tbsp	baking powder	15 mL
1/4 tsp	salt	1 mL
1/2 cup	cold unsalted butter, cut into 1/2-inch (1.25 cm) pieces	125 mL
1	egg, beaten	1
3/4 cup	light cream	175 mL
1 1/2 cups	whipping cream	375 mL

1. Preheat the oven to 400°F (200°C). Butter an 8-inch (20 cm) round cake pan.

2. Slice the strawberries, reserving eight of the nicest berries for garnish. Place the berries in a bowl and sprinkle with 2 tbsp (25 mL) sugar.

3. In a large bowl, sift the flour, 3 tbsp (45 mL) sugar, baking powder and salt. Cut in the butter until the mixture resembles coarse meal.

4. In a separate bowl, combine the egg and light cream. Stir into the dry ingredients with a fork, until the mixture is completely moistened.

5. Scrape the dough onto a lightly floured board. Knead very briefly, once or twice only. Pat the dough into the bottom of the prepared pan. Bake on the center rack of the oven until golden-brown and firm, about 20 to 30 minutes.

6. Remove the pan to a wire rack; cool the shortcake in the pan until lukewarm, about 15 minutes.

7. Remove the shortcake from the pan. Split the cake into two layers with a long serrated knife. Set the bottom half, cut side up, on a serving plate. Spoon about two-thirds of the fruit (and any juice) on top.

8. In a chilled bowl with chilled beaters, whip the whipping the cream until stiff. Spoon in mounds over the fruit. Top with the other half of shortcake. Top with the remaining fruit and spread the cream thickly over the cake. Top with the whole strawberries.

Serves 8

7
July

Summer is at its height, and all kinds of berries are flooding the market. This is a month for simple salads and palate-refreshing ice creams made from the abundance of fresh fruit. Picnics, too, take advantage of the beautiful weather.

In season
apricots
black currants
blueberries
cherries
cucumbers
gooseberries
lettuce
radishes
raspberries
red currants
strawberries

Holidays
Canada Day

Menu
Mediterranean Picnic for Eight

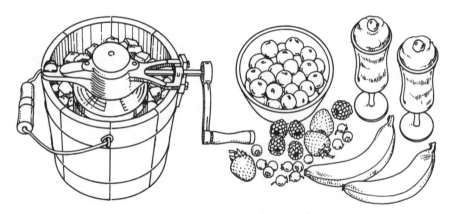

ICE CREAM

Marco Polo was not only responsible for bringing the noodle to Italy; he also brought a recipe for a frozen dessert made with ice and milk. The Italians immediately began to experiment with the combination, eventually producing the first ice cream.

Although store-bought ice cream can be sensational, there are advantages to making your own. You can control the quality of the ingredients, eliminate artificial emulsifiers and stabilizers, produce low-calorie versions and use fresh produce in season.

Ice Cream Machines

• There are a variety of ice cream machines on the market, to suit different needs and wallets. The most expensive are freon gas-cooled electric churns that don't require refrigeration. The machine takes 20 minutes to make a superior product, and with newer models you can remove the bowls for washing.

• There is a reasonably priced

machine with a cylinder that goes in the freezer for 8 hours before making the ice cream. The custard is poured into the frozen cylinder and is then hand-churned occasionally for 15 to 20 minutes. Good ice cream results from this method, too.

• There are several types of machines that use the ice and salt method to lower the temperatures in the containers. Some are electrically churned, while others are hand-churned. Ice and salt are layered in a ratio of about eight parts ice to one part salt in an outer container, while the ice cream mixture is placed in an inner container. The salt lowers the temperature at which the ice will freeze, keeping the outer container very cold. (Because of the identical chemical reaction, don't get any salt in your ice cream mixture, because the salt will prevent it from freezing.)

• Successful ice cream can also be made without a machine, although the texture will not be as creamy. Make a base, cool it, then freeze it in a covered metal bowl, stirring occasionally to break up the ice crystals. When the mixture is frozen, beat it in a processor or mixer until smooth (this breaks down the crystals again and adds air to the mixture), cover and refreeze. Using this method, the ice cream should be transferred from the freezer to the refrigerator for 30 minutes before it is needed to let it soften slightly. The final texture will not be as smooth or velvety as machine-made ice cream.

Ingredients

• Ice cream is essentially a mixture of milk, sugar, eggs and flavoring, cooked, chilled and churned.

• Milk is the basis of most ice cream. For a richer flavor, use light cream or whipping cream. For fewer calories, use skim milk or low-fat yogurt.

• Use granulated sugar. If the ice cream base is uncooked, beat the sugar well with the other ingredients to avoid a granular texture. Honey can be substituted for sugar, but the taste will change.

• Eggs serve as a thickening agent for custard-based ice creams. Whole eggs produce a lighter ice cream; egg yolks will result in a richer one. Never bring the custard to a boil, or the egg yolks will curdle.

• To make the best ice cream, slowly simmer the egg yolks, sugar and milk in a heavy pot on the stove, until the mixture lightly coats a spoon. Flavor and chill the custard, then freeze it.

• In the unlikely event that there is some ice cream left over, store it in a sealed plastic container in the freezer until needed. Ice cream takes on freezer flavors, so make sure it is well sealed. Although homemade ice cream will keep for a few months, the texture becomes more granular as it sits, due to fluctuations in freezer temperature.

• Before serving, all homemade ices and ice creams should sit out of the freezer for 30 minutes in the refrigerator, or for 20 minutes at room temperature, to soften them slightly. They contain no artificial stabilizers to keep them soft.

• Homemade ices and ice creams have the best texture when freshly made and eaten directly out of the ice cream machine.

A custard base produces the richest and best ice cream, but a simple ice cream can be made by beating cream, sugar and fruits together, then freezing until firm.

Ices

- Ices are intensely flavored mixtures of fruit puree and sugar syrup, which are then frozen. They have no milk or eggs in them. Most have added lemon juice, and often a liqueur is added for extra flavor (although adding too much alcohol will prevent ices and ice creams from freezing properly). Technically, sherbets or sorbets are fruit ices with the addition of stiffly beaten egg whites, although some manufacturers add milk or cream instead.
- When making ices, remember that freezing diminishes flavor. The mixture must be fruity enough when it goes into the freezer to allow for some flavor loss.
- You can make ices easily without an ice cream machine, although the texture will not be as light. The mixtures are cooled, frozen, then pureed in a food processor or blender to break up the ice granules before being refrozen. Transfer the ices from the freezer to the refrigerator for 30 minutes before serving to allow the mixture to soften slightly.
- It is helpful to have a light syrup on hand to make ices. Make up a couple of quarts and store in the refrigerator indefinitely. Light syrups avoid the graininess of improperly dissolved sugar in the ice, and you won't have to wait for the sugar syrup to cool before making the ice.
- For the prettiest presentation of ices and ice creams, scoop them out with an oval spoon, placing two or three flavors on one plate. Fresh fruit sauces in corresponding or contrasting flavors and colors turn simple ices into a gourmet dessert.

Old-fashioned hand-churning is fun for families to do together, but make sure there are lots of willing hands, because it's hard work.

Ice Cream Base

This is a rich custard base that can be turned into all sorts of decadent flavors. Use light cream or milk instead of whipping cream for a lighter base. You can also reduce the egg yolks to four for less cholesterol (but a less creamy texture).

To make vanilla ice cream, add 1 tsp (5 mL) vanilla extract to the ice cream base before freezing.

3 cups	whipping cream	750 mL
1 cup	milk	250 mL
6	egg yolks	6
³/₄ cup	granulated sugar	175 mL

1. Heat the cream and milk in a heavy pot on low heat, stirring occasionally, until the mixture is hot.

2. In a large bowl, whisk the egg yolks and sugar together until thick. Still whisking, slowly pour in 1 cup (250 mL) hot liquid. Beat in the remaining liquid.

3. Return the base to the pot and stir constantly until the mixture thickens slightly and coats the back of a spoon. Chill.

4. Strain the custard into the ice cream maker and follow the manufacturer's instructions. To make by hand, strain the mixture into a cold bowl, cool, then freeze. Beat with a mixer, food processor or by hand and return to the freezer.

Makes 4 cups (1 L)

Chocolate Ice Cream

The blend of the two chocolates gives this ice cream a powerful chocolate flavor. The chocolate must be mixed with the hot liquid, otherwise it will coagulate.

3 oz	semisweet chocolate	90 g
1 oz	unsweetened chocolate	30 g
1	recipe hot ice cream base (see page 106)	1

1. Melt the chocolates together in a medium pot over low heat, stirring occasionally until smooth. Remove from the heat.

2. Gradually add small amounts of the hot ice cream base to the chocolate, stirring frequently to keep the chocolate smooth. Cook over low heat until the mixture is well blended. Chill.

3. Pour the mixture into the ice cream maker and freeze according to the manufacturer's instructions.

Makes 4 cups (1 L)

Oreo Ice Cream

Perfect for a children's party, or for adults who like comfort food.

1	recipe ice cream base, chilled (see page 106)	1
12	Oreo cookies, broken into chunks	12

1. Pour the custard base into the ice cream machine. Following the manufacturer's instructions, freeze for 10 minutes.

2. Add the cookies and freeze completely.

Makes about 4 cups (1 L)

Coffee Ice Cream

For a mocha flavor, mix coffee and chocolate ice cream together.

1	recipe ice cream base (see page 106)	1
1/4 cup	instant coffee granules	50 mL

1. In a heavy pot, mix 1 cup (250 mL) ice cream base with the coffee over low heat, stirring until the granules dissolve. Mix in the remaining base. Chill.

2. Pour the mixture into an ice cream maker and freeze according to the manufacturer's instructions.

Makes 4 cups (1 L)

Quick Strawberry Ice Cream

4 cups	strawberries, hulled	1 L
1/2 cup	granulated sugar	125 mL
	Juice of 1 lemon	
1 1/2 cups	whipping cream	375 mL

1. Puree the strawberries, sugar and lemon juice in a food processor. Stir in the whipping cream.

2. Pour the mixture into the ice cream machine and freeze according to the manufacturer's instructions.

Makes about 4 cups (1 L)

Easy Maple Walnut Ice Cream

If you make this ice cream without a machine, don't add the walnuts until you have pureed the base in the food processor.

1 cup	maple syrup	250 mL
2 cups	whipping cream	500 mL
1/2 cup	milk	125 mL
3/4 cup	walnut pieces	175 mL

1. In a bowl, combine the maple syrup, whipping cream and milk. Stir in the nuts.

2. Pour the mixture into an ice cream machine and freeze according to the manufacturer's instructions.

Makes about 4 cups (1 L)

Quick Raspberry Ice Cream
Combine two 10-oz (300 g) packages frozen raspberries in syrup in a food processor with 2 cups (500 mL) whipping cream. Freeze for 2 hours, or until firm. Makes 4 cups (1 L).

Honeydew Melon Ice with Anisette

Peel a cantaloupe or honeydew melon and puree the flesh in a food processor. If no licorice-flavored anisette or Pernod is available, use any orange or passionfruit liqueur. Cut up more melon and serve it with the ice.

2 cups	honeydew melon puree	500 mL
1/4 cup	anisette	50 mL
1/3 cup	granulated sugar	75 mL

1. Mix the puree with the liqueur and sugar. Pour into a metal bowl, cover and freeze.

2. Beat the mixture until fluffy, or puree in the food processor. Return to the metal bowl, cover and freeze until firm.

3. Serve a scoop of melon ice with a piece of melon.

Makes about 3 1/2 cups (875 mL)

Elderflower Sorbet

This recipe was taught by Toronto caterer Allison Cumming in one of my cooking courses. As well as being a summer dessert, it is perfect for "cleansing the palate" between courses of a special dinner. Use a spotlessly clean, greaseless pot. If necessary, clean the pot first with half a lemon and salt. Dried elderflowers are available at health food stores.

2 1/2 cups water		625 mL
	Finely grated rind and juice of 1 orange	
	Finely grated rind and juice of 2 lemons	
1 cup	granulated sugar	250 mL
4 tsp	dried elderflowers	20 mL
1	egg white	1
	Fresh mint sprigs	

1. Place the water, orange rind and juice, lemon rind and juice, sugar and elderflowers in a pot on high heat. Bring to a boil, lower the heat to medium-low and simmer for 12 minutes.

2. Strain into a metal bowl. Cover and cool. Transfer to the freezer and leave overnight.

3. Remove the mixture from the freezer and beat well with a mixer or puree in a food processor.

4. In a bowl, beat the egg white until stiff. Quickly stir the beaten egg white into the elderflower mixture. Cover and refreeze for about 4 hours or overnight. Serve garnished with fresh mint sprigs.

Makes about 4 cups (1 L)

Fresh Strawberry Ice

A tingling, fresh ice with orange overtones. A great end to a fashionable dinner party or a super treat in the evening. Substitute water instead of the orange and lemon juice, if desired.

4 cups	strawberries, hulled	1 L
2 cups	granulated sugar	500 mL
1½ cups	fresh orange juice	375 mL
½ cup	fresh lemon juice	125 mL
¼ cup	orange liqueur	50 mL
Garnish:		
1 cup	strawberries	250 mL
	Fresh mint leaves	

1. In a food processor or blender, combine 4 cups (1 L) berries with the sugar and fruit juices. Blend until smooth.

2. Stir in the liqueur. Pour into a metal bowl, cover and freeze until firm.

3. Let sit for 20 minutes at room temperature before serving. Garnish with the whole berries and mint leaves.

Makes about 4 cups (1 L)

Lemon Sorbet

A simple, delightful way to end a barbecue or heavy meal, and it's light in calories, too. If you have a light syrup, use it instead of the water and sugar.

1 cup	water	250 mL
	Grated rind and juice of 3 lemons	
1 cup	granulated sugar	250 mL
1	egg white	1
1 cup	sliced strawberries	250 mL

1. Bring the water, lemon rind and juice and sugar to a boil in a pot. Simmer for 5 minutes. Strain and cool.

2. Place the mixture in a metal bowl, cover and freeze for 12 hours. Remove from the freezer and process in a food processor or beat until smooth.

3. Beat the egg white until it holds its shape. Stir into the ice. Place in a serving bowl or mold and return to the freezer until frozen.

4. Remove the sorbet from the freezer to the refrigerator 30 minutes before serving. Serve topped with the strawberries.

Makes 4 cups (1 L)

Light Sugar Syrup
In a pot, combine 4 cups (1 L) water with 4 cups (1 L) granulated sugar. Bring to a boil, then simmer for 2 minutes. Cool and refrigerate. Makes about 5 cups (1.25 L). Use in place of the water and sugar quantities in the recipes for ices, if desired.

CHERRIES

Cherries are my favorite summer treat. Their season passes so quickly, perhaps I feel I have to eat a year's worth in three short weeks!

Popular Varieties

• **Bings** are the number one cherry in Canada. They are large, firm, sweet and juicy. Buy plump, shiny, dark-red fruit with stems attached. The stems should be green; dark-colored stems usually mean the fruit is not freshly picked.

• **Royal Anne** are yellow, heart-shaped cherries with a red blush. They have a fine flavor, but they are softer and more perishable than red cherries.

• **Red, tart** or **sour** cherries are used for pies, canning and processing, and some people like them for eating (including myself).

• Sour cherries can be bought pitted and frozen from fruit stands and supermarkets in cherry-growing areas. They are excellent for pies and jams. Look for cherries that have been frozen without sugar; they will have a better flavor.

• Look for plump, glossy fruit with the stems on. (The stems help to keep the cherries fresh longer.)

• Treat cherries gently, because they bruise easily.

• Don't wash cherries until just before eating or cooking, because they go soggy easily.

Cherries must be pitted for most recipes. There's nothing worse than trying to delicately discard the pits at a dinner party! Sour cherry pits can be squeezed out with your fingers, but sweet cherries require a cherry pitter, available at kitchen shops.

Cherry Custard Pie

This pie can be made with plums, cherries or peaches. You can substitute whipping cream for sour cream for a richer taste. Don't fill the pie shell right to the top, because the custard puffs up.

1	partially baked 10-inch (25 cm) pie shell	1
1	egg white, beaten	1
1/2 cup	fresh breadcrumbs	125 mL
3 cups	tart red cherries, pitted	750 mL
1 cup	sour cream	250 mL
2	eggs	2
1	egg yolk	1
1/2 cup	granulated sugar	125 mL

1. Preheat the oven to 425°F (220°C).

2. Brush the pie shell with the egg white and sprinkle with the breadcrumbs. Scatter the cherries on top.

3. Beat together the cream, eggs, egg yolk and sugar. Pour over the cherries.

4. Bake for 25 minutes, or until the filling is browned and slightly puffy.

Serves 6

Cherry Meringues

The cherry sauce is also excellent over ice cream.

3	egg whites	3
3/4 cup	granulated sugar	175 mL
1/2 tsp	vanilla extract	2 mL
Cherry Sauce:		
1/2 cup	granulated sugar	125 mL
1 cup	water	250 mL
3 cups	Bing cherries, pitted	750 mL
1 tbsp	cornstarch	15 mL
2 tsp	kirsch, optional	10 mL
2 cups	vanilla ice cream	500 mL

1. Preheat the oven to 225°F (108°C).

2. To make the meringues, in a large bowl, with an electric beater, whisk the egg whites until they form soft peaks. Beat in ³/₄ cup (175 mL) sugar, 1 tbsp (15 mL) at a time. Continue beating until the mixture is thick and glossy. Beat in the vanilla.

3. Spoon 2 tbsp (25 mL) of meringue mixture onto a baking sheet lined with parchment paper. Repeat with the remaining mixture. You should have 8 to 10 mounds.

4. Bake for 1 hour, or until the mixture has dried out. Cool and remove from the parchment paper.

5. To make the sauce, combine ¹/₂ cup (125 mL) sugar with the water in a large pot. Bring to a boil and boil for 2 minutes. Add the cherries and simmer for 10 minutes, or until soft. Remove half the cherries and reserve.

5. Place the remaining cherries and liquid in a food processor or blender. Puree.

6. Return the puree to the pot. Combine 2 tbsp (25 mL) puree with the cornstarch. Stir into the remaining puree and bring to a boil. Add the remaining whole cherries and kirsch. Cool.

7. Sandwich ¹/₂ cup (125 mL) ice cream between two meringues. Pour the sauce on a serving plate. Place the meringue sandwich on top and coat with extra sauce. Repeat with the remaining meringues, ice cream and sauce.

Serves 4

Cherry Relish

Serve this relish with cold meats or chicken.

1 cup	dry red wine	250 mL
¹/₂ cup	granulated sugar	125 mL
	Grated rind and juice of 1 orange	
4 cups	tart red cherries, pitted	1 L

1. In a large pot, place the wine, sugar, orange rind and juice. Bring to a boil on high heat. Boil for 2 minutes, turn the heat to low and simmer for 10 minutes.

2. Add the cherries and simmer 10 minutes longer. Remove the cherries and reserve in a bowl.

3. On high heat, reduce the liquid until slightly thickened, about 5 minutes. Combine with the cherries and chill.

Makes about 4 cups (1 L)

Cherry Vinegar

Use to marinate chicken or pork before barbecuing, or sprinkle it on fruit or salads for a different flavor. Buy pretty bottles and give the cherry vinegar as a hostess gift.

1 cup	tart red cherries, pitted	250 mL
1 cup	white wine vinegar or rice vinegar	250 mL

1. In a blender or food processor, puree the cherries with the vinegar. Transfer to a stainless steel or enamel bowl and cover with plastic wrap. Set in a cool place for 7 to 10 days.

2. Strain through a coffee filter-lined sieve. Pour the vinegar into sterilized bottles. Discard the cherries.

Makes about 1¹/₂ cups (375 mL)

RASPBERRIES

Raspberries are the quintessential summer fruit. Luscious and juicy, their short but sweet season is splendid.

• Raspberries usually range in color from bright-red to purple; elegant apricot-colored raspberries are beginning to make an appearance, but they taste the same as the red ones.

• Raspberries are fragile and delicate. They should be purchased the day you want to eat them for maximum flavor. Look for firm, dry fruit that is a good color. Avoid boxes that are stained with juice — a sign that the berries are either past their prime or damaged.

• Don't wash the berries until you use them. Water causes mold to form. Wash them in a sieve, making sure you shake off all the excess water.

• Freeze raspberries on baking sheets until firm, then bag them in freezer bags. They should keep for about six months.

• Frozen raspberries can be substituted for fresh in most recipes that call for them to be cooked or pureed.

When raspberries are ripe, the fruit drops off the vine, leaving a little hollow cup in each berry. If raspberries have their stems still attached, they are not ripe.

Raspberries with Sabayon

Sabayon is a light, custard-like cream which can be eaten on its own or spooned over fresh fruit. Strawberries, raspberries and blueberries are excellent with it; or try poached pears or apples. Although this dessert should be made at the last minute, if all the ingredients are measured and on hand, it should be ready within 5 minutes.

4 cups	raspberries	1 L
1/2 cup	granulated sugar	125 mL
4	egg yolks	4
1/2 cup	dry white wine	125 mL
2 tbsp	orange liqueur	25 mL

1. Place the raspberries in a bowl. Sprinkle with 2 tbsp (25 mL) sugar.

2. In a large, heavy pot on low heat, whisk together the egg yolks and remaining sugar until the mixture doubles in volume and holds its shape. Whisk in the wine and liqueur. Continue to whisk until the mixture is thick and creamy and has almost tripled in volume.

3. Divide the raspberries among six plates. Spoon the warm sabayon over. Serve immediately.

Serves 6

Lemon Tartlets with Raspberries

An elegant dessert that I once ate in a restaurant in Washington, where I was told that it was Nancy Reagan's favorite!

Pastry:		
1 1/2 cups	all-purpose flour	375 mL
1/4 cup	granulated sugar	50 mL
pinch	salt	pinch
3/4 cup	unsalted butter	175 mL
1	egg yolk	1
1 tbsp	lemon juice	15 mL
Lemon Curd Filling:		
1 cup	granulated sugar	250 mL
1/2 cup	unsalted butter	125 mL
5	eggs, beaten	5
	Grated rind and juice of 3 lemons	
Raspberry Sauce:		
3 cups	fresh raspberries	750 mL
1/2 cup	light sugar syrup (see page 109)	125 mL

1. To make the pastry, in a bowl, mix together the flour, sugar and salt. With your fingers, cut in the butter until the mixture resembles fine breadcrumbs.

2. In a small bowl, beat together the egg yolk and lemon juice. Stir into the flour mixture and form into a ball. Wrap in plastic wrap and refrigerate for 1 hour.

3. Preheat the oven to 400°F (200°C).

4. With your fingertips, pat the pastry into twelve 3-inch (7.5 cm) tart tins or muffin cups.

5. Bake the pastry for about 8 minutes, or until it is pale gold. Cool and remove from the tins.

6. To make the filling, place the sugar, butter, eggs, lemon rind and juice in a heavy pot. Cook over low heat, whisking constantly, until the mixture thickens and coats the back of a spoon. Remove from the heat and dip the base of the pot into cold water to stop the cooking. Transfer to a chilled bowl and cool.

7. Spoon the cool filling into the pastry shells and smooth the surface. Chill.

8. Reserve 1 cup (250 mL) raspberries. In a food processor or blender, puree the remaining raspberries with the sugar syrup to make a smooth sauce. Press the sauce through a sieve to remove the seeds.

9. To assemble the dessert, top the tarts with raspberries. Place a pool of sauce on each serving plate and top with the raspberry/lemon tarts.

Serves 8

BLUEBERRIES

Tiny wild blueberries are a fleeting treat in July and August. They are picked in areas with an acidic but not fertile soil. The Maritimes supply the rest of Canada with the vast majority of our blueberries, but there are large crops in Quebec and around Sudbury, too. The tiny ones have much more flavor than the larger cultivated berries and are excellent eaten raw by the handful or cooked in muffins, pies and pancakes.

• Look for small, dark-blue berries with a sheen to them. They should be plump and firm. Avoid underripe, green berries.

• Blueberries are very perishable, so pick out any that are moldy or overripe; refrigerate the berries in a plastic container for no more than three days.

• Blueberries freeze well. Freeze them in a single layer on a baking sheet until firm, then store in freezer bags or plastic containers for up to six months. Use for pies and muffins.

Blueberry Yeast Cake

This cake is adapted from an old recipe from the Alsace region of France, where yeast was often used instead of baking powder as a leavener in cakes. The texture of this cake has to be firm in order to stand up to the blueberry juices that run through it. This is my mother's very favorite cake. Serve it with whipped cream.

Blueberries grow wild in Europe, Russia and North America. Because they are available in so many different places, they are called by many different names — huckleberries, bilberries and wartleberries.

1¹⁄₃ cups	all-purpose flour	325 mL
1 tsp	active dry yeast	5 mL
pinch	salt	pinch
4	eggs	4
¹⁄₂ cup	granulated sugar	125 mL
1 tsp	vanilla extract	5 mL
4 cups	blueberries	1 L
Caramel Syrup:		
¹⁄₂ cup	granulated sugar	125 mL
1 tbsp	water	15 mL
1 tbsp	boiling water	15 mL
2 tbsp	orange liqueur	25 mL
Glaze:		
2 tbsp	granulated sugar	25 mL

1. Preheat the oven to 350°F (180°C). Butter a 9-inch (23 cm) springform pan and line it with parchment paper.

2. In a bowl, sift together the flour, yeast and salt.

3. In a large bowl, beat together the eggs and ¹⁄₂ cup (125 mL) sugar until thick and glossy and triple in volume. Quickly fold in the vanilla and flour/yeast mixture.

4. Place half the blueberries in the bottom of the springform pan. Spread over half the batter. Cover with the remaining blueberries and top with the remaining batter.

5. Bake for 40 minutes, or until a cake tester comes out clean.

6. Meanwhile, in a small pot, make the syrup by boiling together ¹⁄₂ cup (125 mL) sugar and 1 tbsp (15 mL) water until the mixture is an amber color. Do not stir. Remove from the heat, cool slightly, then pour in the boiling water and the orange liqueur.

7. Remove the cake from the oven and unmold onto a rack over a serving plate. Pour the warm caramel syrup over. Sprinkle on the remaining 2 tbsp (25 mL) sugar.

8. Place the cake under the broiler until the sugar becomes golden.

Serve 8 to 10

Blueberry Cobbler

A cobbler is a fruit-based dessert with a biscuit topping that looks like cobblestones when baked.

4 cups	blueberries	1 L
¹⁄₄ cup	granulated sugar	50 mL
1 tbsp	all-purpose flour	15 mL
1 tbsp	grated lemon rind	15 mL
Topping:		
1¹⁄₂ cups	all-purpose flour	375 mL
1 tbsp	baking powder	15 mL
4 tbsp	granulated sugar	60 mL
¹⁄₂ tsp	salt	2 mL
¹⁄₂ cup	unsalted butter, at room temperature	125 mL
¹⁄₂ cup	light cream or milk, approx.	125 mL

1. Preheat the oven to 375°F (190°C).

2. Combine the blueberries with ¹⁄₄ cup (50 mL) sugar, 1 tbsp (15 mL) flour and lemon rind. Place in a buttered 12 × 8-inch (3 L) ovenproof baking dish.

3. To make the topping, in a large bowl, combine 1¹⁄₂ cups (375 mL) flour, baking powder, 3 tbsp (45 mL) sugar and salt. Cut in the butter with your fingertips until the mixture looks like fine breadcrumbs. Mix in the cream until a soft dough forms, adding more cream if necessary.

4. Drop the topping by spoonfuls onto the blueberries. Sprinkle with the remaining 1 tbsp (15 mL) sugar.

5. Bake for 25 to 30 minutes, or until the mixture is lightly browned on top and the blueberries have formed a bubbling syrup.

Serves 6

Blueberry Sauce

Serve this over ice cream, pancakes and meringues.

4 cups	blueberries	1 L
¹/₂ cup	granulated sugar	125 mL
¹/₂ cup	water	125 mL
	Grated rind and juice of 1 lemon	
2 tbsp	cornstarch	25 mL
2 tbsp	water	25 mL
1 tbsp	unsalted butter	15 mL
2 tbsp	cassis	25 mL

1. In a pot, combine 2 cups blueberries with the sugar, ¹/₂ cup (125 mL) water, lemon rind and juice. Bring to a boil on high heat and cook for 5 minutes. Puree in a food processor or blender and return to the heat.

2. In a cup, combine the cornstarch and 2 tbsp (25 mL) water. Add the cornstarch mixture and butter to the pot and stir until thickened. Remove from the heat and cool.

3. Add the cassis and fold in the remaining blueberries.

Serves 8

Mediterranean Picnic for Eight

With the long hot days strung out in front of us, going on a picnic is a pleasurable way to spend a day in July. Although picnicking is fun, the menu has to be well thought out so that it stays cool, doesn't spoil and is easy to eat.

• Freeze boxes of juice the day before the picnic. The frozen boxes will act as ice packs in the picnic hamper, keeping the food cool. By the time you picnic, the drinks should be defrosted but still chilly.

• Don't take green salads; they are usually wilted by the time you are ready to eat. Marinated vegetables and dips are better.

• Pack a cooler full of ice bags — it's not as pretty as the portable wicker baskets, but a lot more practical.

• Stay away from food that can spoil. Anything with whipping cream can be a problem. Contrary to what most people think, commercial mayonnaise does not spoil easily; it is homemade mayonnaise that you should worry about.

• Make sure that the food can be eaten with fingers or with a plastic fork. Fighting food with a knife and fork on a plastic or paper plate is no fun.

• Bring a container of water to rinse off freshly picked fruit.

• If you want to bring pies to a picnic, leave them in their original baking pan and invert another on top. Tape the pans together and the pastries should travel without falling apart.

If olives are very salty, soak them in water for 10 minutes before using.

If you wrap wine in several layers of newspaper, it should stay cool.

Tapenade

For an appetizer nibbly, spread tapenade on chunks of fresh French bread. It tastes like the south of France. Use French or Italian olives if you can for this dish; they give it a sunny taste. A couple of tablespoons of canned tuna fish can be added to the recipe for an interesting variation. If you do not have a food processor, chop all the ingredients finely with a knife.

¹/₂ cup	pitted black olives	125 mL
2 tbsp	drained capers	25 mL
1	clove garlic, chopped	1
¹/₄ tsp	dried thyme	1 mL
¹/₂ tsp	freshly ground pepper	2 mL
1	2-oz (50 g) can anchovy fillets, drained	1
¹/₄ cup	olive oil	50 mL
1 tbsp	lemon juice, or to taste	15 mL

1. Add the olives, capers, garlic, thyme, pepper and anchovies to the bowl of a food processor. Turn the processor on and pour the olive oil down the feed tube. Process until the mixture is smooth. Stir in the lemon juice and more olive oil if the mixture is too thick. Refrigerate.

2. Spread on bread or crackers to serve.

Makes about 1 cup (250 mL)

Rustic Torta

An earthy, layered, pizza-like pie that is perfect for picnicking. Bake the pie a day ahead so that the flavors mingle, then refrigerate until needed.

Eggplant Layer:		
1	eggplant	1
1 tsp	salt	5 mL
2 tbsp	olive oil	25 mL
Pepper Layer:		
2 tbsp	olive oil	25 mL
2	cloves garlic, finely chopped	2
1	red pepper, sliced	1
1	green pepper, sliced	1
1 tbsp	finely chopped fresh basil, or 1 tsp (5 mL) dried	15 mL
Spinach Layer:		
2	10-oz (300 g) packages fresh spinach, cooked	2
1 tsp	ground nutmeg	5 mL
	Salt and freshly ground pepper to taste	
Pastry:		
1 lb	puff pastry, fresh or frozen	500 g
Ham Layer:		
8 oz	smoked ham, sliced	250 g
Cheese Layer:		
8 oz	mozzarella cheese, sliced	250 g
Glaze:		
1	egg, beaten	1

1. To make the eggplant layer, slice the eggplant thinly and sprinkle with the salt. Let sit for 30 minutes; wipe dry.

2. Preheat the broiler. Brush the eggplant slices with oil and broil for 3 minutes on each side, or until brown. Reserve.

3. To make the pepper layer, heat the olive oil in a frying pan on medium heat. Sauté the garlic, peppers and basil until the peppers are limp, about 3 minutes. Reserve.

4. To make the spinach layer, squeeze the cooked spinach to remove any moisture. Sprinkle with the nutmeg, salt and pepper. Reserve.

5. Preheat the oven to 425°F (220°C).

6. Roll out three-quarters of the puff pastry into a 12-inch (30 cm) circle. Line the sides and bottom of a 9-inch (23 cm) springform pan. Prick the base.

7. Layer half the eggplant slices, ham, cheese, peppers and spinach in the pastry shell, seasoning each layer with salt and pepper. Repeat with the remaining eggplant, ham, cheese, peppers and spinach.

8. Roll out the remaining pastry. Lay over the filling to cover, sealing the edges. Decorate with any leftover pastry.

9. Brush the pastry with the beaten egg. Bake on the lower rack of the over for 10 minutes. Lower the heat to 375°F (190°C) and bake for 30 minutes longer, or until the pastry is golden-brown. Serve hot or cold.

Serves 8

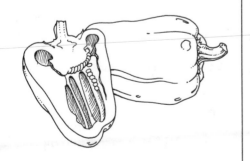

Grilled Marinated Tuna

Slice the tuna and wrap it well before taking it on a picnic. You can substitute boneless chicken breasts or beef filet, but cook the filet for about 10 minutes, or until red juices begin to appear on the surface of the meat.

	Juice of 1 lime	
1 lb	fresh tuna steak	500 g
1 tsp	dried rosemary	5 mL
1 tsp	dried thyme	5 mL
1 tsp	dried basil	5 mL
2 tbsp	olive oil	25 mL
1 tbsp	balsamic vinegar	15 mL
	Salt and freshly ground pepper to taste	
1	lime, thinly sliced	1

1. Sprinkle the lime juice over the tuna. Marinate for 30 minutes.

2. Combine the herbs and the olive oil.

3. Preheat the broiler. Place a baking sheet under the broiler for 5 minutes, or until very hot.

4. Brush the herbed oil over the tuna on both sides and place on the hot baking sheet. Broil about 3 inches (7.5 cm) from the heat for 4 minutes, or until the fish is firm to the touch. Do not turn the fish over. Remove from the oven. Pour over the balsamic vinegar and cool.

5. Season well with salt and pepper and slice into ¼-inch (5 mm) slices. Garnish with lime slices before serving.

Serves 8 as part of a picnic; serves 4 as an appetizer

Farfalle with Mint Pesto

Although pesto is traditionally made with basil, using mint leaves gives a fresh, exciting taste. Many gardens are overrun with mint in July, so this is an excellent way to use it up. If you make mint pesto for the freezer, omit the cheese and add it after defrosting. Try this salad for a summer lunch, or add shrimp and serve as a main course.

1 lb	farfalle (butterfly pasta) or other short pasta	500 g
1/2 cup	pine nuts	125 mL
4	cloves garlic	4
3 cups	fresh mint leaves	750 mL
1 cup	olive oil	250 mL
1/2 cup	grated Parmesan cheese	125 mL
	Juice of 1 lemon	
	Salt and freshly ground pepper to taste	
1/2 cup	peas, defrosted	125 mL
1 cup	diced English cucumber	250 mL
4	green onions, sliced	4

1. Cook the pasta according to the package directions. Drain and rinse with cold water. Drain again.

2. In a food processor or blender, process the pine nuts, garlic and mint leaves until finely chopped. With the processor running, pour in the olive oil until combined. Add the cheese, lemon juice and salt and pepper.

3. Toss the pesto with the pasta. Mix in the peas, cucumber and green onions. Serve garnished with mint leaves.

Serves 8

Belgian Endive and Pecan Salad

For a picnic, pack the dressing separately and dip the Belgian endive leaves in as you eat. Munch on the pecans separately.

6	Belgium endives	6
1 cup	pecan halves	250 mL
3 tbsp	raspberry vinegar	45 mL
1 tbsp	plain yogurt	15 mL
1/2 cup	olive oil	125 mL
1 tbsp	walnut oil, optional	15 mL
	Salt and freshly ground pepper to taste	

1. Separate the endives into leaves. Spread on a platter and scatter with the walnuts.

2. In a small bowl, combine the raspberry vinegar with the yogurt. Slowly beat in the olive and walnut oils. Season with salt and pepper. Pour the dressing over the endives.

Serves 8

Cherries with Sour Cream Dip

Although pitting cherries is extra work, it makes them more luscious to eat. If you love cheese, serve the cherries with a slice of ripe, oozing Brie instead of the dip.

1 lb	cherries	500 g
1/2 cup	sour cream	125 mL
2 tbsp	brown sugar	25 mL
1/4 tsp	almond extract	1 mL

1. Wash the cherries, but do not remove the stems. Combine the sour cream, brown sugar and almond extract. Dip each cherry into the sour cream before eating.

Serves 8

8
August

*With fall on its way, August delivers us some special gifts —
tomatoes and corn. Who hasn't thought lingeringly of juicy
red beefsteaks when looking at the anemic winter tomato
crop? And corn straight from the field into the pot — it
practically makes the end of summer bearable.*

In season
apricots
beans
beets
blueberries
broccoli
cauliflower
celery
corn
cucumbers
peaches
peppers
tomatoes
zucchini

Menu
Elegant and Easy
Dinner for Six

PRESERVING THE SUMMER

Every year my garden becomes over-grown with herbs. I like to preserve this summer bounty, because there is nothing more agreeable than using your own herbs in the cold of winter. They smell better, taste better and are certainly cheaper than the store-bought version.

Through the years I've tried to bring herbs indoors and grow them in pots in a sunny window. Usually within three weeks they are brown and droopy; within a month they are dead. So I've had to think of other ways to preserve them.

Using the following methods, you can have a bountiful supply of garden herbs all winter long.

Preserving Herbs in Oil

• Flavor oils with your favorite herb or a combination of herbs; the more herbs you add, the stronger the oil will be.

• Use whole stalks, because they have lots of flavor. Cover the stalks with either a good-quality vegetable oil or olive oil (it is not necessary to use premium extra-virgin olive oil). Leave for one week, then remove the herbs. (Make sure the herbs are completely covered by the oil, otherwise they will turn rancid.)

• Try mixing several different herbs together, and add a clove of garlic or a chili pepper for extra zest.

• Use flavored oils for salad dressings, marinades, sautéing, or sprinkling on pizzas. Prettily bottled, they make attractive gifts.

Pears are the only fruit that cannot be frozen, because their texture changes to mush.

Preserving Herbs in Vinegar

• Use single herbs on their stalks, or a combination of herbs. Fill half the jar with herbs. Do not pack tightly.

• Use either a white wine vinegar or rice vinegar because their mild flavor will give you a less acidic, more mellow product.

• Place the herb stalks in a bottle or jar, cover with vinegar and leave in the sunlight for two weeks to draw out the flavor from the herbs.

• Remove the herbs and add a single fresh stalk for presentation. Store in a cupboard.

Drying and Freezing Herbs and Spices

• To dry herbs, pick them just before they start to flower.

• Do not wash the herbs before drying them, unless they are very dusty. If you have to wash them, dry them well with a paper towel.

• The easiest way to dry herbs is to tie a bunch loosely with string and hang upside down in an airy place for four to five days, or until the herbs are completely dry. Shake the leaves into a paper bag and discard the stems. Store the leaves in jars in a dark, cool place and use as needed.

• If you are growing spices which form into seeds (such as coriander, caraway, fennel and cumin), harvest them as soon as the seed heads droop. Cut away the seeds, discarding any stalks, and place on a baking sheet. Dry the seeds naturally in the air for two days. (If the sun is out, the seeds should dry in a couple of hours.) Place the seeds in jars and store in a dark place.

• If you see any signs of moisture in the jars once the seeds have been bottled, pop the seeds in a 150°F (65°C) oven for an hour to make sure they are completely dry.

• Some herbs can be successfully frozen. Chives, dill, tarragon and cilantro should chopped, scattered on a baking sheet, frozen, then packed into a jar or freezer bag and kept in the freezer. Use the frozen herbs in sauces, stews and other wet mixtures, but don't thaw them before using.

• Marjoram, mint and sage should be frozen in sprigs in freezer bags. Their flavor is better preserved frozen than dried.

Freezing Fruits and Vegetables

• Most fruits and vegetables can be frozen successfully. Tomatoes, peaches, red tart cherries, raspberries and blueberries freeze well, and you cannot find good-quality fresh versions of these fruits and vegetables in the winter. Use the frozen produce for pies, sauces, soups and puddings.

• To freeze fruits and vegetables, leave them whole, rinse and dry well. Lay on a baking sheet and freeze, then pack in freezer bags and containers. Do not peel tomatoes or peaches — the skins will fall off easily when they defrost.

• Fruit can be frozen packed in sugar. Some people prefer this method because the added sugar allows the fruits to retain their flavor for a longer period of time. A rule of thumb is to use ³/₄ cup (175 mL) sugar for 4 cups (1 L) sliced fruit and ¹/₂ cup (125 mL) sugar for 4 cups (1 L) whole fruit or berries. When using this fruit, cut back on the sugar in the recipe.

• Frozen fruit should keep in the freezer for up to one year.

Oregano Basil Oil

Use for salad dressings, sautéing vegetables or veal in Italian dishes, or sprinkling on pizzas. Brush on chicken before grilling or use to flavor pizza dough. If you have to rinse the herbs because they are dirty, shake them and dry thoroughly in paper towels; otherwise, any water will cause the oil to spit when heated. Remove the herbs when the oil is ready and replace with a garnish of fresh ones. Other possible herb combinations include tarragon-mint, marjoram-sage and rosemary-thyme. Experiment with your own favorite combinations; you'll find they give new life to your recipes.

2 cups	olive oil	500 mL
3	stalks fresh basil with leaves	3
3	stalks fresh oregano with leaves	3

1. In a bottle or jar, cover the basil and oregano with the oil. Leave for one week before using.

Makes 2 cups (500 mL)

Tarragon Vinegar

All herb vinegars are made by the same method. I make a chervil, dill and tarragon vinegar that gives a lovely lift to salad dressings. You can easily double or triple these recipes.

2 cups	white wine vinegar	500 mL
1 cup	fresh tarragon	250 mL

1. Pour the vinegar over the tarragon leaves in a glass jar. Cover and leave in a sunny window for two weeks. Strain the vinegar, if desired. Store in a cool, dark cupboard. Keeps indefinitely.

Makes 2 cups (500 mL)

Pesto

Don't add Parmesan to pesto before freezing; beat ¹/₄ cup (50 mL) Parmesan cheese and 2 tbsp (25 mL) olive oil into the defrosted pesto just before using. Try pesto over fresh fettuccine noodles, or beat into butter as a topping for grilled pork or veal chops. Other non-traditional forms of pesto can be made with parsley, sage, dill or mint.

2	cloves garlic	2
2 cups	packed fresh basil leaves	500 mL
2 tbsp	pine nuts	25 mL
¹/₂ cup	olive oil	125 mL
	Salt and freshly ground pepper to taste	

1. Place the garlic, basil, pine nuts and olive oil in a food processor or blender. Process until smooth. Season with salt and pepper.

2. Place in freezer bags or jars and freeze.

Makes 1¹/₂ cups (375 mL)

Basil Leaves in Oil

This method preserves the herbs for use later in the season. Any large-leafed herb like sage or mint can be preserved by this method. Sprinkle 1 tsp (5 mL) coarse salt in the bottom of a jar. Pack in basil leaves until the jar is half full. Sprinkle another ¹/₂ tsp (2 mL) salt over the leaves. Continue to layer in the leaves until the jar is full. Pour in the oil until the leaves are completely covered. Cover tightly and leave in a cool place for up to one year. Use the leaves for flavoring dishes and the oil for cooking.

Pesto Salad Dressing

To use pesto as a salad dressing, whisk ¹/₄ cup (50 mL) pesto with 2 tbsp (25 mL) lemon juice and ¹/₄ cup (50 mL) olive oil.

CORN

Yellow cobs of freshly picked corn slathered with butter — it's the best August treat. Corn starts to lose its freshness as soon as it is picked — the sugar content turns to starch — so look for locally grown corn and rush it to the pot.

- Don't buy partially exposed tips; the corn deteriorates even faster when exposed to light.
- Look for bright-green husks that tightly encircle the kernels. Reject wilted-looking, yellowing husks.
- The silk at the end of the husk should be bright, moist and silky-looking. The drier the silk, the older the corn.
- To check corn for freshness, pull back the husk to expose about 2 inches (5 cm) of corn. The kernels should be even-sized, glossy, plump and resistant to the touch. Or, hold the husk tightly at the silk end. If the corn is ripe, you should be able to feel the kernels through the husk.
- To store husks after buying, place in a sealed plastic bag and refrigerate. Corn likes a cold, moist atmosphere.
- To remove kernels from the ear, first slice between the rows with a knife. Then, using the back of the knife, scrape the kernels with their milky liquid into a bowl. Leftover corn can also be cut off the cobs and frozen for another use.
- To boil corn on the cob, remove the cob from its husk and place in a large pot of salted boiling water. Boil for 5 to 7 minutes, or until the kernels are tender.
- To steam corn, place the cobs on a rack over about 2 inches (5 cm) boiling water. Steam, covered, for 5 to 7 minutes.
- To microwave corn, wrap the corn in plastic wrap and cook at High (100%) for 5 minutes.
- One ear of corn yields about 1/2 cup (125 mL) kernels.

For a quick topping for corn on the cob, combine 1/4 cup (50 mL) softened butter with 1 tbsp (15 mL) each chopped fresh chives and basil. This should make enough for four cobs. Or mix together 1/2 cup (125 mL) cream cheese with 1 tbsp (15 mL) mayonnaise, 1 tsp (5 mL) lemon juice, 1/2 tsp (2 mL) chili powder and hot pepper sauce to taste.

Corn Chowder

Spicy cornbread* goes well with this chowder. Serve before steaks, lamb chops or hamburgers.

1 tbsp	olive oil	15 mL
2	slices bacon, chopped	2
1	onion, chopped	1
1/2	red pepper, diced	1/2
1/2	green pepper, diced	1/2
1	large potato, peeled and diced	1
1 cup	chicken stock	250 mL
2 cups	milk	500 mL
2 cups	corn kernels	500 mL
1	bay leaf	1
	Salt and freshly ground pepper to taste	

1. In a large pot, heat the oil and add the bacon and onion. Sauté until soft and slightly browned. Add the red and green peppers and the potato. Sauté for 1 minute.

2. Pour in the chicken stock and milk. Add the corn and bay leaf and simmer for 30 minutes, or until the vegetables are tender.

3. Remove the bay leaf and season with salt and pepper to taste.

Serves 4

*See *Lucy Waverman's Cooking School Cookbook*, page 116.

Succotash

Succotash, a creamy melange of vegetables, is an old Indian dish made with fresh corn. Serve with barbecued chicken, spareribs or fish.

2 tbsp	butter	25 mL
1	red onion, chopped	1
2	cloves garlic, finely chopped	2
1	red pepper, chopped	1
2 cups	corn kernels	500 mL
2 cups	cooked lima beans	500 mL
1/2 cup	whipping cream	125 mL
	Salt and freshly ground pepper to taste	

1. In a frying pan on medium heat, melt the butter. Add the onion, garlic and red peppers. Sauté gently for 2 minutes, or until softened. Add the corn and continue to sauté until the corn is tender, about 4 minutes.

2. Stir in the lima beans and reheat. Pour in the whipping cream and simmer for a few minutes, or until the cream has thickened. Season well with the salt and pepper.

Serves 6

TOMATOES

In August, the finest tomatoes will begin to appear in our markets. Their sunny flavor and sweet taste will banish all memories of the Styrofoam tomatoes we eat during the rest of the year.

Popular Varieties

• **Beefsteak** tomatoes are the most popular tomatoes in Canada. They are large, slightly flattened and have fleshy walls. Beefsteaks are stars in cooking and make excellent eating. They freeze well.
• There are many varieties of **round** tomatoes, all with similar tastes. Most are medium-sized, globe-shaped and good for eating and freezing.
• **Plum** or **Roma** tomatoes are elongated, thick-fleshed and less juicy than other tomatoes. Because of their texture, they are excellent for cooking, canning and drying.
• **Cherry** tomatoes are small, round and good for eating, barbecuing and garnishes. The trendy tomato today is the yellow, pear-shaped cherry

Corn has about 83 calories per ear (not counting the butter!), and it contains lots of dietary fiber.

There is a delicious variety of corn called Peaches and Cream, which has both yellow and white kernels.

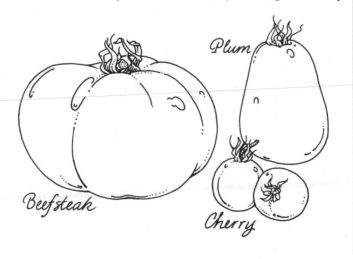

tomato, which makes a beautiful garnish on a plate as well as a spectacular nibble.

Buying and Preparing

• Look for tomatoes that are heavy for their size; they are usually the juiciest. They should be firm and unblemished, with no cracks on the surface. A few scars on the stem end are acceptable, but yellow or green scars are not.

• Field tomatoes are sun-ripened tomatoes grown outdoors; hot-house tomatoes are grown in a controlled climate under glass. The best-tasting tomatoes are vine-ripened field tomatoes, so buy them while they are available. Eat them fresh while they are plentiful, or preserve them by drying, freezing or using in sauces and soups.

• Always store tomatoes at room temperature. Storing them in the refrigerator can be detrimental to both their taste and texture. Unripe tomatoes should be placed on a sunny window sill until they redden. Do not refrigerate unripe tomatoes, or they can become mealy.

• Slice tomatoes with a serrated knife, which will grip the skin more easily. The best way to slice is to place the tomato stem side up and cut through the tomato vertically. The slices retain more juice than cutting the more traditional horizontal way.

• Peel tomatoes by making a small slit in the skin, then immersing them in boiling water for 30 seconds. Run under cold water. Slide the tip of a knife under the skin; it should peel off easily. Most cooked tomato dishes call for peeled tomatoes, because the skin comes off during the cooking and becomes chewy and unattractive.

Most green tomatoes will not ripen on a sunny window sill, but they do have other delicious uses. Fry them with lots of garlic and use as a garnish for steaks. Make a green tomato chutney or use in a ratatouille instead of green peppers.

• Core tomatoes by cutting around the stem and removing it. Seed tomatoes by cutting them in half crosswise. Squeeze the halves gently over a bowl; the seeds should fall out.

Drying Tomatoes

Today sun-dried tomatoes pop up on pizzas, in sauces and salads, as a nibble with cheese and on antipasto platters. They are an expensive luxury, and the quality varies in direct proportion to the price. There appears to be no such thing as a bargain sun-dried tomato that is edible.

But tomatoes are easy to dry at home. It is essential to use plum tomatoes because of their thick flesh and strong flavor. The traditional method of sun-drying — leaving tomatoes on racks in the sun for a few days — doesn't work in Canada because of the humidity and uncertainty of rain. Instead, tomatoes can be dried in dehydrators or by the following home method.

• Preheat the oven to 200°F (100°C). Line baking sheets with wire cake racks. Wash and dry the tomatoes. Cut them in half lengthwise. (You can remove the seeds, if desired.) Lay on racks, cut side up, and lightly sprinkle with salt. Place in the oven.

• Bake for 30 minutes, lower the heat to 150°F (65°C) and bake for another 12 to 14 hours, or until the tomatoes are leathery but not hard. Keep checking, because the size and thickness of the tomatoes will affect the cooking time. Occasionally press the tomatoes down with a spatula to try to keep them flat. They will reduce in weight by about 90 percent.

• Remove from the oven and cool to

room temperature. If there is any sign of dampness, return to the oven until completely dry. Place the cooled tomatoes in clean jars and completely cover with olive oil. You can tuck a sprig of rosemary or a chili pepper into each jar if desired. Cover tightly and store in a cool place. The tomatoes should keep for one year, and the oil is wonderful for marinades or frying tomatoes or other vegetables.

Sun-dried Tomato Bread with Provolone Cheese

This is Clare Hymas's recipe, developed for a special summer barbecue. It is my favorite quickbread to serve with an Italian meal or a barbecue. Substitute mozzarella if you cannot find provolone.

2¹/₂ cups	all-purpose flour	625 mL
2 tsp	baking powder	10 mL
1 tsp	salt	5 mL
¹/₂ tsp	baking soda	2 mL
1 cup	grated provolone cheese	250 mL
¹/₂ cup	chopped green onion	125 mL
2 tbsp	finely chopped parsley	25 mL
2 tsp	dried rosemary	10 mL
¹/₄ tsp	freshly ground pepper	1 mL
¹/₄ cup	chopped sun-dried tomatoes	50 mL
¹/₄ cup	sun-dried tomato oil or olive oil	50 mL
2 tbsp	granulated sugar	25 mL
2	cloves garlic, finely chopped	2
2	eggs	2
1¹/₄ cups	buttermilk	300 mL
¹/₃ cup	pine nuts	75 mL

1. Preheat the oven to 350°F (180°C). Grease two 9 × 5-inch (2 L) loaf pans.

2. In a large bowl, combine the flour, baking powder, salt, baking soda, grated cheese, green onion, parsley, rosemary, pepper and tomatoes.

3. In a separate bowl, combine the oil, sugar, garlic, eggs and buttermilk.

4. Stir the wet ingredients into the dry until combined. Stir in the pine nuts.

5. Pour the mixture into the prepared pans and bake for 45 to 50 minutes, or until a toothpick comes out clean.

6. Cool in the pans for 5 minutes, then remove to a wire rack.

Makes two loaves

Sun-dried Tomato and Olive Sauce

Serve this Italian-style sauce to top a grilled tuna or swordfish steak, chicken breasts or veal. Or thin it with extra olive oil and toss it with pasta.

1 cup	black olives, pitted	250 mL
¹/₂ tsp	dried thyme	2 mL
2	cloves garlic, chopped	2
10	sun-dried tomatoes, chopped	10
¹/₄ cup	olive oil	50 mL

1. In a food processor, combine all the ingredients except the olive oil. With the machine running, pour the olive oil through the feeder tube. Process until the mixture is slightly chunky.

Makes 1¹/₂ cups (375 mL)

Best Summer Sandwich
When beefsteaks are at their finest, spread two slices of bread generously with mayonnaise. Lay thick slices of beefsteak tomatoes on top. Season with salt and pepper and a few basil leaves.

Tomato Sauce

To freeze tomatoes in sauce form, prepare the following simple recipe. It may be necessary to reseason the sauce when it is thawed, because freezing can cause the seasoning to deteriorate slightly. Pureeing the tomatoes means they don't have to be peeled.

2 tbsp	olive oil	25 mL
1	onion, chopped	1
2	cloves garlic, finely chopped	2
8	large tomatoes, pureed	8
¼ cup	tomato paste	50 mL
3 tbsp	finely chopped fresh basil, or 1 tbsp (15 mL) dried	45 mL
pinch	granulated sugar	pinch
	Salt and freshly ground pepper to taste	

1. Heat the oil in a large frying pan over medium heat. Add the onion and garlic and sauté until softened, about 3 minutes.

2. Stir in the tomatoes, tomato paste, basil and sugar.

3. Simmer, uncovered, for 30 to 45 minutes, or until the sauce has thickened slightly. Season with salt and pepper. Cool and freeze in freezer containers or freezer bags.

Makes about 3½ cups (875 mL)

PEACHES

I remember eating a perfect peach when my father returned from the war. As a present he brought me a beautiful blushing golden peach. I had never seen or eaten such a fruit before. To this day I remember its sweet juiciness and full peachy smell. Jane Grigson, a famous English food writer, tells of her journey to find the perfect peach in France. She had heard of the famous French Montreuil peaches that Louis XIV was addicted to. But after a long search she found that these magnificent peaches were no more. The trees had been chopped down. ''The French are more careless of their past than we are,'' she commented.

Why the obsession with the perfect peach? Perhaps because with its golden, downy skin and warm succulent flesh, it is nature's most flawless fruit.

Popular Varieties

• There are two basic types of peaches. In **clingstone** peaches, the peach flesh adheres to the pit. Clingstones are used for canning and processing.
• In **freestone** peaches, the flesh separates easily from the pit. Red Havens are one of the best freestone varieties, and they are excellent for eating. A crossbreed variety, the **semi-freestone**, usually the first available eating peach in July, can be used for both canning and eating.

Buying and Storing

• A good peach has a creamy yellow background color and a peachy smell. The deeper and more uniform the color, the riper the peach. The pink or red blush indicates variety, not the ripeness.

• Peaches should be firm to the touch and have a smooth, unwrinkled skin. Don't buy bruised peaches.

• Softness, which people sometimes use to indicate ripeness, usually means the peach is stringy inside.

• If you are poaching peaches, leave the skin on, because it improves the color of the syrup and can easily be removed afterwards.

• Store ripe unwashed peaches in the refrigerator for up to one week.

• Place unripe peaches on the kitchen counter away from the sun. Refrigerate them as they ripen.

• To peel peaches, drop them into boiling water for 30 seconds. Rinse with cold water, and the skins should slip off easily.

• Toss peeled peaches with lemon juice to prevent browning.

Peach Cake

A moist, buttery cake topped with juicy peaches. Serve as a dessert or at tea time.

3	large peaches, peeled and pitted	3
1/2 cup	unsalted butter, at room temperature	125 mL
3/4 cup	granulated sugar	175 mL
2	eggs	2
1/2 cup	plain yogurt	125 mL
	Grated rind of 1 lemon	
1 tsp	vanilla extract	5 mL
pinch	salt	pinch
1 tsp	baking powder	5 mL
1/2 tsp	baking soda	2 mL
2 cups	all-purpose flour	500 mL
Topping:		
1/4 cup	granulated sugar	50 mL
2 tbsp	unsalted butter	25 mL

1. Preheat the oven to 350°F (180°C).

2. Butter and flour a 9-inch (23 cm) springform pan. Slice the peaches about 1/8 inch (3 mm) thick.

3. In an electric mixer or food processor, cream 1/2 cup (125 mL) butter until softened, then beat in 3/4 cup (175 mL) sugar until thick and fluffy.

4. Add the eggs one at a time, beating well after each addition. Beat in the yogurt, lemon rind and vanilla.

5. In a separate bowl, sift together the salt, baking powder, baking soda and flour. Beat into the batter until just combined.

6. Spread the batter in the prepared pan. Top with the peaches, overlapping the slices. Sprinkle on the remaining 1/4 cup (50 mL) sugar and dot with the remaining 2 tbsp (25 mL) butter.

7. Bake for 55 to 60 minutes, or until a cake tester comes out clean. Serve warm or cold.

Serves 8

You don't see much fuzz on peaches anymore. It is mechanically removed when the peaches are picked.

When baking peach pies, the juice can make the pastry soggy. To avoid this, brush the pastry with a lightly beaten egg white before adding the filling, or a sprinkle cookie crumbs over the base of the tart to absorb the juices. (Ginger cookies are my favorite.)

Peach Soup with Champagne

This refreshing soup was the hit of a charity dinner that I planned for three hundred people at the King Edward Hotel in Toronto.

³/₄ cup	water	175 mL
2	whole cloves	2
¹/₄ cup	granulated sugar	50 mL
1	3-inch (7.5 cm) cinnamon stick	1
pinch	ground nutmeg	pinch
³/₄ cup	Champagne or sparkling white wine	175 mL
4	large peaches, peeled	4
¹/₂ cup	whipping cream Fresh mint leaves	125 mL

1. Combine the water, cloves, sugar, cinnamon and nutmeg in a medium pot. Bring to a boil on high heat. Lower the heat and simmer for 10 minutes. Strain and cool. Add the Champagne and chill the mixture.

2. Pit the peaches. Puree in a food processor or blender. Gradually add the Champagne mixture. Stir in the cream. Refrigerate until serving time. Garnish each serving with a mint leaf.

Serves 4 to 6

Quick Peach Ideas
• Split scones or tea biscuits in half and sandwich with sliced peaches and whipped cream. Top with more peaches and cream.
• Puree peeled peaches with 1 tbsp (15 mL) lemon juice and a sprinkling of nutmeg and cinnamon. Use to top ice cream or as a sauce for crêpes.
• Drop a whole peeled peach into a glass of Champagne or sparkling white wine. Eat the wine-bathed peach, then drink the Champagne. (This is the forerunner of the Bellini — a combination of pureed peach and Champagne.)

Peach Schnitz Pie

This is a traditional and excellent Mennonite recipe with peaches nestled in a pie crust, topped with cream and crumble. The filling should be slightly runny.

¹/₂ cup	brown sugar	125 mL
3 tbsp	all-purpose flour	45 mL
pinch	salt	pinch
2 tbsp	unsalted butter	25 mL
1	unbaked 9-inch (23 cm) pie shell	1
4 cups	thickly sliced, peeled peaches	1 L
2 tsp	lemon juice	10 mL
¹/₄ cup	whipped cream	50 mL
1	egg yolk	1

1. Preheat the oven to 425°F (220°C).

2. In a medium bowl, combine the sugar, flour and salt. Cut in the butter until the mixture is crumbly. Sprinkle one-third of the mixture on the bottom of the pie shell to absorb the peach juices.

3. Add the peaches and sprinkle with the lemon juice.

4. In a small bowl, combine the cream and egg yolk and pour evenly over the peaches. Cover with the remaining crumbs.

5. Bake for 10 minutes. Lower the heat to 375°F (190°C) and bake for a further 30 to 35 minutes, or until the pastry is golden-brown and the filling is bubbly. Cool before serving.

Serves 6

Peach Ginger Pie

As no pastry is involved in this pie, it is a snap to make. Process ginger cookies to make the cookie crumbs.

1¹/₂ cups	gingersnap cookie crumbs	375 mL
¹/₂ cup	melted unsalted butter	125 mL
¹/₄ cup	granulated sugar	50 mL
2 tbsp	cornstarch	25 mL
¹/₄ cup	peach nectar	50 mL
¹/₄ cup	apricot jam	50 mL
1 tbsp	lemon juice	15 mL
6	large peaches, peeled and pitted	6
2 tbsp	unsalted butter	25 mL
2 tbsp	peach schnapps	25 mL

1. Preheat the oven to 375°F (190°C).

2. Combine the cookie crumbs and melted butter in a bowl. Press evenly over the bottom and sides of a 9-inch (23 cm) flan pan.

3. Bake for 8 minutes, or until lightly browned. Cool.

4. In a medium pot, combine the sugar and cornstarch. Stir in the peach nectar, apricot jam and lemon juice.

5. In a food processor or blender, puree 2 peaches. Add to the pot. Cook and stir over medium heat until the mixture comes to a boil; boil for 1 minute. Remove from the heat and stir in the butter and peach schnapps.

6. Slice the remaining 4 peaches into ¹/₄-inch (5 mm) slices. Stir into the sauce.

7. Mound the filling into the pie shell. Chill for about 3 hours, or until set.

Serves 8

PLUMS

Contrary to what many people believe, a prune is not a dried version of a plum. Most plums ferment if they are dried with their pits; only a special variety — prune plums — can be dried with the pits in them. Because farmers were afraid of the public's reaction to the name "prune" plums, they are marketed as blue or purple plums.

But the prune plum is only one of a vast variety of plums on the market. From the almost-black varieties to the yellow-fleshed fruit, plums come in many shapes, colors and tastes. They can be round or oval, black, yellow, green or red-skinned. Most are clingstone, but a few are freestone.

Popular Varieties

• **Santa Rosa** is the best-selling plum. It is conical in shape, with a reddish skin and a greenish-yellow flesh. It is slightly tart but quite uninteresting in taste.
• **El Dorado** is a heart-shaped, black-red plum with a greenish-yellow flesh that turns pink when cooked. It has lots of juice and a tart/sweet flavor.
• **Queen Anne** is a refreshingly flavored black plum with an amber-colored flesh.
• The **prune** plum is a small, oval-shaped, dark-blue freestone plum that is excellent for baking and jam.
• **Damson** is a small blue plum not available as much as in the past because its tart flesh is more suitable for making jams and chutney than eating. The few that are available have become expensive and trendy.

• The **greengage** plum is a greenish-yellow plum suitable for eating when very ripe, but it is also excellent for cooking. The Kelseys are the best variety of greengage plums.

Buying and Storing

• Unfortunately, most plums are picked before they are ripe for efficient shipping and storage, and they don't ripen as well off the tree as on. Without a consumer uprising, the days of fresh-picked, ripe, juicy, crisp plums could be over.
• Look for plums that are firm to the touch but give slightly when pressed. The color should be uniform.
• Avoid bruised, shrivelled or split plums.
• Store ripe plums loose in the refrigerator for three to four days. Leave unripe plums on the window sill until they yield slightly to the touch.

Chicken with Plums

An easy chicken dish that is baked in a Chinese-style plum sauce.

8	chicken legs with thighs	8
	Salt and freshly ground pepper to taste	
2 tbsp	butter	25 mL
2 tbsp	vegetable oil	25 mL
1	onion, chopped	1
1	clove garlic, chopped	1
1/2 cup	plum jam	125 mL
1 tbsp	soy sauce	15 mL
1 tsp	dry mustard	5 mL
1 tsp	ground ginger	5 mL
1/2 tsp	cayenne pepper	2 mL
1/4 cup	lemon juice	50 mL
1/4 cup	tomato paste	50 mL
6	black plums, pitted and quartered	6

If you substitute chicken breasts for chicken legs, cook for 10 minutes less than the prescribed cooking time.

1. Preheat the oven to 350°F (180°C).

2. Separate the legs and thighs and season with salt and pepper.

3. On medium heat, melt the butter and oil in a large frying pan. When sizzling, add the chicken in batches and cook for 3 minutes per side, or until golden-brown. Remove to an ovenproof baking dish large enough to hold the chicken in a single layer. Discard all but 1 tbsp (15 mL) of the fat.

4. Add the onion and garlic to the frying pan and sauté until the onion is softened, about 2 minutes. Whisk in the jam, soy sauce, mustard, ginger, cayenne, lemon juice and tomato paste. Bring to a boil and simmer for 15 minutes.

5. Pour the sauce over the chicken. Surround with the plums. Bake, uncovered, for 35 to 45 minutes, basting occasionally, until the juices run clear.

Serves 8

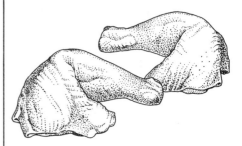

Cinnamon Plum Tart

This is a favorite Scottish tart. It is like a plum quiche with a crunchy cinnamon topping. If you use the small blue plums, increase the number to 12.

8	plums, pitted and quartered	8
1	baked 9-inch (23 cm) pie shell	1
1 cup	whipping cream	250 mL
2	eggs	2
1	egg yolk	1
	Juice of 1 lemon	
1/2 cup	granulated sugar	125 mL
1 tsp	ground cinnamon	5 mL

Topping:

3 tbsp	brown sugar	45 mL
1 tsp	ground cinnamon	5 mL

1. Preheat the oven to 350°F (180°C). Arrange the plums in the pie shell, skin side up.

2. In a bowl, beat together the cream, eggs and egg yolk, lemon juice, granulated sugar and 1 tsp (5 mL) cinnamon. Pour over the plums.

3. Bake for 25 minutes, or until the plums are softened.

4. Mix together the brown sugar and the remaining 1 tsp (5 mL) cinnamon. Sprinkle over the tart. Return to the oven and bake for a further 10 minutes, or until crusty. Serve warm.

Serves 6

ZUCCHINI

Several years ago I decided to have a vegetable patch. I wanted to grow zucchini and tomatoes. I had heard they were easy crops to grow — important for a black thumb like me.

Walking around the garden one summer day, I admired my plump green tomatoes and the slender finger-like zucchini with its glorious yellow flowers. How many more weeks would it be before they were ready for picking, I wondered.

Within two days my garden was overrun by these fast-growing green monsters; they were even nudging the tomatoes out of the way. Because I had to pick these giants immediately, we ate many loaves of zucchini bread that winter. Now I don't grow it any more.

• Zucchini is a green summer squash of Italian origin. The seeds and skin are edible.

• Look for smaller ones, which are sweeter and less seed-filled than the large. They should be a brightly colored vibrant green. Yellow zucchini have the same flavor as green, and the two colors look good together on a plate.

• Avoid mushy, bruised or overlarge zucchini, because they can be bitter.

• Store zucchini in the refrigerator; they spoil quickly.

• Some zucchini have a bitter taste, which can be removed by salting them lightly and letting them drain for 30 minutes. Wipe them dry before cooking.

Zucchini Watercress Soup

Use a tart apple such as a Granny Smith or Spy in this soup. The watercress adds a sharp, interesting taste and the apple is used as a thickener. Garnish the soup with grated curls of zucchini.

¹/₄ cup	butter	50 mL
1	onion, chopped	1
1	apple, peeled and diced	1
4 cups	chopped zucchini	1 L
4 cups	chicken stock	1 L
2 cups	watercress leaves	500 mL
1 cup	milk	250 mL

1. In a large pot, heat the butter on medium heat. Sauté the onion and apple until soft but not brown, about 5 minutes.

2. Stir in the zucchini and sauté for 1 minute. Pour in the chicken stock and bring to a boil. Cover and simmer for 20 minutes, or until the zucchini is tender.

3. Add the watercress leaves and simmer for 5 minutes. Cool slightly, then puree in a food processor or blender. Return the soup to the pot and add the milk. Heat through but do not boil, to avoid curdling the mixture.

Serves 8

Zucchini Rice Casserole

For an attractive presentation, scoop out the cooked zucchini from its skin, complete the dish and stuff the casserole mixture back into the zucchini shells before baking. Serve as a side dish with steaks, chicken, pork or lamb.

If you have copious amounts of zucchini and don't feel like cooking, chop it up and freeze in containers. Use it to make soups or vegetable dishes at a later date.

4	zucchini	4
4	slices bacon, diced	4
1	onion, chopped	1
2	cloves garlic, finely chopped	2
2 cups	cooked rice	500 mL
1 tbsp	finely chopped fresh tarragon, or 1 tsp (5 mL) dried	15 mL
1 tbsp	finely chopped fresh basil, or 1 tsp (5 mL) dried	15 mL
2 tbsp	finely chopped parsley	25 mL
¹/₄ cup	grated Parmesan cheese	50 mL
	Salt and freshly ground pepper to taste	
¹/₂ cup	grated Cheddar cheese	125 mL

1. In a large pot of boiling water, boil the zucchini until tender, about 8 minutes. Drain and refresh with cold water until cool. Dice the zucchini.

2. In a large frying pan on medium heat, cook the bacon until limp. Add the onion and garlic and sauté until softened, about 2 minutes. Stir in the rice, tarragon, basil, parsley and Parmesan cheese. Remove from the heat.

3. Preheat the oven to 350°F (180°C).

4. Add the zucchini to the rice mixture. Season with salt and pepper to taste.

5. Oil a 12 × 8-inch (3 L) ovenproof baking dish and pack with the rice/zucchini mixture. Sprinkle with the Cheddar cheese. Bake for 20 minutes, or until the casserole is hot and the cheese is melted and bubbly.

Serves 6

Zucchini Charlotte

A Charlotte is delicate vegetable custard that is good with grilled chicken, veal and fish. It can be served as a first course with a tomato sauce, or as a side dish.

3	zucchini, cut in chunks	3
3	eggs	3
½ cup	whipping cream	125 mL
	Salt and freshly ground pepper to taste	
¼ cup	chopped fresh basil	50 mL
1	clove garlic, chopped	1
2 tbsp	grated Parmesan cheese	25 mL
2 tbsp	olive oil	25 mL

1. Bring a pot of water to a boil. Add the zucchini and cook until soft, about 5 minutes. Refresh under cold running water and set aside.

2. Preheat the oven to 350°F (180°C).

3. Put the eggs and the cream into the food processor and combine together. Add the cooled zucchini. Puree and season to taste with salt and pepper. Pour into a greased 8-inch (2 L) baking pan.

4. Chop the basil with the garlic and Parmesan until very fine. Transfer to a bowl and whisk in the olive oil.

5. With a spoon, drizzle six lines of the garlic/basil mixture over the zucchini mixture. With the point of a clean knife, draw through the lines of garlic/basil mixture at right angles, six times. This will give the Charlotte a marbled effect. You can also spread the garlic mixture over the top.

6. Place the Charlotte in a larger pan half filled with hot water. Bake for 25 minutes, or until set.

Serves 6

Elegant and Easy Dinner for Six

When it's hot outside, the last thing I want to do is spend time in the kitchen. But families still have to be fed and friends still come over, so closing down the kitchen entirely is not an option. Instead, try this menu that takes less than an hour to prepare. Remember that summer is the time of our own homegrown produce and fresh herbs, with garden flowers to decorate plates — a time when food can look and taste original and creative without too much effort.

Onion Soup with Pesto

Monkfish Provençal

Zucchini Linguine

Peaches Princess of Wales

Onion Soup with Pesto

This soup is a beautiful porcelain color highlighted with green swirls.

2	potatoes, peeled and chopped	2
1	Spanish onion, thinly sliced	1
2	cloves garlic, finely chopped	2
4 cups	chicken stock	1 L
1/2 cup	whipping cream	125 mL
	Salt and freshly ground pepper to taste	
1/3 cup	pesto (see page 121)	75 mL

1. In a pot, combine the potatoes, onions, garlic and chicken stock. Bring to a boil, turn the heat to low and simmer, covered, for 20 minutes, or until the potatoes and onions are tender.

2. Place in a food processor or blender and puree until smooth. Return to the pot, stir in the whipping cream and simmer for 5 minutes. Season with the salt and pepper.

3. Pour the soup into soup bowls and swirl the pesto on top.

Serves 6

Monkfish Provençal

Monkfish, sometimes called poor man's lobster because of its similar texture, is excellent when combined with the strong flavors of sunny Provence — tomatoes, garlic and olive oil. You can make this recipe a day ahead, then cover and refrigerate. Just before serving time, reheat, covered, in a 350°F (180°C) oven for 15 minutes, or until heated through.

1/3 cup	all-purpose flour	75 mL
1/2 tsp	salt	2 mL
1/2 tsp	freshly ground pepper	2 mL
1/2 tsp	dried thyme	2 mL
2 lb	monkfish fillets	1 kg
1/4 cup	olive oil	50 mL
1	large onion, finely chopped	1
2	cloves garlic, finely chopped	2
3 tbsp	brandy	45 mL
1 cup	dry white wine	250 mL
6	tomatoes, peeled, seeded and chopped	6
1/2 tsp	granulated sugar	2 mL
1 tsp	dried thyme	5 mL
1	bay leaf	1
1/4 tsp	salt	1 mL
pinch	cayenne pepper	pinch
1/4 cup	finely chopped parsley	50 mL

1. In a large bowl, season the flour with salt, pepper and 1/2 tsp (2 mL) thyme. Cut the monkfish into 1-inch (2.5 cm) cubes and roll in the seasoned flour.

2. In a large frying pan, heat 2 tbsp (25 mL) oil over medium-high heat. Add the onion and garlic and sauté for 2 to 3 minutes, or until softened. Remove from the pan and reserve.

3. Pour in the remaining oil and add the monkfish, in batches if necessary. Sauté for 3 to 5 minutes, or until lightly browned. Pour in the brandy and reduce by half. Remove the fish and reserve.

4. Return the onions and garlic to the frying pan. Add the wine. Cook, stirring, over medium-high heat for 3 to 5 minutes, or until reduced to ¼ cup (50 mL).

5. Add the tomatoes to the frying pan with the sugar, 1 tsp (5 mL) thyme, bay leaf, salt and cayenne. Bring to a boil, reduce the heat and simmer until the sauce has thickened, about 15 minutes.

6. Return the fish (with any accumulated juices) to the frying pan and simmer for 10 to 15 minutes, or until cooked through. Sprinkle with the parsley before serving.

Serves 6

Zucchini Linguine

The tiny baby zucchini are great just sautéed with a little lemon juice, but the larger ones can be stringy and have less flavor. Here is a good way to use up some of the larger zucchini.

2	large zucchini	2
2 tbsp	olive oil	25 mL
1 tbsp	butter	15 mL
1	clove garlic, finely chopped	1
	Salt and freshly ground pepper to taste	

1. Using the grater blade of a food processor (or a hand grater), grate the zucchini into long shreds.

2. In a frying pan, heat the oil and butter on medium-high heat. When the butter sizzles, add the zucchini and garlic. Sauté until the zucchini

is limp. Season with the salt and pepper.

Serves 6

Peaches Princess of Wales

Purported to be a favorite of Princess Di's, this easy dish adds an elegant summer touch to a sophisticated dinner.

3 tbsp	raspberry jam	45 mL
3 tbsp	red currant jelly	45 mL
3 tbsp	apricot jam	45 mL
¼ cup	Amaretto	50 mL
6	peaches, peeled and sliced	6
4 cups	vanilla ice cream	1 L
1 cup	toasted slivered almonds	250 mL

1. Combine the jams in a large frying pan. Cook on low heat until the jams are liquefied.

2. Pour in the Amaretto. Bring to a boil, add the peaches and stir together until the peaches are warmed through.

3. Place the ice cream on serving plates and top with the peaches, some sauce and almonds.

Serves 6

9
September

Summer may be over, but Mother Nature still offers fine fare for those enjoying all that fall has to offer — eggplants, peppers, and a new season of entertaining.

SHELLFISH

People are eating more shellfish these days, because it is low in fat and calories, cooks quickly and is adaptable to lots of different cooking methods.

In Canada, we are blessed with excellent shellfish. The Atlantic provinces produce mussels, clams, oysters, lobster and scallops. The Pacific produces Dungeness crab, oysters, shrimp, mussels and clams.

Shellfish are at their peak in September because the water temperature begins to cool and triggers changes in the shellfish. They change their feed and begin to have the characteristic sweetness that turns people into shellfish lovers.

Clams

• The **softshell clam**, or **steamer**, is abundant in the Atlantic waters. The clam has a protruding, hose-like neck called a siphon, which it uses to burrow into the ground. Traditionally steamers are served steamed in a bucket with butter and vinegar. You remove the neck and eat the body.

• The Atlantic or **hardshell clam** is often called by its Indian name, **quahog**. It is sold by size. In Canada we simply grade them as small, medium or large, but Americans name the sizes. The smallest **little neck** clam measures about 2 inches (5 cm) in diameter. It is the best type for eating raw because it is the most tender. The **cherrystone** is the middle size. It is known as an all-purpose clam because it can be eaten raw or used in cooking. The largest and most mature hardshell clams are called **chowder** clams because they are used for clam chowder or fritters.

• The west coast clams are the **Manila** — a small, hardshell clam prized by the Japanese (who consume a large percentage of them). The **butter** clam, another variety of softshell clams, are also fished there.

• Clams in the shell must be alive when bought. The shell should be tightly closed. If it is open, tap it; if the shell does not close or the neck contract, the clam is dead and must be discarded.

• Avoid clams with broken shells.

• Look for even-sized clams that will require the same cooking time.

• If the clams are already shucked, looked for plump clams with a clear liquor and no shell particles.

• Store clams in a bowl with ice in the refrigerator, covered with a damp cloth, for up to three days.

• Wash all clams before cooking to remove the sand.

• To open or shuck a clam, place it in the palm of your hand with the hinged end down. Using pressure, insert a small heavy knife between the two shells and lever open. Serve the clam on the larger half shell.

• To steam clams, place them in a pot with about 1-inch (2.5 cm) water or wine. Cover the pot and steam on high heat until the clams open, about 5 minutes. If any shells do not open, discard the clam.

Lobsters

Our lobsters are highly prized because lobsters thrive best in colder water. Many of our lobsters are exported to Europe, where they are considered a luxurious delicacy.

• Buy lobsters live. When you see them in a tank, look for the frisky ones, which are often the freshest. If they are on ice in a refrigerated counter, pick one up by its tail. If the tail curls up, the lobster is alive.

• The lobster shell is dark-green and can look mottled or spotted. The shell turns red when the lobster is cooked.

• Make sure the lobster claws are pegged or banded before picking one up, otherwise you may get slashed.

• Buy live lobsters the day you want to cook them, or refrigerate overnight covered with wet towels.

• To cook a lobster whole, plunge it head first into boiling water. It dies instantly.

• To cook a lobster in parts, first you must sever the spinal cord. Plunge a chef's knife into the joint where the body and the tail section meet. This severs the spinal cord. Running the lobster's head under warm water for about thirty seconds will act as an anesthetic. Split the lobster in half from head to tail. Cut up into the desired number of pieces.

• Lobster is at its best when poached or steamed, which leaves the flesh sweet and juicy. Broiled or baked lobster is invariably overdone and dry.

Long antennae are one sign of a fresh lobster, because when lobsters have been in holding tanks for long periods of time, their antennae are eaten by other lobsters.

Bivalves are shellfish with two shells or "valves" — oysters, mussels, scallops and clams.

• To eat a cooked lobster, you need a nutcracker, a small lobster fork, a bowl for shells and a dish of melted butter with a sprinkle of lemon in it. First snap off the two claws and crack open with the nutcracker. Remove the meat with the fork. Twist the tail off and pull off the tail fins. Push the meat out with your fork or fingers. Before eating the body meat, remove the intestinal tract, gills and stomach sac found near the head. Finish by sucking the juice and meat from the thin legs.

Mussels

Mussels are one of the best of the bivalves. Their creamy orange, tender flesh is succulent and lean. Blue mussels, with their blue-black shells, are considered the finest. They grow in colonies attached by their feathery "beards" to rocks near the shore. Today these wild mussels have lost some of their appeal because of the new cultivated varieties, which have more meat, a more delicate flavor and are much cleaner. These cultured mussels are grown in long sleeves or "stockings" hung from log rafts in bays. They grow more quickly than the wild ones; aquacultured mussels are a large Maritime industry today.

• Mussels in the shell must be alive when bought. The shells should be tightly closed or close when you tap them.

• Discard mussels with broken shells.

• If you are not using fresh mussels right away, place them in a bowl with some ice, covered with a damp cloth. Store in the refrigerator for up to three days.

• To clean mussels, rinse them with cold water and pull away the feathery beards.

• Mussels are usually steamed. In a large pot, bring 1 inch (2.5 cm) of water or wine to a boil. Add the mussels, cover and steam for 1 to 2 minutes, shaking the pot occasionally. Remove the mussels with tongs as they open. Discard any that do not open.

Oysters

See pages 197 to 199.

Scallops

Scallops are the only bivalves that swim. White, fan-shaped shells with thirty-six tiny green eyes skitter through the water searching for food. Scallops are the only molluscs not sold alive. Because these shellfish die very quickly when fished, fishermen usually remove the shells on the boat and place the scallops on ice before shipping them to shore. Unfortunately, our fishermen also throw out the coral-colored roe, which is considered a delicacy in both Europe and Asia.

• There are two kinds of scallops — **bay** and **sea**. The smaller bay scallops, fished from inshore bays and estuaries, are considered the sweetest and juiciest, with a buttery texture, while the larger deep-sea scallops have a slightly chewier texture.

• Scallops should have no fishy aroma. They should be firm to the touch, glistening and fresh-looking. Avoid scallops that are sitting in a pool of water; they are sometimes soaked in water to increase their weight.

• Sea scallops should be white in

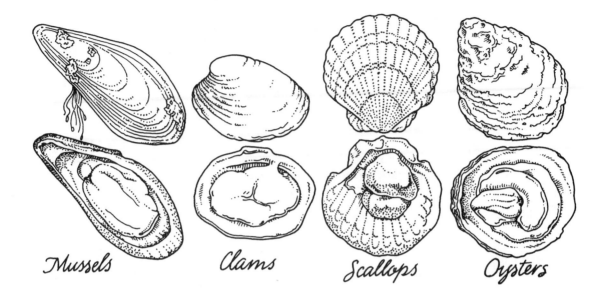

Mussels   Clams   Scallops   Oysters

color; bay scallops are creamy or pinkish.

• Scallops are very perishable — keep them for up to one day in the refrigerator in a bowl, covered with a damp towel.

• Before cooking scallops, remove the tiny white muscle on the side where the scallop was attached to the shell. (Sometimes these muscles have already been removed.)

• Scallops can be sautéed, poached, fried, barbecued or eaten raw. One pound (500 g) should feed three people.

Shrimp

The cooler the water, the smaller and often the more succulent the taste of the shrimp. Very little fresh shrimp comes on the market, because most of it is frozen directly on the fishing boats. The shrimp sold at the fishmonger are usually defrosted ones. Fresh shrimp will always be labeled, and the price will be higher.

• Shrimp come in a variety of colors — pink, brown, green or gray. After cooking, all shrimp turn pink.

• Shrimp are sold by the number of headless shrimp per pound, rather than by size. Sixteen to 20 shrimp per pound are extra-large shrimp; 21 to 25 are large; over 30 per pound are medium shrimp.

• If you find fresh shrimp, buy the ones that have shells tightly enclosing the meat.

• If you are buying packages of frozen shrimp, check for freezer burn (the shrimp will look dried out) or ice inside the package. The ice means the contents have been thawed and refrozen.

• If you are buying frozen shrimp, buy them with the shell on; the shell helps the shrimp retain flavor. Always defrost shrimp overnight in the refrigerator, never at room temperature.

• If you are buying defrosted shrimp, check that they are springy and that

Calico scallops, a small, inferior-tasting variety found in deep ocean water near the southern United States, are sometimes sold as bay scallops. Ask your fishmonger where scallops have come from before buying.

the shells have an even color. They should have no odor.

• To shell shrimp, use a pair of kitchen shears. Cut through the soft undershell and pull it off. The black vein can be removed if you wish, but this is not necessary. You can also remove the tiny legs on the underside before pulling the shell off with your fingers.

• Cook shrimp only until they turn pink and curl, so they will keep their flavor and texture. Overcooked shrimp is dry and tasteless.

• Never boil shrimp; they become tough. Gently simmer them in flavored liquid or sauté, barbecue, bake or deep-fry them.

Lobster Boil

To gauge the correct amount of time needed to boil the lobsters, add up the weight of all the lobsters going into the pot. Boil for 8 minutes for the first pound (500 g); then boil for 2 minutes for each succeeding pound.

12 cups	water	3 L
3 tbsp	sea salt	45 mL
2	stalks celery, chopped	2
2	onions, chopped	2
2	carrots, chopped	2
2	10-oz (341 mL) bottles beer	2
1 tsp	Tabasco	5 mL
4	1¹/₂-lb (750 g) lobsters	4

1. Combine the water and sea salt in a large pot. Add the celery, onions, carrots, beer and Tabasco. Bring to a boil on high heat.

2. Add the lobsters, head first. Cover, reduce the heat to a simmer and simmer for 8 minutes for the first pound (500 g), then 2 minutes per pound (500 g) thereafter (for this recipe it will be 18 minutes all together).

3. Remove the lobsters from the pot and rinse under cold water to stop the cooking. Serve immediately.

Serves 4

Baked Clams

This has been my favorite clam dish ever since I lived in Boston, where it was served at the famous Legal Sea Foods Restaurant. Serve the clams as an appetizer.

¹/₂ cup	chopped bacon	125 mL
¹/₂ cup	finely chopped onion	125 mL
¹/₂ cup	finely chopped celery	125 mL
¹/₄ cup	fresh breadcrumbs	50 mL
¹/₄ cup	finely chopped parsley	50 mL
¹/₄ tsp	Tabasco, or to taste	1 mL
	Salt to taste	
24	clams on the half shell	24

1. Preheat the oven to 450°F (230°C).

2. In a frying pan, sauté the bacon until it is cooked but not crispy. Stir in the onion and celery and cooked until softened. Remove from the heat and mix in the breadcrumbs and parsley. Season with the Tabasco and salt.

3. Place the mixture on top of the clams and bake for 5 minutes, or until the mixture is browned and the clams are hot.

Serves 6

Placing clams in the freezer for 15 minutes will make them easier to open, because it relaxes the muscle.

Steamer clams can be sandy inside. There are various ways of removing the sand, but I soak them in water with a couple of tablespoons of vinegar for an hour before cooking to help them dislodge the grit. If you are steaming them, strain the liquid before using, if it appears gritty.

Female lobsters are more flavorful and tender than males, and they contain the prized pinky-red coral or eggs. To check its gender, turn the lobster on its back and look just behind the last pair of legs where two little protrusions jut out. If they are thick and hard, you have a male lobster; if soft and feathery, the lobster is female. A female lobster also has broader "hips" than a male.

Malaysian Mussels

These tangy, flavorful mussels have an Oriental flavor. If you don't have coconut milk, use whipping cream.

1 tbsp	vegetable oil	15 mL
2 tbsp	chopped fresh ginger	25 mL
2	green chilies, chopped	2
4	cloves garlic, chopped	4
2	shallots, chopped	2
	Grated rind of 2 limes	
2 tsp	ground coriander	10 mL
1 cup	dry white wine	250 mL
1/2 cup	water	125 mL
2 cups	coconut milk	500 mL
40	mussels, cleaned	40
2 tsp	soy sauce	10 mL
1 tbsp	dried basil	15 mL
2 tbsp	finely chopped fresh coriander	25 mL
1	tomato, peeled, seeded and chopped	1
	Salt to taste	

1. Heat the oil in a deep frying pan on high heat. Sauté the ginger, chilies, garlic and shallots until softened, about 1 minute. Stir in the grated lime rind and ground coriander.

2. Add the wine, water and coconut milk. Reduce the liquid until thick and syrupy, about 5 minutes.

3. Add the mussels and cook, covered, until they open, about 1 to 2 minutes. Remove the mussels and place them in serving dishes.

4. Strain the sauce and return to the pan. Add the soy sauce, basil, fresh coriander and tomato. Simmer for 2 minutes. Season with the salt and pour over the mussels.

Serves 4

Moules Marinières

This is the classic French preparation for mussels, with one difference — the garlic cloves are left whole and are cooked in the broth with the mussels, until they lose their strong flavor and become mellow and delicious. Serve in soup bowls with plenty of bread to mop up the sauce.

2	onions, chopped	2
2 tsp	dried thyme	10 mL
12	cloves garlic, peeled	12
1 tsp	freshly ground pepper	5 mL
1 cup	dry white wine	250 mL
1 cup	water	250 mL
40	mussels, cleaned	40

1. Place the onions in the bottom of a large pot. Add the thyme, garlic cloves, pepper, wine and water. On high heat, bring to a boil and cook for 2 minutes.

2. Add the mussels, cover and cook until the mussels open, 1 to 2 minutes. Remove the mussels. Reduce the liquid by boiling for a further 2 minutes. Pour the finished sauce over the mussels.

Serves 4 as an appetizer

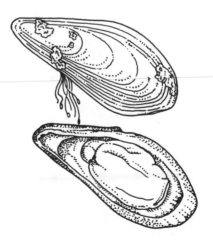

There are two kinds of clam chowder — the New England type and Manhattan. The original New England chowder uses milk or cream, potatoes and bacon, while the Manhattan uses a tomato-based broth.

The Pacific coast geoduck (pronounced gooeyduck) clam is the largest clam in North America. It grows to about 3 lb (1.5 kg), although they can be as heavy as 13 lb (6 kg)! It is used in fritters and chowders.

Tangy Mussel Salad

This recipe is good for a buffet table or as an appetizer.

¹/₄ cup	water	50 mL
40	mussels, cleaned	40
1	lemon	1
2	limes	2
1	large red onion, chopped	1
¹/₄ cup	mayonnaise	50 mL
2 tbsp	finely chopped fresh coriander	25 mL
1	head Boston lettuce, separated into leaves	1

Fresh coriander, which looks a little like Italian parsley, is also known as cilantro or Chinese parsley. It has a fragrant, flowery, lemony flavor and is used in Chinese, Mexican and East Indian dishes.

1. Add the water to a large pot. Bring to a boil, add the mussels, cover and steam over high heat until the shells open, about 1 to 2 minutes.

2. Remove the pot from the heat as soon as the shells open. Cool and reserve the cooking liquid. Remove the mussels from their shells.

3. Squeeze the juice from the lemon and limes into a large bowl. Add the mussel juice, red onion, mayonnaise, coriander, and the mussels. Toss and refrigerate for 1 hour before serving. Serve on a bed of Boston lettuce.

Serves 4

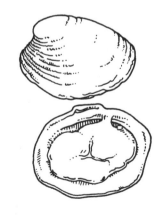

Pasta with Seafood

Use dried pasta for this dish so that the sauce coats the pasta and is not absorbed. Any combination of shellfish or fish can be used. Prepare all the seafood ahead of time and reheat in the sauce when needed.

18	mussels	18
12	clams	12
8 oz	shrimp	250 g
8 oz	scallops	250 g
1 cup	dry white wine	250 mL
2 cups	tomato sauce (page 126)	500 mL
1 lb	spaghetti	500 g
	Salt and freshly ground pepper to taste	

1. Wash and scrub the mussels, pulling off any beards. Wash the clams. Shell the shrimp; remove any little muscles on the sides of the scallops.

2. Pour the wine into a large pot. Bring to a boil on high heat. Add the mussels, cover the pan and steam until just opened, about 1 to 2 minutes. Remove the mussels to a large bowl.

3. Add the clams to the pot, cover and steam until they open, about 5 minutes. Reserve with mussels.

4. Strain the liquid through a fine strainer to remove any bits of shell or grit. Return to the pot. Lower the heat to medium and add the shrimp and scallops. Poach until the shrimp are pink and curled and the scallops are firm to the touch. Add the seafood to the mussels and clams.

5. Meanwhile, bring a large pot of salted water to a boil. Add the spaghetti and boil until *al dente* (tender but firm), about 7 to 10 minutes. Drain.

6. Pour the tomato sauce into the

poaching liquid. Bring to a boil and simmer for 5 minutes. Add all the shellfish. Simmer for 2 to 3 minutes. Season to taste and toss with the spaghetti.

Serves 6

Sautéed Scallops with Orange Butter

The taste of orange goes well with scallops. Serve a little twist of orange rind as a garnish. If blood oranges are available, their juices will make the sauce a beautiful red/orange color. I prefer the smaller bay scallops for this dish, but you can also use sea scallops. Serve as an appetizer or as a main course with fresh linguine.

¹/₃ cup	butter	75 mL
1 lb	scallops	500 g
	Juice of 2 oranges	
2 tbsp	finely chopped fresh dill	25 mL
	Salt and freshly ground pepper to taste	

1. Heat 2 tbsp (25 mL) butter in a frying pan over medium-high heat. Add the scallops and sauté for 2 minutes, or until opaque. Pour in the orange juice and sprinkle on the dill. Bring to a boil.

2. Remove the pan from the heat and whisk in the remaining butter. Season with salt and pepper.

Serves 4 to 6

Scallops and Mushrooms

Mushrooms have a real affinity for scallops. If you can't find the meaty shiitake mushrooms, use regular. Serve this as an appetizer with Cheddar sticks (see page 186), or as a main course with rice.

2 tbsp	butter	25 mL
¹/₄ cup	chopped green onion	50 mL
4 oz	shiitake mushrooms, sliced	125 g
1 lb	scallops	500 g
¹/₄ cup	dry white wine	50 mL
¹/₂ cup	fish or chicken stock	125 mL
¹/₄ cup	whipping cream	50 mL
	Salt and freshly ground pepper to taste	

1. In a large frying pan on medium-high heat, heat the butter until sizzling.

2. Stir in the onions and sauté for 1 minute. Add the mushrooms and sauté 1 minute longer.

3. Add the scallops and cook for 1 minute on each side, or until they are opaque.

4. Pour in the wine and reduce until 1 tbsp (15 mL) remains. Add the stock and the cream, stir together and bring to a boil.

5. Place the scallops on serving plates. Reduce the sauce until slightly thickened, about 2 minutes. Season with salt and pepper, if needed. Pour over the scallops.

Serves 4 to 6

The terms shrimp and prawns are used interchangeably, but the difference is usually in size. Prawns are larger. Technically they have different-shaped heads.

Shrimp Chimichangas

Chimichangas are deep-fried flour tortillas. They usually contain a boring ground meat filling, but this updated version makes a great first course served with guacamole (see page 185) or spicy salsa (see page 148). Or serve it as a main course with guacamole, grilled pepper salad (see page 148) and sliced tomatoes. Excellent salsa can be bought in supermarkets or gourmet shops, or you can make your own.

2	leeks, white part only, thickly sliced	2
1/3 cup	whipping cream	75 mL
2 oz	goat cheese, crumbled	60 g
1 lb	medium shrimp, shelled	500 g
	Salt and freshly ground pepper to taste	
4	medium flour tortillas	4
1/4 cup	vegetable oil	50 mL

1. Bring a pot of water to a boil. Add the leeks and boil for 3 minutes. Remove and drain well.

2. In a frying pan on medium heat, combine the leeks and the cream. Bring to a boil. Stir in the goat cheese. Remove from the heat and stir in the shrimp. Season well with salt and pepper.

3. Divide the filling into four. Pile on the upper third of each tortilla skin. Roll over, fold in the ends and continue to roll until the tortilla forms a cylinder.

4. On medium-high heat, add the oil to the frying pan. When it is hot, fry the tortillas in batches for 2 to 3 minutes, or until golden-brown on each side. Remove and drain on paper towels.

Serves 4

Spanish Shrimp

This is an excellent spicy shrimp appetizer, or main course served with rice.

2 tbsp	butter	25 mL
1 tbsp	olive oil	15 mL
2	shallots or green onions, chopped	2
2	cloves garlic, finely chopped	2
1	dried red chili pepper, chopped	1
1 lb	medium shrimp, shelled	500 g
3	tomatoes, peeled, seeded and chopped	3
2 tbsp	finely chopped parsley	25 mL
2 tbsp	fresh breadcrumbs	25 mL
	Salt and freshly ground pepper to taste	

1. Heat the butter and oil in a frying pan on medium heat. Add the shallots, garlic and chili pepper. Sauté until softened, about 2 minutes.

2. Stir in the shrimp and sauté until they just turn pink, about 2 minutes.

3. Add the tomatoes, parsley and breadcrumbs. Stir everything together and bring to a simmer. Season with salt and pepper.

Serves 3 to 4

EGGPLANT

Eggplant is a wonderful vegetable to use in cooking, because its blandness absorbs the flavor of the herbs and spices cooked with it. My mother, who used to try to disguise food we hated, cut eggplant into French fry shapes, deep-fried it, sprinkled on salt and vinegar and told us they were chips. We believed her!

I love eggplant now; in fact, it is one of my favorite vegetables. It has to be properly handled to remove its bitter juice, but once this is done, it is a delight to eat.

Many European and Asian countries use eggplant as a staple in their cooking. Eggplant Parmesan from Italy, moussaka from Greece and the Middle Eastern eggplant spreads, loaded with garlic and lemon, are some of the best. In China, eggplant stars in spicy vegetable stir-fries; and Indian eggplant curry is a staple in vegetarian cuisine.

Canadians are finally finding a place for eggplant in their kitchens, and it is the darling of new wave restaurants, which feature it simply grilled with olive oil and herbs.
• Eggplants come in various sizes and colors. The deep-hued, oblong, purple ones are the most common.
• The small, finger-like Oriental eggplant has masses of taste, never needs to be peeled, is great for stir-frying but is usually only available in Chinese grocery stores. The more bulbous, small Italian varieties are good for barbecuing and stuffing.
• Look for a deep purple color and a firm texture, with a slight springiness when you touch the flesh. If the stem end is brown, not green, the eggplant is past its prime. Avoid shrivelled or wrinkled-looking eggplants. Young, small eggplants are preferable since they have fewer seeds.
• Store eggplants in the refrigerator for up to 10 days.
• Before cooking eggplant, the stem end must be removed. If the eggplant has a tender skin, don't peel it, because the skin has lots of vitamins. Slice in rounds, then sprinkle salt on the rounds to draw out the bitter juices (Italian or Oriental eggplants don't need this step). Either sauté, grill, bake or deep-fry.

Fried Eggplant

Fried eggplant is served in the Middle East as a vegetable with a main course, or as an appetizer with hummus (see page 47) as part of a Middle Eastern appetizer selection. This is my mother's version of the recipe.

1	eggplant	1
1 tsp	salt	5 mL
1/2 cup	all-purpose flour	125 mL
1/4 cup	vegetable oil	50 mL

1. Slice the eggplant into slices 1/8 inch (2 mm) thick. Salt the slices and leave in a colander to drain for 30 minutes.

2. Dry the slices completely and dust with the flour.

3. In a frying pan, heat the oil on high heat. Add the eggplant a few slices at a time and fry until golden-brown on each side. Remove from the oil and drain on a rack. Continue until all the slices are fried.

Serves 2 to 3

The pristine white eggplants are supposed to be the originals of the species, hence the name eggplant; they look rather like ostrich eggs.

Eggplant Curry

This recipe is adapted from the Taj Hotel restaurant in Bombay, but with one difference — they add three green chilies for an intense heat! The secret is cooking the onions slowly for a sweet, rich flavor.

1	large eggplant	1
1 tsp	salt	5 mL
1/4 cup	butter	50 mL
1	onion, chopped	1
1 tbsp	chopped fresh ginger	15 mL
2 tsp	finely chopped garlic	10 mL
1	dried red chili pepper, chopped	1
1 tbsp	cumin seeds	15 mL
3	tomatoes, peeled and chopped	3
	Salt and freshly ground pepper to taste	
2 tbsp	finely chopped fresh coriander, optional	25 mL

1. Peel the eggplant and cut in 1/2-inch (1.25 cm) cubes. Sprinkle with the salt and leave in a colander for 30 minutes.

2. Heat the butter in a frying pan over medium-low heat. Add the onion, ginger, garlic, chili and cumin seeds. Sauté until the onion softens and begins to color, about 8 to 10 minutes.

3. Stir in the eggplant, cover the pan and cook for 15 minutes, or until the eggplant is nearly tender. Add the tomatoes and season with salt and pepper.

4. Continue to cook, covered, until the eggplant is completely tender, about 15 to 20 minutes more. Stir occasionally to make sure nothing sticks to the bottom of the pan. Serve sprinkled with the coriander.

Serves 4

Eggplant Caviar

Sometimes called poor man's caviar because of a similarity in appearance, this spread is great as an appetizer served with pumpernickel bread, or as a topping for grilled fish.

1	large eggplant	1
1/4 cup	olive oil	50 mL
1	onion, finely chopped	1
1	green pepper, finely chopped	1
2	cloves garlic, finely chopped	2
3	tomatoes, peeled, seeded and chopped	3
pinch	granulated sugar	pinch
	Salt and freshly ground pepper to taste	
2 tbsp	lemon juice	25 mL

1. Preheat the oven to 425°F (220°C).

2. Place the eggplant on a baking sheet and bake for 45 to 60 minutes, turning once, until it is soft and the skin is charred.

3. In a frying pan on medium heat, heat 2 tbsp (25 mL) oil. Sauté the onions until soft, about 3 minutes. Add the green pepper and garlic and sauté for 5 minutes longer, or until the vegetables are tender. Reserve in a bowl.

4. Peel the eggplant and chop the pulp finely. Stir into the onion mixture along with the tomatoes, sugar, salt and pepper.

5. On medium-low heat, heat the remaining 2 tbsp (25 mL) oil in the frying pan. Add the eggplant mixture and cook for 40 minutes, or until the mixture is very thick. Stir in the lemon juice and season to taste.

Serves 6

SWEET AND HOT PEPPERS

A profusion of sweet peppers tumbles into the marketplace in September. Red, green, yellow and purple bell peppers and the long, slender shepherd peppers fill bushel baskets as farms begin their pepper harvest.

Peppers are a versatile vegetable. Try them raw in salads, grilled, stuffed or pureed into a sauce. The red and yellow peppers are sweeter than the green; the purple are disappointing. They look good uncooked, but when cooked, they turn a drab olive color.
• Buy firm, even-colored, shiny peppers.
• Check the stem end, where decay and softening start; avoid wilted or soft peppers.
• Green and red peppers are actually the same species; a red pepper is a fully ripened green one. But if you are looking for red peppers, don't buy green peppers that have red blushes on them. Peppers have to ripen on the stalk, otherwise they will be bitter.

Chili Peppers

With the interest in Mexican and Sichuan food and the recent rise of Southwestern cooking, chilies are appearing in more and more dishes. Some varieties of chilies are hot; others have more depth of flavor and less sting. As a rule, the smaller, narrower and darker the chili, the more lethal the impact.

The easiest chilies to find in our markets are the long, slender, yellow banana pepper, which has flavor but not too much heat; the smaller oval-shaped green jalapeño, which packs a lot of punch; and the tiny red or green incendiary pequin, which is a staple in Asian food.
• Always look for a shiny, smooth, tight skin. Avoid any chilies that have blemishes or are soft or shrivelled.
• To prepare chilies, use rubber gloves to prevent the oil from burning your skin. Cut the chili in half. For less heat, discard the seeds and the membranes. After preparing the chilies, wash your hands and the chopping area well. Be careful not to rub your eyes when working with chilies.

After peeling peppers, you can preserve them for months by placing them in a clean container and pouring olive oil over until they are covered. Refrigerate and use whenever you wish.

Make a pepper sauce by pureeing grilled and skinned peppers in the food processor or blender with twice the amount of whipping cream. Place in a pot, bring to a boil and boil until slightly thickened. Try the sauce with fish, veal and chicken.

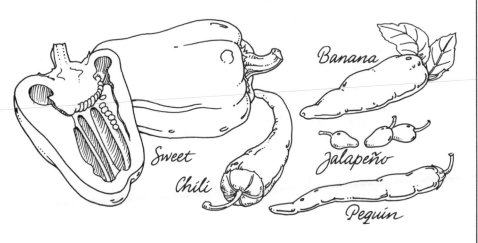

Sweet

Chili

Banana

Jalapeño

Pequin

Green Pepper Soup

This soup is a pale mint color and has a tangy taste. It's a good way to use up peppers that are past their prime. Don't boil the soup after the milk is added, or it will curdle. You can also use red peppers instead of green. The parsnip adds sweetness to the soup.

3	green peppers	3
3	slices bacon, chopped	3
1	onion, chopped	1
1	clove garlic, finely chopped	1
1	parsnip, peeled and chopped	1
2 cups	chicken stock	500 mL
2 cups	milk	500 mL
1 tsp	dried basil	5 mL
pinch	cayenne pepper	pinch
	Salt and freshly ground pepper to taste	

1. Core and seed the green peppers. Chop coarsely, reserving ¼ cup (50 mL) as garnish.

2. In a pot on medium heat, sauté the bacon until the fat begins to run. Add the onion, garlic, parsnip and green pepper. Sauté until the onion is softened, about 2 minutes.

3. Add the stock, milk, basil and cayenne. Turn the heat to low and cook gently for 30 minutes, or until the vegetables are tender.

4. Puree the soup in the food processor or blender until smooth. Return to the pot, season well with salt and pepper and reheat gently. Garnish with the reserved green pepper.

Serves 4 to 6

Quick Salsa

Combine 3 chopped canned tomatoes, 1 chopped small onion, 2 chopped canned jalapeño peppers, 1 tbsp (15 mL) chopped fresh coriander, salt, pepper and a pinch of sugar. The sauce should keep for about 2 weeks. Makes about 1 cup (500 mL).

There are all sorts of chili pepper products. The Chinese use chili peppers ground to a paste and sell it as Chinese chili paste. They also use chili oil. Liquid sauces such as Tabasco or Pick-a-pepper sauce are also made with chilies. Harissa, the Moroccan spice paste, is chili-pepper based.

Grilled Pepper Salad

Grilling peppers changes the taste and texture of the vegetable. They become mellow, soft and luscious. Serve this salad with lamb or beef or add slivers of fontina cheese and serve as a first course.

3	red peppers	3
3	green peppers	3
1 tsp	Dijon mustard	5 mL
1	clove garlic, finely chopped	1
2 tbsp	wine vinegar	25 mL
⅓ cup	olive oil	75 mL
1 tbsp	finely chopped fresh basil	15 mL
	Salt and freshly ground pepper to taste	

1. Cut the peppers in half. Grill, on high heat, skin side down on the barbecue until the skin is blackened, about 5 minutes. (If using the broiler, broil skin side up.)

2. Place in a paper bag for 10 minutes, or until cooled. Peel the skin off; it should slip off easily. Cut the peppers into strips and place in a bowl.

3. In a small bowl, whisk together the mustard, garlic and vinegar. Slowly whisk in the oil.

4. Season the dressing with the basil, salt and pepper. Pour over the peppers.

Serves 6 to 8

Fall Buffet for Twenty

If you are planning a buffet, here are some hints that will make your life easier.

• The golden rule for a successful buffet is to keep it simple. Serve make-ahead recipes that only need reheating, and salads that can be dressed several hours beforehand.

• Don't have too many choices, because people tend to try everything, and different tastes can clash.

• Start cooking several days ahead. It always takes longer than you think. Don't leave yourself too much to do on the day of the party, or you'll be too tired to enjoy yourself.

• Make sure there is no last-minute cooking, but have garnishes ready in the refrigerator to be placed on the platters before serving. Have everything oven-ready, preferably in their serving dishes (which avoids transferring the contents and losing heat).

• Keeping food hot on a buffet table is difficult. If you have candle warmers, use these on dishes that need to be hot. Some dishes are acceptable served at room temperature.

• Serve bite-sized food so guests don't have to use a knife and fork.

• Don't serve anything that has to carved at the table. It ties up a person who might help you serve wine.

• Make sure the logistics of the space and the number of people invited will work for you. Too many people may be cozy but very difficult to feed comfortably.

• For comfort, try to have seating for most of the guests.

• When setting the buffet table, place the plates at the beginning and the forks and knives, if needed, rolled up in a napkin at the end. This way, guests will not have to carry a fork and napkin around while they are serving themselves.

• Place the main course near the plates, then the starch, vegetables and salads, with the breads at the end. Butter some bread, but not all.

• Serve wine, beer and mineral water — not a full bar. Have poured wine in glasses at the end of the buffet, or pass a tray of wine after people are seated.

• Clear the main course off the table before serving dessert and coffee. Place desserts, coffee, coffee cups, teaspoons, milk and sugar on the table. Serve tea, too, if there are tea drinkers.

• For a final luxurious touch, serve chocolate truffles with the coffee.

Seafood Basque

Mediterranean Chicken

Fall Salad

Three Pepper Salad

Provençal Rounds

Blueberry Apricot Flan

Chocolate Roulade

If you are reheating a dish, remove it from the refrigerator one hour before putting it in the oven, to allow it to come back to room temperature.

Seafood Basque

Although the ingredient list is long, this is a simple dish to make. Prepare it up to one day ahead of time; to reheat, place the fish and vegetables in a large shallow serving dish. Cover with foil and reheat in a 350°F (180°C) oven for 20 minutes, or until hot.

⅓ cup	olive oil	75 mL
1	onion, diced	1
3	leeks, cleaned and thinly sliced	3
1	green pepper, diced	1
1	red pepper, diced	1
3	cloves garlic, finely chopped	3
1	green chili pepper, seeded and chopped	1
4	tomatoes, peeled, seeded and chopped	4
1 tsp	paprika	5 mL
½ tsp	saffron threads, optional	2 mL
	Salt and freshly ground pepper	
1 lb	monkfish, cut in ½-inch (1.25 cm) cubes	500 g
⅓ cup	dry white wine	75 mL
1 cup	fish or chicken stock	250 mL
1 lb	scallops	500 g
1 lb	shrimp, shelled	500 g
48	mussels, cleaned	48

1. In a large wide pot on medium heat, heat 2 tbsp (25 mL) oil.

2. Stir in the onion, leeks, green and red peppers and garlic. Sauté for 2 minutes, or until the vegetables are coated with oil. Add the chili, tomatoes, paprika and saffron. Turn the heat to medium-low and cook, stirring occasionally, until the vegetables are softened, about 10 minutes. Season well with salt and pepper. Reserve in a large bowl.

3. Wipe out the pot and add the remaining oil. On high heat, sauté the monkfish until browned on all sides. Pour over the wine and stock, bring to a boil, lower the heat to medium-low and simmer the fish for 10 minutes, or until cooked through. Remove the fish with a slotted spoon and reserve with the vegetables.

4. Add the scallops and poach until barely cooked, about 2 minutes. Remove to the bowl with a slotted spoon. Add the shrimp to the pot. Poach until just pink and curled. Remove and add to the vegetables.

5. Raise the heat to high and stir in the mussels. Cover the pan and steam until the mussel shells open, about 2 minutes. Remove to a separate bowl and reserve.

6. Strain the liquid through cheesecloth to remove any grit and return to the pan. Bring to a boil and reduce by half. Add the vegetables, fish, scallops and shrimp to the pan, season well and reheat.

7. Place on a large serving platter and surround with the mussels.

Serves 16 to 20

Mediterranean Chicken

An exciting, full-flavored dish with the taste of the sun in it. Prepare the dish until it is ready for the oven, refrigerate and bake when needed. You can buy sliced smoked ham at the meat counter in many supermarkets.

3	heads garlic	3
8	whole boneless chicken breasts, skin on	8
¾ cup	all-purpose flour	175 mL
1 tsp	salt	5 mL
1 tsp	freshly ground pepper	5 mL
3 tbsp	finely chopped fresh rosemary, or 1 tbsp (15 mL) dried	45 mL
½ cup	olive oil	125 mL
1 lb	smoked ham, thickly sliced	500 g
4	red onions, thickly sliced	4
½ cup	brandy	125 mL
2	bay leaves	2
1 cup	sliced black olives	250 mL
½ cup	finely chopped parsley	125 mL

1. Preheat the oven to 400°F (200°C).

2. Add the garlic to a pot of cold water and bring to a boil. Boil for 3 minutes, drain and peel the garlic cloves.

3. Cut each chicken breast in half, then cut each half in thirds.

4. In a shallow dish, combine the flour with the salt, pepper and 1 tbsp (15 mL) fresh rosemary. Coat the chicken pieces with the flour.

5. Heat the olive oil in a large frying pan on high heat. Brown the chicken in batches, about 1 to 2 minutes per side. Remove with a slotted spoon to a large ovenproof casserole.

6. Turn the heat to medium-low. Dice the ham and add it to the frying pan with the onions, garlic and remaining rosemary. Sauté until the onions are golden-brown, about 10 minutes. Pour in the brandy and bring to a boil.

7. Scrape the contents of the frying pan over the chicken breasts, add the bay leaves and olives and bake, uncovered, for 15 to 20 minutes, or until the chicken is cooked through. Sprinkle with the parsley.

Serves 16 to 20

When you cook garlic cloves whole, they lose their characteristic pungency and become soft and mellow.

Fall Salad

For this recipe, cut the Parmesan into fine slices with a knife. Grated Parmesan can be used, but the salad will not have such a defined Parmesan flavor.

2	red onions, thinly sliced	2
2 tbsp	balsamic or cider vinegar	25 mL
2	heads Romaine lettuce	2
2	heads red leaf lettuce	2
4	Belgian endive	4
1	large bunch watercress	1
8 oz	Parmesan cheese	250 g
Vinaigrette:		
$1/3$ cup	wine vinegar	75 mL
1 tbsp	Dijon mustard	15 mL
2 tbsp	finely chopped fresh basil, or 2 tsp (10 mL) dried	25 mL
1 cup	olive oil	250 mL

1. Marinate the onion slices in the balsamic vinegar for 1 hour to remove the strong flavor. Discard the vinegar.

2. Wash and tear the Romaine and red leaf lettuce into bite-sized pieces. Slice the Belgian endive into $1/2$-inch (1.25 cm) slices. Separate the watercress into leaves. Combine all the greens in large salad bowl.

3. Cut the Parmesan into crumbly slices. Reserve.

4. In a small bowl, whisk together the wine vinegar, Dijon mustard and basil. Slowly add the olive oil, whisking constantly. Reserve.

5. Just before serving, toss the salad with the reserved onion slices, Parmesan and vinaigrette.

Serves 16 to 20

Three Pepper Salad

If you can find them, use the three colors of peppers for the most effective presentation.

2	red peppers	2
2	green peppers	2
2	yellow peppers	2
3	red onions	3
Vinaigrette:		
$1/3$ cup	wine vinegar	75 mL
2 tsp	Dijon mustard	10 mL
1 tsp	dried oregano	5 mL
$2/3$ cup	olive oil	150 mL
	Salt and freshly ground pepper to taste	

1. Cut the peppers in half and remove the cores and seeds. Slice into thin strips. Cut the onions in half, then slice thinly.

2. In a bowl, mix together the peppers and onions.

3. In a small bowl, whisk together the vinegar, mustard and oregano. Slowly whisk in the olive oil. Season to taste with salt and pepper. Pour over the pepper mixture and marinate for 1 hour before serving.

Serves 12

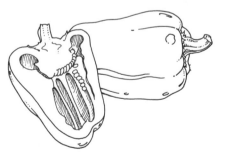

Provençal Rounds

A savory bread to serve with both the chicken and seafood dishes.

4	baking potatoes, peeled	4
1/2 cup	olive oil	125 mL
8	anchovies, crushed	8
2	cloves garlic, finely chopped	2
1	pimento, finely chopped	1
	Salt and freshly ground pepper to taste	
1	French stick, thinly sliced	1

1. Fill a pot with cold water. Boil the potatoes until tender. Drain well and mash.

2. While the potatoes are still hot, slowly whisk in the olive oil. Beat in the anchovies, garlic, pimento, salt and pepper. Cool.

3. Toast the French bread rounds. Spread each round with a thin layer of the potato mixture.

Serves 20

Blueberry Apricot Flan

This custard may look lumpy when you are cooking it, but the lumps should disappear when the mixture boils. If you still notice lumps, sieve the custard before spooning it into the pastry.

2 cups	milk	500 mL
5	egg yolks	5
1/2 cup	granulated sugar	125 mL
1/4 cup	all-purpose flour	50 mL
1 tsp	vanilla extract	5 mL
1	9-inch (23 cm) baked sweet pastry shell*	1
3 cups	blueberries	750 mL
3 cups	ripe apricots, peeled, pitted and halved	750 mL
1 cup	red currant jelly	250 mL

1. In a heavy pot, bring the milk to a boil. Set aside.

2. In a large bowl, whisk together the egg yolks and sugar until pale. Beat in the flour.

3. Gradually add the hot milk to the egg-yolk mixture while whisking. Return to the pot.

4. On medium heat, bring the mixture to a boil, stirring. Boil for 1 minute, stirring constantly, until the mixture thickens. Beat in the vanilla. Cover the surface of the custard with plastic wrap to prevent a skin from forming. Cool.

5. Spoon the custard into the pastry. Arrange the blueberries and apricots (cut side down) on top of the custard.

6. In a small pot, bring the red currant jelly to a simmer. Stir until liquid. Cool slightly, then brush on top of the fruit.

Serves 6 to 8

Glazing flans with melted jellies or jams gives them a professional finish. However, do not refrigerate the flans after glazing, since refrigerator dampness is absorbed by the glaze, and it will run.

*See *Lucy Waverman's Cooking School Cookbook*, page 95.

Chocolate Roulade

A chocolate roulade is a dense chocolate soufflé mixture baked in a jelly roll pan. There is no flour to interfere with the chocolate. Roll it up while warm to help it keep its shape. When cool, fill the cake with the rich mocha filling. Sweetened whipped cream also makes a good filling. When my daughter Katie bakes this, she cuts the flat sheet into three or four strips, spreads the cake with the filling, assembles it in layers, and cuts it into fingers to serve. She says you get more filling this way!

Cake:

6 oz	bittersweet chocolate	180 g
2 oz	unsweetened chocolate	60 g
8	eggs, separated	8
1 cup	granulated sugar	250 mL

Filling:

4 oz	bittersweet chocolate	125 g
1/3 cup	strong black coffee	75 mL
1 1/2 cups	whipping cream	375 mL
1/4 cup	icing sugar	50 mL

1. Preheat the oven to 350°F (180°C).

2. Butter and flour a 15 1/2 × 10 1/2 × 3/4-inch (2 L) jelly roll pan. Cut a sheet of parchment paper to fit the base and place it over the flour.

3. To make the cake, combine the chocolates in a heavy pot and melt over low heat. When melted, remove and cool.

4. Using an electric mixer or whisk, beat the egg yolks and 3/4 cup (175 mL) sugar until thick. With a spatula, fold in the chocolate mixture.

5. Using a clean electric mixer or whisk, beat the egg whites until stiff peaks form. Beat in the remaining 1/4 cup (50 mL) sugar.

6. Using a large spoon, stir one-quarter of the beaten egg whites into the egg yolks. Fold in the remaining egg whites.

7. Spoon the mixture onto the prepared baking sheet and spread evenly. Bake for 15 to 18 minutes, or until puffed and dry-looking.

8. Let the cake cool on the baking sheet for 5 minutes. Turn out onto a clean tea towel. Roll up immediately, from the long edge, and cool.

9. To make the filling, in a heavy pot on low heat, melt the 4 oz (125 g) bittersweet chocolate in the coffee until smooth. Cool.

10. In a large bowl, whip the cream, gradually adding the icing sugar. Fold in the chocolate mixture.

11. To assemble, unroll the cake and spread with half of the filling. Reroll the cake and use the remaining filling to decorate the top. Chill overnight or for 4 hours. Cut into slices for serving.

Serves 12

10
October

October is a unique month. Winter's bite is far away, and the bittersweet days of Indian summer are still with us. The air is soft, and the distinctive tastes and textures of autumn are everywhere.

In season
apples
broccoli
Brussels sprouts
cauliflower
celery
cranberries
leeks
onions
pumpkins
squash

Holidays
Thanksgiving
Halloween

Menu
Thanksgiving Dinner for
Twelve

SAUSAGES

Sausages were the earliest convenience food. Sausage-making is a very old technique that was originated to use up bits and pieces from a butchered carcass. These leftovers were ground up, seasoned and stuffed into the clean intestines — to make the whole far better than the sum of the parts! As there was no refrigeration, usually the sausages were smoked so they could be stored and used over long periods of time.

Each country developed its own sausage and, with our immigrant population, we are fortunate that almost every type is available in Canada.

For a long time I avoided making my own sausages, because I thought the process would be messy and difficult. But one day after a fruitless hunt for a decent spicy Italian sausage, I decided to try. What a revelation! Sausage-making is easy and fun, and the end result is far superior to the store-bought product. And, once you learn the technique of sausage-making, you can create your own textures and flavors.

There are three basic types of sausage:

Fresh sausages are made with fresh meat (often pork or a mixture of pork and veal). Use them within two days or freeze them.

Smoked sausages are smoked to give them a unique taste, ranging from mild to highly smoked. The heavier the smoke, the darker and more full-flavored the sausage will be. Chorizo and pepperoni are two common varieties of smoked sausage.

Dried sausages, such as the Mennonite air-dried summer sausage and salami, are often smoked before being dried. They are safe to eat uncooked and should last for several months.

Popular Varieties

Bologna: An indifferent, bland sausage that is sometimes mildly smoked; often made with finely ground pork or beef with indistinctive seasonings. Well loved by children.

Boudin blanc: A white French sausage made with veal or chicken.

Bratwurst: A fresh pork sausage of German origin, made for frying or roasting. It usually contains caraway.

Chorizo: A spicy smoked, air-dried sausage originally from Spain. It is used in soups, paellas, etc., to add a spicy, full flavor.

Country sausage: A coarsely ground, mildly seasoned sausage, usually made with pork.

Kielbasa: A smoked and cooked Polish sausage usually seasoned with garlic and paprika. It is formed into long rolls and sold by the chunk.

Lop chong: A dried, very fatty Chinese sausage with a hint of sweetness. It is used in noodle and rice dishes.

Pepperoni: The air-dried, spicy Italian pork sausage that usually garnishes pizza.

Equipment

• A meat grinder is good but not essential, because you can buy pre-ground meat or ask the butcher to grind it for you.

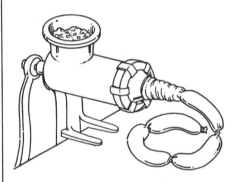

• A sausage funnel, either attached to a grinder or bought separately, makes filling the casings easier, but a piping bag will work well as long as the mixture is smooth. Hand-held sausage stuffers are often available at kitchen stores and stores that sell sausage casings. In a pinch you can push the sausage meat into the casings with the end of a wooden spoon, but this method is time-consuming.

Stuffing Casings

• Sausage casings are usually available at Italian, Portuguese or Hungarian butchers, or on special order from others.

• Rinse the casings to remove the salt, then attach them to the rim of a water faucet and run water through them. Soak the casings overnight to make them more pliable.

There are two kinds of sausage casings — natural and artificial. The natural casings are made from pork or beef intestines. Artificial casings are made from cellulose. They are thicker and less tender than natural casings.

If the stuffed casings have air bubbles, prick them with a needle and push more filling into the air spaces.

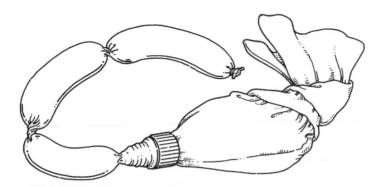

- To make sausages juicy and tasty, you need fat in the ratio of three parts meat to one part fat. Some of this fat will cook out, but without it, your sausages will be dry. It's better to eat fewer sausages than to try to use less fat.
- If you are grinding your own meat, remove all sinews and tendons before grinding. Combine the ground meat with seasonings. Use about 1 tsp (5 mL) salt, ½ tsp (2 mL) freshly ground black pepper and 2 tsp (10 mL) dried herbs for every 1 lb (500 g) meat.
- To give sausages a smooth texture, beat the ground meat well with an electric mixer or a wooden spoon. If you want a chunkier texture, mix the ingredients together but don't beat.
- For the best flavor, leave the meat in the refrigerator overnight to marinate.
- Before filling the casings, fry up a little of the mixture and taste to adjust the seasonings.
- If you use a sausage funnel, stuffing casings is extremely simple. Attach the funnel to the grinder and push the entire length of casings onto the funnel, tying a knot at the end. Add the ground meat, turn the grinder on and gently ease the casings off as they automatically fill.

- The casings will burst if overfilled. To test for the correct consistency, pinch the casings with your thumb and forefinger. The casings should feel full but not taut.
- If you don't have a grinder funnel, use either a hand-held sausage funnel or a piping bag with a large tube. Pull the casings over the tube and fill the bag by gently squeezing the meat into the casings.
- Twist or tie off the casings at 3-inch (7.5 cm) intervals, or any desired length.

Cooking

- An old Scottish sausagemaker told me never to prick my sausages because the fat, juices and taste would run out. If you are starting with a good-quality homemade sausage, there is no need to prick them. If you do, the texture will be drier. In mass-produced store-bought sausages, the fat quantity is probably higher and the sausages should be pricked to release the fat.
- My favorite method of cooking sausages is to place them in a frying pan, unpricked, adding enough water to film the bottom of the pan. Cover tightly, turn the heat to medium and let the sausages simmer for 3 to 5 minutes or until they start to release

If sausage casings are unavailable, you can still make excellent sausages. Form the filling into sausage shapes or patties, flour lightly and fry. They will have a similar taste to stuffed sausages but the texture won't be as compact and firm.

Commercial sausages often contain nitrites — a salt that helps to preserve the color. Don't use them in homemade sausages because they may be a health hazard.

Head cheese, which is considered a kind of sausage, is made from pieces of pork, usually from the cheek or tongue area, which are bound together by the gelatinous cooking liquid. Head cheese is always eaten cold, otherwise it disintegrates.

fat. Uncover, pour off any water, add 1 tbsp (15 mL) oil if needed, and fry until the sausages are brown.

• Sausages can also be baked at 400°F (200°C) for 20 to 30 minutes, or until they are cooked through. By using this method you can cook a large number of sausages at the same time.

• If you are barbecuing sausages, simmer them for 5 minutes before barbecuing, to prevent too much flare-up from dripping fat.

• I don't recommend broiling sausages; they have a tendency to burst under the broiler because of the intense heat, covering the oven with grease.

Spicy Italian Sausage

Restaurant entrepreneur Freddy Locicero's mother, Maria, makes these dynamite spicy sausages for his restaurants. This sausage is great barbecued, or sliced and tossed with pasta.

8 oz	ground pork	250 g
8 oz	ground veal	250 g
1 tsp	salt	5 mL
1 tsp	coarsely ground pepper	5 mL
1 tbsp	crushed dried fennel seeds	15 mL
1 tsp	dried chili flakes	5 mL

1. Combine the ground meats, salt, pepper, fennel seeds and chili flakes. Cover and refrigerate overnight.

2. Stuff the meat into the sausage casings, tying off at 3-inch (7.5 cm) lengths.

Makes about 8 sausages

Spiced Pork Sausages

These sausages have a good depth of flavor but are not hot. Serve them for breakfast with hash browns.

1 lb	fatty ground pork	500 g
1	clove garlic, finely chopped	1
1 tsp	salt	5 mL
1/2 tsp	granulated sugar	2 mL
1/2 tsp	freshly ground pepper	2 mL
pinch	ground cloves	pinch
1/4 tsp	ground ginger	1 mL
1/4 tsp	ground nutmeg	1 mL

1. Combine the pork, garlic, salt, sugar, pepper, cloves, ginger and nutmeg. Cover and refrigerate overnight.

2. Stuff the mixture into the sausage casings, tying off at 3-inch (7.5 cm) intervals.

Makes about 8 sausages

Claire's Lamb Sausages

Claire Hymas, who helped develop the recipes for this book, produced this incredible lamb sausage. Fry, then serve with heaps of mashed potatoes, fried onions and minted mustard.

1 lb	ground lamb	500 g
1 tsp	dry mustard	5 mL
1 tsp	salt	5 mL
1/2 tsp	freshly ground pepper	2 mL
1/2 tsp	dried thyme	2 mL
1 tsp	dried rosemary	5 mL

1. Combine the ground lamb, mustard, salt, pepper, thyme and rosemary. Cover and refrigerate overnight.

2. Stuff the mixture into the sausage casings and tie off at 3-inch (7.5 cm) intervals.

Makes about 8 sausages

Seafood Sausages

This is my favorite sausage — rich, juicy and low in fat. Serve as an appetizer with sautéed mushrooms and a beurre blanc*, or slice and use in a seafood risotto. You can also serve these as a main course with rice and a salad.

Don't prick these sausages, or valuable juice will be lost.

6 oz	salmon, boned	180 g
6 oz	turbot or halibut, boned	180 g
1	egg white	1
1/2 cup	whipping cream	125 mL
2 tbsp	chopped fresh dill	25 mL
1/2 tsp	salt	2 mL
1/4 tsp	freshly ground pepper	1 mL
4	large sea scallops, diced	4
4	large shrimp, peeled and diced	4
	Fish stock or water	
2 tbsp	butter	25 mL

1. In a food processor or blender, puree the salmon and turbot. With the machine running, pour the egg white and whipping cream through the feed tube until just combined.

2. Remove the mixture to a large bowl and stir in the dill, salt, pepper, scallops and shrimp.

3. Stuff the mixture into the sausage casings. Do not prick.

4. Fill a large, deep frying pan with 2 inches (5 cm) of fish stock or water. Bring to a simmer. Add the sausages, cover and simmer for 5 to 7 minutes, or until the sausages are cooked through. Drain.

5. Dry the frying pan and return it to the burner on low heat. Melt the butter, add the sausages and cook them gently until the casings are browned, about 2 to 3 minutes.

Makes about 6 sausages

Oktoberfest Sausages

The German-influenced sausage that comes from the Kitchener area in Ontario.

8 oz	ground pork	250 g
8 oz	ground veal	250 g
1 tbsp	paprika	15 mL
1 tbsp	caraway seeds	15 mL
1 tsp	dried sage	5 mL
1	clove garlic, finely chopped	1
1 tsp	salt	5 mL
1/2 tsp	freshly ground pepper	2 mL

1. Combine the pork, veal, paprika, caraway seeds, sage, garlic, salt and pepper. Cover and refrigerate overnight.

2. Stuff into the sausage casings and tie off at 3-inch (7.5 cm) intervals.

Makes about 8 sausages

Minted Mustard
Combine 1/4 cup (50 mL) Dijon mustard with 2 tbsp (25 mL) finely chopped fresh mint. If fresh mint is unavailable, use 2 tsp (10 mL) dried mint. Makes about 1/4 cup (50 mL).

*See *Lucy Waverman's Cooking School Cookbook*, page 50.

WINTER SQUASH

Squash has been growing in North America for over five thousand years. In great-grandmother's day, winter squash was one of the few fresh vegetables available through the long hard winter, because its unique hard outer shell kept it fresh for months. Today winter squash is available all year round, but it is at its best through the fall and winter.

Popular Varieties

Acorn: A dark-green, fluted variety with a distinctive orange flesh. Its large seeds are similar to a pumpkin's. Because of its size and flavor, it is the perfect squash for splitting and baking. It weighs about 1 to 2 lb (500 g to 1 kg).

Butternut: The most popular squash today, sometimes packaged precut. It looks like a yellow pear-shaped club. Its flavor is superb, and its texture is smooth and not stringy.

Hubbard: The big daddy of squashes, it can weigh up to 100 lb (50 kg). The rind is ridged and bumpy and ranges in color from dark-green to orange. The flesh is orangey and tender, but it is less popular today because of its size.

Pumpkin: The familiar Halloween pumpkin is a squash and can be used for cooking, although 99 percent are sold for decorative purposes. The texture is slightly stringy; the taste mild and indistinctive.

Spaghetti: This squash was more popular a few years ago when people were looking for new and exciting vegetables. It is oval, yellow, and has a semi-hard outer shell. When baked, the pale-yellow flesh separates into strands, giving it a spaghetti-like appearance.

Buying and Storing

• Look for a hard, strongly colored squash that feels heavy for its size.
• Don't buy any squash that has a bruised or scarred skin, because it is subject to decay if the outer layer is damaged.
• Winter squash should keep for two

Summer squash such as zucchini, patty pan and crookneck are usually small, with soft, thin outer skins. They should be sautéed for the best results. If these squash are allowed to grow, they become monstrous in size and lose much of their flavor.

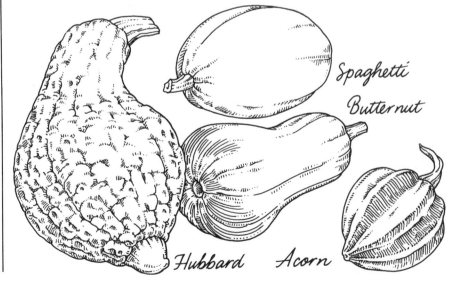

Spaghetti

Butternut

Hubbard   Acorn

to three months if stored in a cool dark place.

• Squash can be baked whole or in wedges. It can be steamed, boiled and even grilled. Its shape also makes it a good receptacle for stuffings, ranging from sausage meat and onions to butter and sugar.

• Because squash has a sweet flavor, it has an affinity for sweet spices such as cinnamon, nutmeg and allspice.

Baked Squash

All winter squash bakes well, but I prefer butternut or acorn.

This recipe is from Patricia Hymas. Serve it with poultry dishes.

2 lb	butternut or acorn squash	1 kg
1/4 cup	butter	50 mL
1/4 cup	brown sugar	50 mL
1	small onion, chopped	1
1/2 cup	thick applesauce	125 mL
1 tsp	ground nutmeg	5 mL

1. Preheat the oven to 350°F (180°C).

2. Cut the squash in half, or if it is large, into wedges. Scoop out the seeds. Cut a thin slice off the rounded side of the squash halves so they will sit in a baking dish.

3. Place the squash halves in a large baking dish. Dot with the butter and sprinkle with brown sugar.

4. In a small bowl, combine the onions and applesauce. Fill the squash cavities with the applesauce mixture and sprinkle with nutmeg.

5. Bake for 1 hour, or until the flesh is tender.

Serves 4 to 6

Squash Casserole

A rich squash dish with a luxurious texture and taste. Serve it with Thanksgiving dinner or on other special occasions. You can use milk instead of cream, but the dish will not be as rich.

2 lb	acorn or butternut squash, peeled, seeded and diced	1 kg
2 cups	chicken stock or water	500 mL
1 tsp	ground nutmeg	5 mL
	Salt and freshly ground pepper to taste	
1	egg	1
1/2 cup	whipping cream	125 mL
2 tbsp	butter	25 mL
1/4 cup	grated Parmesan cheese	50 mL

1. Preheat the oven to 375°F (190°C).

2. Place the squash and stock in a large pot on high heat. Bring to a boil, turn the heat to low, cover and cook for 10 minutes, or until the squash is tender.

3. Drain the squash and mash with a potato masher or fork. Mix in the nutmeg, salt, pepper, egg and whipping cream.

4. Place the squash in a lightly greased 8-cup (2 L) ovenproof baking dish. Dot with the butter and sprinkle with Parmesan cheese.

5. Bake for 20 minutes, or until the squash is hot.

Serves 6

Although a hatchet might seem the best tool for cutting squash, take the point of a chef's knife, lever it through the hard outer skin, then plunge the heel end down to split the squash open. With a thinner-skinned squash, peel off the outer skin with a paring knife.

A half cup (125 mL) boiled, mashed squash has about 38 calories.

Spaghetti Squash with Herb Sauce

A low-calorie "pasta" dinner.

1	spaghetti squash	1
1 tbsp	olive oil	15 mL
1	onion, chopped	1
2	cloves garlic, finely chopped	2
1	28-oz (796 mL) can tomatoes, drained and chopped	1
2 tsp	dried basil	10 mL
1 tsp	dried oregano	5 mL
1/2 tsp	salt	2 mL
1/4 tsp	freshly ground pepper	1 mL
1/4 cup	grated Parmesan cheese	50 mL

1. Preheat the oven to 400°F (200°C).

2. Place the squash on a baking sheet and bake for 1 hour, or until the squash is soft to the touch. Cool for 10 minutes.

3. Meanwhile, in a frying pan, heat the oil on medium heat. Add the onions and garlic and sauté until onions soften slightly, about 2 minutes.

4. Add the tomatoes, basil, oregano, salt and pepper. Bring to a boil, turn the heat to low and simmer, covered, for 30 minutes.

5. Slice the squash in half and remove the seeds. With a fork, pull out the strands of flesh.

6. To serve, place the squash strands on a plate and top with the tomato sauce. Sprinkle with Parmesan cheese.

Serves 4

APPLES

Apples have both a biblical and cultural heritage. Although the Bible does not say what fruit Eve consumed, scholars believe it was an apple. Newton propounded his laws of gravity after watching an apple in motion. And the Pilgrims transported apple seeds and cuttings to the New World to make them feel at home. Apples have been around since time began.

Unfortunately many of these tastier, older apples have dropped into obscurity, the victims of economic planning. Juicy sweet apples such as Pippin and Pearmain are hardly ever cultivated now. Instead we produce easily grown, good-looking but not necessarily tastier apples such as Red Delicious, Golden Delicious, Spy, McIntosh and Ida Red.

Canada is famous for McIntosh apples, first bred and grown by John McIntosh in Dundas, Ontario. We export them all over the world. Our best apple-growing areas range from Nova Scotia's Annapolis Valley and the Saint John River Valley in New Brunswick through the St. Lawrence Valley in Quebec, the lower Great Lakes region of Ontario to the Okanagan Valley in British Columbia.

Popular Varieties

Different apples have different characteristics, making certain varieties better for eating, cooking and storage.

Cortland: A cross between a McIntosh and an old variety called Ben Davis. The flesh is firm and white.

The Cortland is aromatic and mildly acidic, but its best characteristic is its ability to stay white when cut. An excellent choice for salads.

Empire: The new darling of the apple set is a cross between a McIntosh and a Red Delicious. Empires are tastier, firmer and have a better red color than the Macs; they also have a longer storage life. They are primarily an eating apple, but cook well like the McIntosh.

Golden Delicious: This is a good apple for baking because it holds its shape, but it is bland. Add lots of lemon juice to give it a bit of punch.

Granny Smith: A popular variety, though not grown in Canada, since our growing season is not long enough. Its color, firm texture and tart flavor make it good for both eating and cooking.

Ida Red: An apple with a solid, bright-red skin, firm white flesh and a somewhat acidic taste. Good for eating and cooking; best after Christmas because the flavor mellows with storage.

McIntosh: The fine Ontario apple is very versatile. It is juicy, crisp and sweet. A good eating apple, it can also be used for baking, though it falls to applesauce if cooked too long.

Mutsu: Also called Crispin, this is a newer apple — a cross between a Golden Delicious and a crisp Japanese variety. It is firm, dense, juicy and bakes well.

Northern Spy: The best cooking apple and highly recommended for those who like a tart eating apple. It has a tart, acid flavor and holds its shape when cooked, which makes it ideal for pies. Highly prized by apple processors because it gives apple juice a distinctive flavor.

Red Delicious: An elongated, elegant-looking apple. The flesh is creamy and the crunch is good, but the taste has been exorcised. It will also fall apart in cooking.

Red Rome: Often called a hardware apple, because it looks good, packs well and doesn't bruise or blemish. However, it has virtually no flavor. Stores well because it is bred to be indestructible.

Buying and Storing

• Buy the apple that fits your needs for both cooking and eating. Look for unblemished, brightly hued, firm-textured apples, but don't press them too hard because they bruise easily.

• Store in the refrigerator loose or in perforated plastic bags. Apples ripen ten times more quickly at room temperature. If you've picked a bushel and want to store them over the winter, wrap the apples individually in newspaper and store in a cool place. Delicious apples are the best keepers; McIntosh go soft easily in storage.

• Apples darken when they are cut and left to sit. To avoid this, after peeling, coring and slicing apples for recipes, drop them into 4 cups (1 L) water with 1 tsp (5 mL) salt or 1 tbsp (15 mL) lemon juice.

My Personal Apple Choices
Best apples for pies are Spys, Granny Smiths, Golden Delicious and Mutsus. The best apple for apple cakes and applesauce is McIntosl,. Best apples for salads are Cortlands. Best apples for eating are Granny Smiths, McIntosh, Mutsus, Empires and Spys.

While stored in the refrigerator, apples give off ethylene gas, a ripening agent which causes lettuce to go brown and other fruits and vegetables to ripen more quickly. This is a definite benefit to unripe avocados but not great for ripe peaches, etc.

Pork Tenderloin with Glazed Apples

Use two or three pork tenderloins, depending on their weight. If you like a spicier dish, add one crushed chili pepper to the marinade. Serve with buttered noodles and red cabbage for color.

⅓ cup	apple juice	75 mL
¼ cup	liquid honey	50 mL
2 tbsp	soy sauce	25 mL
2 tbsp	vegetable oil	25 mL
1 tbsp	Dijon mustard	15 mL
4	green onions, chopped	4
2	cloves garlic, finely chopped	2
2 tbsp	grated fresh ginger	25 mL
¼ tsp	freshly ground pepper	1 mL
2 lb	pork tenderloin	1 kg
4	apples, peeled, cored and cut into wedges	4
2 tbsp	lemon juice	25 mL
2 tbsp	butter	25 mL
½ cup	whipping cream	125 mL

1. In a large dish, whisk together the apple juice, 2 tbsp (25 mL) honey, soy sauce, vegetable oil and mustard. Stir in the green onions, garlic, ginger and pepper. Place the tenderloins in the marinade and coat well. Cover and marinate for 4 hours or overnight, refrigerated.

2. Preheat the oven to 350°F (180°C). Remove the tenderloins from the refrigerator and allow to come to room temperature. Place in an ovenproof baking dish large enough to hold all the tenderloins in one layer. Spoon over half of the remaining marinade.

3. Bake for 45 to 50 minutes, or until the pork is no longer pink. During cooking, baste frequently with the remaining marinade.

4. Meanwhile, toss the apples with the lemon juice. Just before serving, melt the butter in a frying pan over medium-high heat. Add the apples, drizzle with the remaining honey and sauté until the apples are softened and glazed, about 3 minutes.

5. Slice the tenderloins into slices 1 inch (2.5 cm) thick and top with apple wedges.

6. In a small pot, reheat any remaining marinade. Add the cream and boil together until thickened slightly. Pour over the tenderloins.

Serves 6

Pita Sandwiches with Apples and Cheese

A recipe created by my daughter Emma for her school lunches; this also becomes a super supper sandwich.

3	pita breads	3
⅓ cup	honey mustard	75 mL
⅓ cup	mayonnaise	75 mL
8 oz	old Cheddar cheese, sliced	250 g
3	tart apples, peeled and thinly sliced	3

1. Slice the pita breads in half and spread the insides with mustard and mayonnaise.

2. Stuff each pita with a layer of cheese and apples.

Serves 3

Apple Kuchen

Apple kuchen is basically a creamy apple square. It is good for lunch boxes, picnics and as a snack with a cup of coffee. Use Spy apples for the best flavor. This cake freezes well.

1 cup	all-purpose flour	250 mL
1/4 tsp	baking powder	1 mL
1 tbsp	granulated sugar	15 mL
1/4 tsp	salt	1 mL
1/2 cup	unsalted butter	125 mL
4	Spy apples	4
1/2 cup	granulated sugar	125 mL
1/2 tsp	ground cinnamon	2 mL
1	egg yolk	1
3 tbsp	whipping cream	45 mL

1. Preheat the oven to 350°F (180°C).

2. In a bowl, sift together the flour, baking powder, 1 tbsp (15 mL) sugar and salt. Cut in the butter until the mixture resembles coarse crumbs. With your fingers, pat the dough into a 9-inch (23 cm) square baking dish.

3. Peel, core and slice the apples. Arrange in rows on top of the dough.

4. Combine the sugar and cinnamon. Sprinkle over the apples.

5. In a small bowl, beat the egg yolk and cream together. Drizzle over the apples.

6. Bake for 45 minutes, or until the crust is golden and the fruit is soft. Serve warm or cool.

Serves 6

Baked Apples

A homey dessert best made with Spy, Mutsu or Granny Smith apples. Serve warm with custard, whipped cream or ice cream.

4	apples, cored	4
1/4 cup	brown sugar	50 mL
2 tbsp	unsalted butter	25 mL
1 tsp	ground ginger	5 mL
1/4 cup	chopped dried figs or apricots	50 mL

1. Preheat the oven to 350°F (180°C).

2. Run a knife around each apple, between the flesh and the peel, about one-third of the way down the apple.

3. In a frying pan, combine the brown sugar, butter and ginger. Stir on medium heat until the mixture becomes foamy, about 2 minutes.

4. Stir in the figs and cook for 5 minutes, or until slightly soft.

5. Place the apples in a buttered baking dish. Fill the cored centers with the fig filling. Bake for 45 minutes, or until the apples are soft. Remove the loosened peel around the top of the apples (the remaining apple peel will look like a cup holding the apple).

Serves 4

A medium apple has about 70 calories. It adds bulk to the diet and supplies minerals and vitamins — no wonder it keeps the doctor away!

CRANBERRIES

Cranberries grow wild in acid, sandy bogs, especially around Bala on Lake Muskoka, Ontario, and in the Maritimes. They are harvested and shipped raw all over Canada, or they are processed into sauces or juice. These hard, dark-red, sour berries are a wonderful addition to other foods. They can be slowly cooked into exciting relishes, compotes or chutneys, or they can be tossed into sauces at the last minute to add a tart zing and a pretty color. As an added benefit they are rich in vitamin C.

Because of their excellent keeping qualities, cranberries were the first native North American fruit to be exported to Europe.

Buying and Storing

• Look for dark or light-red, firm fruit. The lighter the color, the sweeter the berries.
• Avoid cranberries that are shriveled, discolored or moist-looking. Remove any stems or bruised berries before using.
• Because of their high acidity, cranberries will keep, refrigerated, for several weeks; they also freeze well.

Last-Minute Cranberry Relish

The origins of this recipe are lost in the mists of time, but I think James Beard developed a version for the original food processor cookbook. It is quick and delicious.

2 cups	cranberries	500 mL
1	orange, unpeeled, diced	1
¹/₂ cup	granulated sugar	125 mL
2 tsp	orange liqueur, optional	10 mL

1. Place all the ingredients in a food processor and process until pureed. Serve immediately or keep for up to 3 weeks, refrigerated.

Makes about 3 cups (750 mL)

Cranberry Relish

This relish keeps for about three months in the refrigerator. It becomes better as it sits. Serve with chicken, turkey or ham. Spoon into attractive small jars and give away as hostess gifts.

1	large navel orange, unpeeled	1
1	lime, unpeeled	1
4 cups	granulated sugar	1 L
1 cup	water	250 mL
1 tbsp	finely chopped fresh ginger	15 mL
1 cup	raisins	250 mL
3	cinnamon sticks	3
3 lb	cranberries	1.5 kg

1. Dice the orange and lime.

2. Place the sugar and water in a large heavy pot on medium heat. Cook together until the sugar turns a pale gold color.

3. Stir in the diced orange, lime (and any juice), ginger, raisins and cinnamon sticks. Cook in the syrup for 2 minutes, stirring constantly.

4. Fold in the cranberries and continue to cook, stirring occasionally, until most of the cranberries break open.

5. Remove from heat and let the mixture cool. Spoon into sterilized jars, cover tightly and refrigerate.

Makes about 6 cups (1.5 L)

Cranberry Stuffing

Use for a 12-lb (6 kg) turkey or cut the recipe in half and stuff into a roasting chicken. The stuffing looks as if it is studded with red jewels, and it has a real tang to it.

¼ cup	butter	50 mL
1	onion, chopped	1
2 cups	cranberries	500 mL
8 oz	sausage meat	250 g
2 cups	fresh breadcrumbs	500 mL
1 tbsp	chopped fresh parsley	15 mL
	Grated rind and juice of 1 orange	
¼ tsp	ground ginger	1 mL
½ tsp	salt	2 mL
¼ tsp	freshly ground pepper	1 mL
1	egg, beaten	1

1. Melt the butter in a large frying pan over medium heat. Stir in the onion and sauté until softened, about 2 minutes. Add the cranberries and cook until the first few berries pop. Remove from the heat.

2. Transfer the mixture to a large bowl and mix in the sausage meat, breadcrumbs, parsley, orange rind and juice. Season with the ginger, salt and pepper. Stir in the egg.

3. Fry about 2 tbsp (25 mL) mixture in the frying pan and taste for seasoning. Readjust, adding more salt and pepper as needed.

Makes enough for a 12-lb (6 kg) bird

Apple Cranberry Maple Crumble

This could be the definitive Canadian dessert! Its tart/sweet combination is perfect after a heavy meal. In a pinch, you can substitute flour for the tapioca (although the texture will not be as smooth).

4	McIntosh apples	4
1 tbsp	quick-cooking tapioca	15 mL
⅓ cup	maple syrup	75 mL
1 cup	cranberries	250 mL
½ cup	rolled oats	125 mL
¼ cup	all-purpose flour	50 mL
¼ cup	brown sugar	50 mL
¼ cup	unsalted butter	50 mL

1. Preheat the oven to 375°F (190°C).

2. Peel, core and slice the apples into eighths.

3. In a medium bowl, combine the tapioca and maple syrup. Add the apples and cranberries and toss to coat the fruit. Spread in a buttered 4-cup (1 L) baking dish.

4. In the same bowl, combine the oats, flour and brown sugar. Cut in the butter until the mixture resembles coarse breadcrumbs. Sprinkle over the fruit.

5. Bake for 30 minutes, or until the top is golden.

Serves 4

Cranberries are now considered by some scientists to counter the effects of urinary tract infections.

Cranberry Upside-Down Cake with Eggnog Sauce

This is the best upside-down cake ever — moist, tart and sweet. I serve it at Christmas dinner for people who don't like Christmas pudding. It is also a good dessert after a heavy meal because it is light and not too sweet. The recipe also works with blueberries and black currants, but pears and apples have to be sautéed first.

Base:

2 tbsp	unsalted butter, at room temperature	25 mL
1 cup	brown sugar, loosely packed	250 mL
12 oz	cranberries	375 g

Cake:

³/₄ cup	unsalted butter, at room temperature	175 mL
1 cup	granulated sugar	250 mL
2	eggs	2
2 cups	all-purpose flour	500 mL
1 tbsp	baking powder	15 mL
²/₃ cup	milk	150 mL
1 tsp	vanilla extract	5 mL

1. Preheat the oven to 350°F (180°C).

2. Spread 2 tbsp (25 mL) butter on the base of a 9-inch (23 cm) springform pan. Spread the brown sugar over the butter and pat down firmly. Spread the cranberries over the sugar.

3. In a large bowl or electric mixer, beat ³/₄ cup (175 mL) butter and the granulated sugar together until light and fluffy.

4. Add the eggs one at a time, beating well after each addition.

5. In a separate bowl, stir together the flour and baking powder. Add the dry ingredients to the egg/butter mixture alternately with the milk, until well combined. Stir in the vanilla.

6. Spread the batter over the cranberry base. Bake for 1¼ hours, or until the top is light brown and a cake tester comes out clean.

7. Run a knife around the sides of the pan and release. Invert onto a serving platter and lift off the removable bottom of the pan. Serve warm or cold, with eggnog sauce.

Eggnog Sauce

2 cups	whipping cream	500 mL
3	eggs	3
¹/₂ cup	granulated sugar	125 mL
¹/₂ cup	dark rum	125 mL

1. In a small pot, heat the whipping cream to a simmer.

2. In a medium pot, beat together the eggs, sugar and rum.

3. On low heat, whisk the egg mixture until it begins to thicken slightly. Pour in the warm cream and continue to whisk until the mixture is thick enough to coat a spoon. Remove from the heat. Serve hot or cold with the cranberry cake.

Serves 8

Thanksgiving Dinner for Twelve

Thanksgiving is a time for celebration, and it calls for a menu that is truly festive. All the dishes can be assembled or made ahead, except for roasting the turkey. Reheat all dishes at 350°F (180°C), or microwave until hot.

Pears with Melted Cambozola

Turkey with Sausage Stuffing

Creamy Potato and Parsnip Gratin

Baked Onions

Sweet Sugar Snaps (page 98)

Cranberry Relish (page 166)

Pumpkin Pecan Pie

Pears with Melted Cambozola

Cambozola is an Italian cheese that combines Camembert and Gorgonzola. Its mild flavor heightens the taste of pears. If your pears are not fully ripened, poach them first in a sugar syrup until tender, or use apples instead. Serve Cheddar sticks (see page 186) with this warm salad. If Cambozola is unavailable, use Brie.

3	green onions, white part only	3
1	small ripe pear, peeled and cored	1
¹/₃ cup	olive oil	75 mL
3 tbsp	white wine vinegar	45 mL
	Salt and freshly ground pepper to taste	
6	ripe pears	6
¹/₄ cup	chutney	50 mL
12 oz	Cambozola	375 g
1	head Boston lettuce	1

1. Preheat the oven to 375°F (190°C).

2. In a food processor or blender, puree the green onions, small pear, oil, vinegar and salt and pepper until smooth. Reserve.

3. Peel, core and halve the pears. Arrange the pears, cored side up, in a buttered ovenproof dish. (Cut a small slice off the bottom of the pears so they will sit in the dish.)

4. Spread each pear with about 1 tsp (5 mL) chutney. Crumble the Cambozola and sprinkle on top of the pear halves.

5. Bake for 10 minutes, or until the cheese has melted.

6. Meanwhile, drizzle the dressing over 12 individual lettuce-lined salad plates. Place a pear half on each plate and serve immediately.

Serves 12

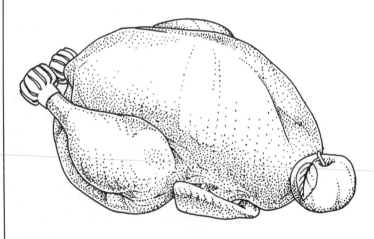

Turkey with Sausage Stuffing

Take some of the pressure off by preparing the stuffing ahead of time.

1	12- to 14-lb (6 to 7 kg) turkey	1
¼ cup	butter	50 mL
Stuffing:		
2 tbsp	vegetable oil	25 mL
1	large onion, chopped	1
12 oz	sausage meat	375 g
2	apples, peeled and chopped	2
2 tbsp	finely chopped parsley	25 mL
2 tsp	dried thyme	10 mL
½ tsp	dried sage	2 mL
2 cups	fresh breadcrumbs	500 mL
2 tbsp	Calvados or brandy	25 mL
1 tsp	salt	5 mL
1 tsp	freshly ground pepper	5 mL
Gravy:		
¼ cup	all-purpose flour	50 mL
4 cups	chicken or turkey stock	1 L
1 tbsp	tomato paste	15 mL
1 tbsp	red currant jelly	15 mL
	Salt and freshly ground pepper to taste	

Do not stuff birds until just before cooking, to prevent any bacteria from growing.

1. Remove the giblets and neck from the turkey and cut off the wing tips; reserve for stock.* Wipe the turkey inside and out with a damp cloth. Dry the skin well.

2. To make the stuffing, in a frying pan, heat the oil on medium heat. Add the onion and sauté until tender.

3. In a large bowl, crumble the sausage meat. Stir in the onion, apples, parsley, thyme, sage, breadcrumbs, brandy, salt and pepper.

4. Loosely stuff the body and neck cavities of the turkey. Skewer the cavities closed. Truss the turkey.

5. Set the turkey, breast side up, on a rack in a roasting pan. Rub the butter into the breast and legs.

6. When ready to roast, preheat the oven to 375°F (190°C). Roast for 2¾ to 3 hours, or until the juices from the thigh run clear when pierced. Baste every 30 minutes with the pan juices.

7. Remove the turkey to a platter. Cover with tea towel and let stand for 10 minutes while you make the gravy.

8. To make the gravy, drain all but ¼ cup (50 mL) fat from the roasting pan. Place the pan over medium heat, stir in the flour and cook, stirring, until the mixture is pale gold. Add the stock and tomato paste. Bring to a boil, stirring, reduce the heat and simmer for 5 minutes. Stir in the red currant jelly and simmer for 5 minutes longer. Season with salt and pepper. Pour the gravy into a warmed sauce boat and serve with the turkey.

Serves 12

*See *Lucy Waverman's Cooking School Cookbook*, page 41.

Creamy Potato and Parsnip Gratin

Parsnips add a delicate sweetness to this fall casserole. Use firm boiling potatoes for the best results, because they absorb the cream. To cut down the calories, use half chicken stock and half cream.

1	clove garlic, halved	1
8	potatoes, thinly sliced	8
1 tsp	dried thyme	5 mL
	Salt and freshly ground pepper to taste	
8	parsnips, thinly sliced	8
2 cups	whipping cream	500 mL

1. Butter a 13 × 9-inch (3.5 L) casserole dish and rub with garlic.

2. Arrange a single layer of potatoes in the dish. Sprinkle lightly with a little of the thyme, salt and pepper. Cover with a layer of parsnips. Sprinkle with the seasonings. Repeat layering with the remaining vegetables.

3. Pour in enough cream to come three-quarters up the side of the dish.

4. When ready to bake, preheat the oven to 375°F (190°C). Place the casserole on a baking sheet and bake, covered, for 30 minutes. Uncover and bake for 30 minutes longer, or until the top is brown and crusty and the potatoes are cooked through.

Serves 12

Baked Onions

The rich color and taste of this dish make it an excellent foil for turkey.

6	red onions, unpeeled, halved	6
	Rind of 1 lemon	
1/2 cup	olive oil	125 mL
1/2 cup	port or sherry	125 mL
1/4 cup	cider vinegar	50 mL
1 cup	raisins	250 mL
1 tbsp	brown sugar	15 mL
	Freshly ground pepper	

1. Place the onions and lemon rind in a large pot. Cover with water. Bring to a boil and boil for 5 minutes. Drain. Refresh the onions under cold running water and drain again. Discard the rind.

2. Peel the onions and arrange in a 13 × 9-inch (3.5 L) baking dish. Pour the olive oil over the onions.

3. When ready to bake, preheat the oven to 375°F (190°C). Bake, uncovered, for 40 minutes, basting occasionally.

4. In a small bowl, combine the port, vinegar, raisins, sugar and pepper. Pour over the onions and bake for 30 minutes longer, or until the juices are syrupy.

Serves 12

Pumpkin Pecan Pie

Pecans add a taste of the South to this traditional pumpkin pie. Double the recipe and make two pies to serve twelve people.

3	eggs, beaten	3
1	14-oz (398 mL) can pumpkin	1
1 cup	packed brown sugar	250 mL
1/2 cup	corn syrup	125 mL
1/3 cup	melted unsalted butter	75 mL
1 tsp	vanilla extract	5 mL
1/2 tsp	ground cinnamon	2 mL
1/2 tsp	ground nutmeg	2 mL
1/4 tsp	salt	1 mL
1	unbaked 9-inch (23 cm) pie shell	1
1 cup	pecan halves	250 mL

1. Preheat the oven to 350°F (180°C).

2. In a food processor or blender, combine the eggs, pumpkin, sugar, corn syrup, butter, vanilla, cinnamon, nutmeg and salt. Process until blended. Pour into the pie shell.

3. Arrange the pecans in concentric circles over the filling.

4. Bake for 45 minutes, or until a tester inserted in center comes out clean.

Makes one 9-inch pie (23 cm)

Pumpkin pies are sometimes made with Hubbard squash, not pumpkin. Once spices are added it is hard to tell the difference. Canned pumpkin also often contains squash.

11
November

In season
Brussels sprouts
cabbage
carrots
kale
leeks
onions

Menu
Classic Cocktail Party for
Twenty

Don't freeze
- potatoes (unless mashed)
- salad greens
- soft or cream cheese
- hard-boiled egg whites
- cream fillings
- Hollandaise sauce

Do freeze on purchasing
- coffee
- nuts
- grated Parmesan cheese

November is a month of anticipation. It is a time to organize yourself for the coming festive season and start freezing dishes for a busy December. The first snowfall teases us, and the first welcoming fires are burning in the fireplace.

FREEZING

Freezing is a great boon to the person who manages a career, kids and other demands of today's busy lifestyle. Freezing enables you to plan menus weeks ahead of time and come home and toss dinner in the oven or microwave. It makes entertaining easier because you can do much of the work ahead. Freezing also helps to keep down the cost of groceries, because specials can be bought and frozen until needed.

Making the Most of Your Freezer

• Freezing is the best way to preserve the flavor, texture and color of most foods. Not everything freezes beautifully, but most dishes will work. Some of the spicing will become milder during freezing, so always season strongly before freezing and taste for seasoning after cooking from the frozen state.
• Make double batches of dishes like lasagna, spaghetti sauce, stews and casseroles and freeze for future use.

If you are single, freeze in meal-sized portions for one and reheat when needed.

• When you bake a cake, make two and freeze one. Make a double batch of pastry and freeze one batch already rolled into a pie plate. When frozen, remove the pastry shell from the pie plate and store in a freezer bag.

• Freeze unbaked rolls of refrigerator cookie dough in airtight freezer bags for up to four months. Let thaw for 5 minutes; slice and bake following the original baking instructions.

• Always label freezer bags with baking times and temperatures.

• Freeze muffins in freezer bags. Reheat from the frozen state in a 350°F (180°C) oven.

• Remember that little things are apt to end up as nameless lumps in the dark recesses of your freezer. Store them towards the front, making sure they are clearly labelled.

• For holiday entertaining, freeze colorful juices (e.g., cranberry) in cubes and place in freezer bags, ready for punches. They won't dilute the punch like regular ice cubes.

• If you have extra cheese on hand, grate it and freeze in freezer bags for up to three months.

• When butter is on sale, buy a quantity, enclose in freezer bags and store for up to one year.

• Throw leftover chicken bones, wing tips and odds and ends of vegetables into a large freezer bag and freeze for stock.

Packaging

• Heavy-duty polyethylene bags are airtight, moisture-proof and vapour-proof. Foods can be frozen directly in them, or they can enclose other forms of packaging for extra protection.

• Plastic freezer containers or recycled dairy-product containers stack nicely and are especially good for liquids.

• Heavy-duty foil can be wrapped around a finished dish or be used for odd shapes such as fish, but be careful not to puncture the foil. Seal by crimping the edges.

Storage

• Good inventory-control techniques will ensure that your freezer foods retain maximum flavor and food value. Label and date frozen foods; prepared dishes can be frozen for up to three to six months. Keep an inventory of freezer contents. Rotate foods from the back to the front of the freezer; use foods from the front first and place new foods at the back (or top and bottom, depending on the type of freezer).

Defrosting

• Poultry or meat products should be defrosted for 24 hours in the refrigerator for optimum taste. If you don't have time, you can thaw food more quickly at room temperature, although this will result in some flavor and juice loss.

• Some foods taste best when transferred directly from the freezer to the oven. Pastries, for example, become soggy if defrosted; pasta dishes may become more liquid.

From Freezer to Oven

• Let the dish sit outside the freezer for 5 to 10 minutes before cooking.

• If a dish has a sauce, cover and

Whatever you freeze, if you don't package properly, the contents will deteriorate. They will develop freezer burn, a condition caused by dehydration as air seeps into the packaging. (Freezer burn cannot be reversed by thawing.)

When freezing food in containers, remember that food expands when frozen. Be sure to allow headspace of at least 2 inches (5 cm), so the container will not burst.

Washed milk bags secured with a twist tie make excellent freezer bags. Store bags of food flat to make the best use of your freezer space.

reheat at 350°F (180°C) until the sauce is bubbly.

• If a dish has a potato or pastry topping, reheat, uncovered, at 350°F (180°C) for 35 to 45 minutes, depending on the size of the dish.

• When reheating, watch for bubbling juices as a signal that the dish is ready.

• All dishes can be reheated in a microwave except those wrapped in foil. A rule of thumb is to cover the dish and use Medium power (50%) for 15 to 30 minutes, stirring occasionally. However, it is best to check the instructions for your specific microwave oven.

Phyllo pastry is a paper-thin pastry used in Middle Eastern countries to wrap savory and sweet fillings. It is available fresh and frozen from supermarkets and delicatessens. If you can find fresh, buy it, because freezing causes the dough to break more easily. Phyllo dries out quickly, so cover unused portions with a damp tea towel.

Chicken and Artichoke Pie

This spectacular pie is excellent hot or cold. Serve it with Hollandaise sauce (see page 53), if desired, and steamed green beans with pine nuts. You can double this recipe and make a large pie in a 13 × 9-inch (3.5 L) casserole dish to serve at buffet parties.

	Rind and juice of ¹/₂ lemon	
1 cup	milk	250 mL
4	whole chicken breasts, skinned and boned	4
2 tbsp	melted butter	25 mL
1	6-oz (180 mL) jar marinated artichoke hearts, drained	1
2 tbsp	butter	25 mL
2 tbsp	all-purpose flour	25 mL
1 tsp	salt	5 mL
pinch	freshly ground pepper	pinch
8	sheets phyllo pastry	8
¹/₄ cup	melted butter	50 mL

1. In a small pot, combine the lemon rind and milk. Bring to a simmer. Remove from the heat and let stand for 30 minutes to flavor the milk. Strain the milk and discard the rind.

2. Brush the chicken breasts with 2 tbsp (25 mL) melted butter. Place on a baking sheet. Broil for 5 minutes on each side. Squeeze lemon juice over the breasts and let cool. Cut the chicken into chunks and combine with the artichokes.

3. In a medium pot, melt 2 tbsp (25 mL) butter; stir in the flour and cook, stirring occasionally, for 1 minute. Pour in the lemon milk and bring to a boil, stirring constantly. Add the salt, pepper and any juices from the chicken. Pour over the chicken mixture and let cool.

4. Place one sheet of phyllo in a buttered 8-inch (1.2 L) round cake pan so the bottom is covered and the phyllo drapes over the edges. Brush lightly with melted butter. Make a quarter-turn of the pan, then repeat with a second sheet of phyllo. But-

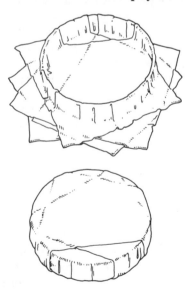

ter lightly. Continue to line the pan with phyllo sheets. Spoon in the chicken mixture.

5. Fold the extended phyllo sheets over the top of the pie and cover with a half sheet of phyllo. Butter the top sheet. Wrap well and freeze.

6. Defrost the pie in the refrigerator overnight. Preheat the oven to 425°F (220°C). Place the pie in the oven, reduce the heat to 375°F (190°C) and bake for 40 minutes, or until the top is golden. Loosen the sides and shake the pan to loosen the bottom. Invert onto a serving platter and cut into wedges.

Serves 6

Baked Lemon Chicken

Bake this dish from the frozen stage, so the breadcrumbs don't become soggy. You can use sautéed spinach or leeks instead of the butter mixture, or use tarragon, basil or marjoram instead of the parsley combination in the filling.

1 cup	butter, at room temperature	250 mL
	Grated rind and juice of 1 lemon	
2 tbsp	finely chopped parsley	25 mL
1 tbsp	finely chopped chives	15 mL
2	cloves garlic, finely chopped	2
1 tsp	salt	5 mL
pinch	freshly ground pepper	pinch
6	whole chicken breasts, boned	6
¹/₄ cup	all-purpose flour	50 mL
¹/₄ tsp	salt	1 mL
¹/₄ tsp	freshly ground pepper	1 mL
3	eggs	3
1¹/₂ cups	dry breadcrumbs	375 mL

1. Beat the butter in a medium bowl until soft. Stir in the lemon rind, lemon juice, parsley, chives, garlic, 1 tsp (5 mL) salt and pinch pepper until well combined. Spread the mixture onto waxed paper in a 4 × 3-inch (10 × 7.5 cm) rectangle, about ¹/₂ inch (1.25 cm) thick. Place in the freezer for about 20 minutes.

2. Cut the chicken breasts in half and place, smooth side down, between two sheets of waxed paper. Flatten with a heavy object until about ¹/₄ inch (5 mm) thick, being careful not to break the meat. Remove the paper.

3. Remove the herb butter from the freezer. Cut lengthwise into six sticks ¹/₂ inch (1.25 cm) wide, then halve each stick to make twelve fingers.

4. Place a finger of herb-butter in the center of each flattened chicken breast. Bring the long sides of the chicken over the butter; then fold the ends over, making sure the butter is completely covered. Fasten with wooden picks.

5. In a shallow dish, combine the flour, ¹/₄ tsp (1 mL) salt and ¹/₄ tsp (1 mL) pepper. Beat the eggs in a separate shallow dish. Place the breadcrumbs in a third dish.

6. Dip each chicken roll in flour, then in beaten egg, then roll in the breadcrumbs to coat completely and with crumbs. Wrap in foil and freeze.

7. To bake, preheat the oven to 425°F (220°C). Unwrap the chicken rolls. Place in a single layer on a jelly roll pan. Bake for 10 minutes. Reduce the heat to 400°F (200°C) and bake for a further 30 minutes, or until chicken juices run clear.

Makes 12 rolls

Do not freeze uncooked mixtures, because they tend to become watery when baked.

Basic Beef Braise

Have this in the freezer, packaged in sizes to suit your needs. Before serving, add one of the variations to the basic recipe to make a more interesting stew.

¹/₂ cup	all-purpose flour	125 mL
2 tsp	salt	10 mL
1 tsp	freshly ground pepper	5 mL
5 lb	stewing beef	2.5 kg
¹/₂ cup	vegetable oil	125 mL
2	large onions, diced	2
2	cloves garlic, finely chopped	2
1 cup	dry red wine	250 mL
6 cups	beef stock	1.5 L

1. Preheat the oven to 325°F (160°C).

2. Combine the flour, salt and pepper in a shallow dish. Roll the meat in the seasoned flour.

3. Heat the oil in a heavy Dutch oven on high heat. Brown the meat in batches on all sides. Remove and reserve.

4. Sauté the onions and garlic in the oil until softened. Pour in the red wine and beef stock and bring to a boil. Return the meat to the pot and cover.

5. Bake in the oven for 2 hours, or until the meat is tender. Cool. Freeze in quantities to suit your family.

6. To reheat, defrost the stew in the refrigerator for 24 hours and reheat in a 325°F (160°C) oven for 30 minutes.

Serves 16 to 20

When you are reheating a dish from the frozen state, use a metal skewer to judge whether the food is hot. Insert the skewer into the center of the dish. If the skewer feels cold, the dish is not cooked through.

Fall Beef Stew

1 tbsp	olive oil	15 mL
2	cloves garlic, finely chopped	2
4	tomatoes, peeled, seeded and chopped	4
¹/₂ cup	pitted green olives	125 mL
2 lb	Basic Beef Braise	1 kg

1. Heat the oil in a frying pan. Sauté the garlic until softened, about 2 minutes. Toss in the tomatoes and olives and stir together. Add to the stew and simmer for 5 minutes.

Beef Orleans

1 tbsp	butter	15 mL
12	small onions, peeled	12
4 oz	small mushrooms	125 g
¹/₂ cup	dry red wine	125 mL
pinch	cayenne pepper	pinch
	Salt to taste	
2 lb	Basic Beef Braise	1 kg

1. Heat the butter in a frying pan. Sauté the onions and mushrooms for 5 minutes, or until the onions are slightly softened.

2. Pour in the red wine and bring to a boil. Simmer for 5 minutes. Season with cayenne and salt. Add to the stew. Simmer together for 15 minutes.

Lemon Torte

Reminiscent of lemon meringue pie, this is a light, refreshing treat after a heavy meal. It is also spectacular on a buffet. Use orange juice and rind instead of lemon, if desired. Freeze for up to one month.

5	egg yolks	5
6	egg whites	6
1¹/₄ cups	granulated sugar	300 mL
³/₄ cup	lemon juice	175 mL
	Grated rind of 2 lemons	
2 cups	whipping cream	500 mL
1	3¹/₂-oz (100 g) package ladyfingers	1
pinch	cream of tartar	pinch

1. In the top of a double boiler, beat together 5 egg yolks, 2 of the egg whites, 1 cup (250 mL) sugar, lemon juice and rind. Cook over medium heat, stirring frequently, until thickened, about 5 minutes. Spoon into a large bowl and refrigerate until cool.

2. In a separate bowl, whip the cream until it holds its shape. Fold into the lemon mixture.

3. Butter an 8-inch (2 L) springform pan and line the sides with ladyfingers. Spoon in the lemon-cream mixture. Freeze for 6 hours, or until firm.

4. In a separate bowl, beat the remaining 4 egg whites with the cream of tartar until frothy. Gradually add the remaining ¹/₄ cup (50 mL) sugar, beating until stiff peaks form. Pile the meringue on top of the frozen lemon dessert.

5. Broil on the bottom rack of the oven until the meringue is brown, about 1 minute. Cover with plastic wrap and foil. Transfer to the freezer.

6. About 1 hour before serving, transfer the torte from the freezer to the refrigerator. Remove the sides of the springform pan.

Serves 12

CABBAGE

The phrase, "From cabbages to kings," gives the cabbage a very lowly status. In fact, cabbage is an easily grown, tasty, cheap and nutritious vegetable.

There are three main types of cabbage — the round, smooth, green variety, which is the most popular; savoy cabbage, which has lacy ruffled leaves and is good for stuffed cabbage leaves; and garnet-colored red cabbage, which braises beautifully and complements duck, goose and pork.

Although cabbage is available all year, dark-green, ruffle-leafed kale is at its best in November. Kale is part of the cabbage family and was the first cabbage cultivated. It grows abundantly in cool, wet climates and has a better flavor after the first frost. Kale has a strong, slightly bitter taste and can be sautéed like spinach, or made into hearty soups.

• Look for cabbage heads that seem heavy for their size. The leaves should be brightly colored and not wilted. If the outer leaves are separating from the head and are flabby and yellow, the cabbage is overmature and won't have a good taste.

• When buying kale, choose crisp-looking leaves with a good dark color.

• Store cabbage in the refrigerator or a cool cupboard; it should keep for a month. Remove any withered leaves before cooking.

• Cabbage has suffered from bad press, probably because of its tendency to give off an odor if overcooked. I prefer it stir-fried, stuffed or in salads rather than boiled.

Cabbage Roses
For a spectacular table centerpiece, spread out the leaves of a Savoy cabbage and insert roses among the leaves.

To shred cabbage, cut into quarters, remove the core, then slice down against the grain with a sharp knife to the desired thickness.

Sautéed Kale
Remove the leaves from the stalks (which are discarded). Wash and dry the leaves thoroughly and slice in strips. In a frying pan, heat ¹/₄ cup (50 mL) butter or four strips chopped bacon per bunch of kale. Add the kale and sauté until softened. Turn the heat to low, cover the pan and cook for 10 minutes, or until the kale is tender.

Cabbage with Juniper Berries and Garlic

Being a cabbage lover, I cook it in many ways, but this is my favorite. If you don't have juniper berries, add 1 tbsp (15 mL) gin before baking.

2	cloves garlic, peeled	2
10	juniper berries	10
¹/₄ cup	olive oil	50 mL
1	head cabbage, shredded	1

1. Preheat the oven to 350°F (180°C).

2. In a small bowl, mash together the garlic and juniper berries.

3. In a large frying pan, heat the oil on high heat. Sauté the garlic/berry mixture for 30 seconds.

4. Add the cabbage and toss to coat with oil. Transfer to an 8-cup (2 L) gratin dish and bake, covered, for 10 minutes.

Serves 6

Kale Soup

The Portuguese touch in this kale and potato soup comes from the sliced sausage and olive oil, which are added to the boiled potatoes. The kale must be chopped finely, because it only cooks for a short time. Use chorizo sausage, pepperoni or Polish sausage. In Portugal, the soup is usually served with a thick piece of maize bread, called broa, *which has a nutty flavor and crumbly texture.*

3	large potatoes, peeled and chopped	3
1	large onion, chopped	1
6 cups	water	1.5 L
2 cups	shredded kale or finely chopped green cabbage	500 mL
4 oz	Polish sausage or chorizo, thinly sliced	125 g
1 tbsp	olive oil	15 mL
	Salt and freshly ground pepper to taste	

1. In a large pot, on medium heat, boil the potatoes and onion in the water until mushy, about 15 minutes.

2. In a food processor or blender, puree the potatoes, onions and 2 cups (500 mL) liquid until fairly smooth. Return the potatoes and liquid to the pot and reheat.

3. Add the kale, Polish sausage and olive oil. Simmer for 15 minutes, or until the kale is softened. Season with salt and pepper to taste.

Serves 6

Savoy

Green

Kale

HOLIDAY FRUIT CAKES AND PUDDINGS

Baking your Christmas cakes in November gives them plenty of time to mature, and leaves you free for other holiday preparations in December.

Ingredients

• Use dried fruits interchangeably. Combine or use separately sultanas, currants, seeded raisins, dried apricots, figs, dates, red and green glace cherries, candied pineapple, dried pears and peaches. Candied orange peel, lemon peel and citron peel (a type of lemon peel) are also interchangeable.
• Include whichever nuts you enjoy. If you prefer not to use nuts, continue making the cake as the recipe instructs. Traditionally, almonds and walnuts are the most popular. Dust the fruit and nuts with some of the flour from the recipe, to prevent them from sinking to the bottom of the cake.
• Sherry, brandy, Scotch, liqueurs, wine and even beer can be used to flavor Christmas cakes. If you prefer not to use alcohol, substitute fruit juice or orange syrup.
• Butter, margarine or shortening are interchangeable, but butter gives the richest taste.
• Use all-purpose flour; cake and pastry flour isn't heavy enough to hold the fruit together.

Equipment

• Baking pans can be any shape or material, but avoid black pans, which absorb heat, tending to caramelize the fruit. Tube pans produce a cake that has an interesting look when sliced. Once, in desperation, I used coffee cans, which worked fine. Small loaf pans are the ideal size for gifts.
• Butter or oil the pans, then line them with brown or parchment paper so that the cake can be removed easily. Commercial cooking sprays also work well.

Baking and Storing

• Fruit cakes are usually baked for long periods of time at low temperatures, so that they cook evenly.
• Cool the cakes, then unmold and wrap in tea towels soaked in liquor. Either wrap in foil for storage or put in cake tins. Every two weeks, resoak the tea towels and rewrap the cakes. The cakes need at least one month to ripen.

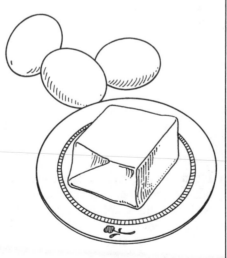

Five-Day Christmas Pudding

This dessert is like a brandied apple pudding. Guests are always delighted with it because it is lighter and tastier than the traditional Christmas puddings.

Make this five days before Christmas or up to two weeks before, and reheat on Christmas Day.

Substitute ground almonds for the hazelnuts or omit the nuts altogether. I often use orange peel instead of mixed peel.

Suet is the very fine, hard fat around the kidneys and loins of beef. It is used in Christmas puddings because it helps to hold them together.

8 oz	beef suet	250 g
1 cup	raisins	250 mL
1 cup	sultanas	250 mL
1/2 cup	currants	125 mL
2 cups	mixed candied peel	500 mL
1/2 cup	ground hazelnuts	125 mL
6	tart apples, peeled and chopped	6
1 1/4 cups	brown sugar	300 mL
1/2 tsp	ground cloves	2 mL
2 tsp	ground cinnamon	10 mL
1 tsp	ground ginger	5 mL
1 tsp	ground nutmeg	5 mL
1 tsp	salt	5 mL
1/2 cup	all-purpose flour	125 mL
3 cups	fresh breadcrumbs	750 mL
	Grated rind and juice of 1 lemon	
	Grated rind and juice of 1 orange	
1 1/2 cups	brandy	375 mL
6	eggs	6

1. In a large bowl, combine the suet, raisins, sultanas, currants, mixed peel, hazelnuts, apples, sugar, spices, salt and flour. Toss well to coat the fruit with the flour.

2. Stir in breadcrumbs, rind, juice and 1/2 cup (125 mL) brandy. Combine everything well.

3. Cover and leave in a cool place (not the refrigerator) for five days, stirring in 1/4 cup (50 mL) brandy each day.

4. On the fifth day, beat the eggs and stir into the fruit.

5. Line a large heatproof bowl with foil. Pour in the pudding. Cover with more foil or tie a cloth over the bowl.

6. Place the bowl on a trivet in a large pot. Add water to the pot, but don't allow the water to touch the bowl. Bring the water to a simmer, cover and steam the pudding on low heat for 5 hours. Check the water level occasionally and add more water if necessary.

7. Remove the pudding from the steamer (reheat when needed by resteaming for 1 hour).

8. Turn out onto a platter, top with holly and flame with 1/4 cup (50 mL) extra brandy.

Serves 12 to 16

Gumdrop Cake

Most kids don't like fruit cake, so I have devised a moist version of the classic gumdrop cake. Freeze the cake until Christmas or refrigerate for up to two weeks.

1 cup	gumdrops	250 mL
1/2 cup	raisins	125 mL
2 cups	all-purpose flour	500 mL
1 tsp	baking powder	5 mL
1/2 tsp	baking soda	2 mL
1 tsp	ground cinnamon	5 mL
1 tsp	ground nutmeg	5 mL
pinch	salt	pinch
1 cup	unsalted butter	250 mL
1 cup	granulated sugar	250 mL
3	eggs	3
1 cup	applesauce	250 mL
	Grated rind of 1 lemon	

1. Preheat the oven to 350°F (180°C).

2. Cut the gumdrops into small pieces. In a small bowl, toss with the raisins and ½ cup (125 mL) flour. Reserve.

3. In a separate bowl, combine the baking powder, baking soda, cinnamon, nutmeg and salt with the remaining flour.

4. In a large bowl, cream the butter until light and fluffy. Gradually beat in the sugar. Beat in the eggs one at a time.

5. Stir in the applesauce, flour mixture and lemon rind. Fold in the gumdrop and raisin mixture.

6. Butter a 9 × 5-inch (2 L) loaf pan and line with buttered waxed or parchment paper. Pour in the batter.

7. Bake for 1 to 1½ hours, or until a knife inserted comes out clean.

8. Turn out the cake and let it cool completely. Wrap well with foil and store for 1 to 2 weeks in the refrigerator. Freeze it if keeping longer than 2 weeks.

Makes one loaf

Grandma Daisy's White Fruit Cake

This is a simple but delicious pure white fruit cake. The recipe comes from my husband Bruce's grandmother, Daisy, who was renowned in the Maxville area of Ontario for her fine baking. Because this cake is delicate, after Christmas I freeze any leftovers. The cake should be refrigerated after baking, because there is no liqueur in the batter.

1 cup	unsalted butter	250 mL
¾ cup	granulated sugar	175 mL
2 cups	all-purpose flour	500 mL
½ tsp	baking powder	2 mL
½ tsp	salt	2 mL
2	eggs, beaten	2
½ cup	milk	125 mL
	Grated rind of 1 lemon	
	Grated rind of 1 orange	
½ tsp	vanilla extract	2 mL
1 cup	mixed candied peel	250 mL
1 cup	glace pineapple, chopped	250 mL
1 cup	glace cherries, chopped	250 mL

1. Preheat the oven to 300°F (150°C).

2. In a large bowl, cream together the butter and sugar until light and fluffy.

3. Reserve 2 tbsp (25 mL) flour. Sift the remaining flour with the baking powder and salt in a separate bowl.

4. Beat the eggs into the butter/sugar mixture one at a time until incorporated. Beat in the milk, lemon and orange rind and vanilla.

5. Mix the fruit together and combine with the reserved 2 tbsp (25 mL) flour. Stir into the batter. Slowly fold in the remaining dry ingredients until incorporated.

6. Oil or butter a 9-inch (23 cm) cake pan and line with parchment paper or brown paper. Spoon in the batter.

7. Bake for about 2 hours, or until a cake tester comes out clean. Cool on a rack and unmold.

8. Wrap well with liqueur-soaked tea towels and foil and refrigerate.

Makes one 9-inch (23 cm) cake

Some people do not use black gumdrops in baking because the color sometimes runs. It depends on the brand of gumdrops. Test by heating one in some water. If the color runs, omit.

Scissors dipped in hot water will cut gumdrops and other sticky candies and dried fruits easily.

Dark Fruit Cake

The leavening in this black, rich, moist cake comes from the creamed butter and sugar mixture; there is no baking powder or baking soda in the cake. Make sure all ingredients are at room temperature.

A well-soaked Christmas cake should keep, unrefrigerated, for one year.

1/2 cup	candied orange peel	125 mL
3 cups	currants	750 mL
3 cups	raisins	750 mL
1 cup	mixed candied peel	250 mL
1 cup	chopped glace cherries	250 mL
3 cups	slivered almonds	750 mL
2 cups	all-purpose flour	500 mL
2 tsp	ground nutmeg	10 mL
1 cup	unsalted butter	250 mL
1 1/2 cups	brown sugar	375 mL
6	eggs	6
1/2 cup	molasses	125 mL
1/2 cup	wine or brandy	125 mL
1/2 cup	orange juice	125 mL

1. Preheat the oven to 250°F (120°C).

2. In a large bowl, combine the fruits, nuts, flour and nutmeg.

3. In a separate bowl, cream the butter. Add the sugar a little at a time, beating until the mixture is light and fluffy. Add the eggs one at a time, beating well after each addition. Beat in the molasses, wine and orange juice. Stir into the fruit/flour mixture.

4. Oil a deep 10-inch (25 cm) cake pan or springform pan. Line with brown paper or parchment. Spoon in the batter and smooth the top.

5. Bake for 2 1/2 to 3 hours, or until a cake tester comes out slightly sticky.

6. Cool, unmold, then wrap with brandy-soaked tea towels and foil.

Makes one 10-inch (25 cm) cake

Classic Cocktail Party for Twenty

Cocktail parties are right back in vogue again, because they are less expensive and require less work and less time than large dinner parties.

If you are having one, here are some tips to ensure success.

• Decide on the date. Send invitations for a more formal party, phone for a casual get-together. Five to seven p.m. or six to eight p.m. are the usual cocktail party hours. On a weeknight, use the later hours because people come from work. On weekends, earlier is better if guests want to go on to something else.

• If you are catering the party yourself, decide on your menu. Choose recipes that can sit on a table and don't have to be passed around, leaving you time to mingle. Make more cold things than hot to avoid tying yourself to the oven. Look for tasty make-ahead recipes that don't require a fork. If you run out of time, butchers will often cook a ham or a turkey, and some caterers will cook individual dishes for you.

• I would highly recommend staff or help even if you are making the food yourself.

• Do a few things well rather than a whole lot poorly. I like to have vegetables and dips scattered around the room for munching and for guests who are watching calories. For the simplest party, cook one big item like a turkey or ham and serve it with good breads, mustards and relishes and let guest make sandwiches.

• Organize the bar. Decide whether you'll have a full bar or just wine or punch. Have plenty of non-alcoholic beverages available (especially important with today's concerns about drinking drivers).

• Make sure you have plenty of serving trays, napkins and ice. Keep the food and bar areas separate; it causes congestion if they are close together.

• If you are having the party fully catered, discuss the menu with the caterer, working around your ideas and her suggestions. Don't be concerned with last-minute logistics such as when to start serving or where to put the boots — the catering staff should handle everything.

• For a cocktail party, don't have too much seating. The idea is for people to mingle. If too many guests sit down, the atmosphere becomes static.

The dishes for our cocktail party are divided into those you can leave around the room and those that need passing. Attractively display the vegetables and dips, the pâté and the Cheddar sticks in baskets or serving dishes, either on a buffet table or around the room. The chicken and the corn cups with guacamole are cold and can either be circulated around the room or left on a buffet table. The hot chili corn cups and the curried beef triangles should be passed around.

Imperial Chicken

Chicken Liver Pâté

Corn Cups with Mexican Fillings

Vegetables with Spicy Dips

Cheddar Sticks

Phyllo Triangles with Curried Beef

Imperial Chicken

The Chinese overtones in this recipe linger pleasantly. The soy sauce acts as a preservative for the chicken, so you can make the dish up to three days ahead of time. Use chicken wings instead of chicken breasts if desired, but remember that the bones will have to be discarded.

1 cup	soy sauce	250 mL
1/2 cup	water	125 mL
1/4 cup	dry white wine	50 mL
1/2 cup	granulated sugar	125 mL
3	1-inch (2.5 cm) slices fresh ginger, the size of a quarter	3
1 tsp	ground cinnamon	5 mL
1/2 tsp	ground nutmeg	2 mL
6	single chicken breasts, boned and skinned	6
1	carrot, slivered	1
2	green onions, slivered	2
1/2 cup	beansprouts	125 mL
1	bunch watercress	1

1. In a large frying pan over high heat, bring the soy sauce, water, wine, sugar and seasonings to a boil. Reduce the heat to a simmer, add the chicken breasts and simmer, uncovered, for 8 minutes on each side. Cool in the liquid.

2. Remove the chicken, slice each breast on the diagonal into five strips and arrange on a round platter in a circular formation.

3. Scatter the carrots, onions and beansprouts on top of the chicken. Pour over 1/4 cup (50 mL) soy liquid to moisten the breasts. Place a bunch of watercress in the center of the platter.

Makes about 3 dozen pieces

Expect your cocktail party to last about one hour longer than the closing time specified on the invitation.

Always ask for an R.S.V.P. on your invitation, because a "regrets only" reply can leave you uncertain about numbers. People often treat a regrets only instruction more casually than a request to R.S.V.P.

Allow six to eight savories per person for a two-hour cocktail party.

Chicken Liver Pâté

This pâté's special flavor comes from the brandy-soaked currants, which give it an undercurrent of sweetness. Serve it with apple and pear slices or on melba toast. Soak the apple and pear slices in cold salted water for 30 minutes before serving, so they will retain their color and crispness.

This pâté can be made three days ahead and covered with melted butter, but don't freeze it.

¹/₂ cup	currants	125 mL
2 tbsp	brandy	25 mL
2 lb	chicken livers	1 kg
1 cup	butter	250 mL
1	onion, finely chopped	1
2	cloves garlic, finely chopped	2
1 tsp	dried thyme	5 mL
¹/₂ tsp	allspice	2 mL
¹/₂ cup	whipping cream	125 mL
	Salt and freshly ground pepper to taste	

1. Soak the currants in the brandy for 1 hour. Cut the chicken livers in half and remove any fat.

2. Heat ¹/₄ cup (50 mL) butter in a frying pan. Sauté the onions and garlic for 1 minute, then add the livers. Sauté for about 5 minutes, or until cooked but slightly pink inside. Scrape into a food processor or blender.

3. Add the remaining butter, thyme, allspice and whipping cream. Process until completely smooth.

4. Stir in the currants and the brandy. Taste for seasoning, adding salt and pepper as needed. Pack into a terrine. Serve surrounded by apple and pear slices and melba toast.

Makes 6 cups (1.5 L)

For a cocktail party, plan to have at least two glasses per person; most guests will use more than one.

Freeze hors d'oeuvres on a baking sheet in the freezer, then transfer them to plastic bags or containers. To reheat, place the frozen pieces on a greased baking sheet and reheat in a preheated 350°F (180°C) oven for 10 minutes, or until cooked through. Do not freeze hors d'oeuvres for longer than one month — they may lose flavor.

Corn Cups with Mexican Fillings

These little pastries are very versatile. You can use them with a variety of fillings, especially ones with Mexican or Italian overtones (the fillings should have lots of oomph to balance the cornmeal flavor). Make the corn cups up to five days ahead of time; the guacamole can be made one day ahead and the chili two days. Double the corn cup recipe if you make both fillings.

1 cup	all-purpose flour	250 mL
¹/₂ cup	cornmeal	125 mL
2 tbsp	finely chopped parsley or fresh coriander	25 mL
pinch	cayenne pepper, optional	pinch
pinch	salt	pinch
¹/₂ cup	butter	125 mL
¹/₂ cup	cream cheese	125 mL

1. Preheat the oven to 350°F (180°C).

2. Place the flour, cornmeal, parsley, cayenne and salt in a food processor or a blender.

3. Cut the butter and cream cheese into four pieces each. Add to the processor. Using the on/off motion, cut the fats into the flour mixture until it resembles coarse crumbs.

4. Remove from the processor and knead the dough together until it forms a ball.

5. Divide the dough into 1-inch (2.5 cm) balls. Pat evenly into small muffin tins.

6. Bake for 20 minutes, or until the pastry is golden.

Makes about 3 dozen pastries

Guacamole Filling

There are as many recipes for guacamole as there are Mexican households. It can be chopped coarsely or pureed; sour cream can be added; the garlic can be increased or omitted; coriander can be used or not; even tomatoes are left out in some versions. The only constant is a ripe avocado. This filling can also be served as a dip with tortilla chips.

1	large avocado, peeled	1
1/4 cup	finely chopped red onion	50 mL
1	clove garlic, finely chopped	1
1	tomato, seeded and chopped	1
1 tsp	chopped jalapeño pepper	5 mL
	Juice of 1 lime	
2 tbsp	finely chopped fresh coriander	25 mL
36	baked corn cups	36

1. Mash the avocado with a potato masher. Fold in all the other ingredients.

2. Fill the corn cups. Serve at room temperature.

Fills 3 dozen corn cups

Sausage Chili Filling

8 oz	spicy sausage meat	250 g
1 tbsp	vegetable oil	15 mL
1	onion, chopped	1
1	clove garlic, finely chopped	1
1 tbsp	chili powder	15 mL
1 tsp	ground cumin	5 mL
2 cups	drained canned tomatoes, chopped	500 mL
1/2 cup	grated Cheddar cheese	125 mL
	Salt and freshly ground pepper to taste	
36	baked corn cups	36

1. Remove the sausage meat from its casings and crumble.

2. Heat the oil in a pot on medium heat. Add the sausage meat and sauté until browned. Discard the excess oil, leaving 1 tbsp (15 mL).

3. Add the onion and garlic and sauté until softened, about 2 minutes. Add the chili powder, cumin and tomatoes. Bring to a boil, lower the heat and simmer for 20 minutes, or until the mixture thickens. Stir in the cheese and season well with salt and pepper.

4. Fill the corn cups. Reheat at 350°F (180°C) for 10 minutes before serving.

Fills 3 dozen corn cups

Avocado is a winter fruit, at its best between November and February. It grows in both Florida and California. The best avocados are the black-skinned, crinkly Haas avocados from California. The green, pear-shaped avocados from Florida do not have as much oil and are less flavorful. Hard, unripe avocados will usually ripen if placed in a paper bag in a dark place for about four days.

Avocados turn brown when exposed to the air. To avoid this, place plastic wrap directly on the surface of the guacamole, leaving no air space. Placing the avocado pit in the guacamole will also retard the browning process a little. Avocados sliced for a salad should be added at the last minute.

Vegetables with Spicy Dips

Fresh glistening vegetables with interesting dips are always a hit at parties, especially with people who are watching their calorie intake. Display the vegetables and dips attractively. Use a variety of vegetables and remember to blanch the harder ones for a better taste and brighter color. The Indonesian flavoring of the satay dip is always popular, and the spiciness of the Delhi dip appeals to people who like hot tastes. The dips can be prepared up to three days ahead of time; the vegetables can be prepared the day before the party and kept crisp in cold water.

1	large cauliflower	1
2	bunches broccoli	2
3	large carrots	3

Satay Dip:

2/3 cup	crunchy peanut butter	150 mL
1/3 cup	brown sugar	75 mL
	Grated rind and juice of 2 limes	
1 tsp	Tabasco	5 mL
1 tbsp	soy sauce	15 mL
1	clove garlic, finely chopped	1
1/2 cup	milk	125 mL
1 tsp	sesame oil, optional	5 mL
1	green onion, chopped	1

Delhi Dip:

1/2 cup	mayonnaise	125 mL
1/2 cup	plain yogurt	125 mL
1/4 cup	finely chopped red onion	50 mL
1 tsp	curry powder	5 mL
1 tbsp	lemon juice	15 mL
1 tsp	granulated sugar	5 mL

1. Divide the cauliflower and broccoli into small florets. Cut the carrots into sticks.

2. Bring a large pot of salted water to the boil. Blanch the broccoli for 2 minutes, or until crisp-tender. Remove with a slotted spoon and refresh with cold water until cold.

3. Blanch the cauliflower in same water for 3 minutes, or until crisp-tender. Remove and refresh with cold water until cold.

4. Blanch the carrots for 2 minutes, or until crisp-tender. Refresh with cold water.

5. To make the Satay Dip, in a medium bowl, beat together all the ingredients except the green onions. Place in a serving bowl. Sprinkle the green onions on top.

6. To make the Delhi Dip, in a small bowl, combine all the ingredients. Place in serving bowl.

7. On a large platters, assemble rings of vegetables, alternating colors. Place the dips in the center of the platter.

Cheddar Sticks

These melt-in-the-mouth bites are simple to make and perfect for bringing out of the freezer and reheating at short notice. At a cocktail party, place in dishes around the room so people can serve themselves. Using old Cheddar gives a more distinctive taste to the sticks.

1/2 cup	butter, at room temperature	125 mL
1 cup	grated old Cheddar cheese	250 mL
1 1/2 cups	all-purpose flour	375 mL
1/2 tsp	baking powder	2 mL
1/2 tsp	salt	2 mL
1/2 tsp	dry mustard	2 mL
pinch	cayenne pepper	pinch
1/4 cup	plain yogurt	50 mL
2 tbsp	grated Parmesan cheese	25 mL
1	egg yolk, beaten	1

1. In a large bowl, cream the butter. Add the cheese and cream together.

2. In a separate bowl, sift together the flour, baking powder, salt, mustard and cayenne.

3. Blend the dry ingredients into the butter/cheese mixture. Using your hands, mix in the yogurt and Parmesan.

4. Roughly form the dough into a rectangle (it will be a bit crumbly). Wrap in plastic wrap and refrigerate for at least one hour.

5. Preheat the oven to 350°F (180°C).

6. Roll the dough into a rectangle ¼ inch (5 mm) thick. Brush the top with beaten egg yolk. With a sharp knife, cut the dough into strips approximately ¼ inch (5 mm) wide and 2 inches (5 cm) long.

7. Transfer to an ungreased baking sheet and bake for about 15 minutes, or until crisp and golden-brown around the edges. Remove to cool on racks.

Make about 3 dozen sticks

Phyllo Triangles with Curried Beef

An interesting hors d'oeuvre with a slightly spicy taste. Freeze the uncooked phyllo triangles and bake from the frozen state, or make one day ahead, refrigerate and bake when needed.

2 tbsp	vegetable oil	25 mL
1	onion, finely chopped	1
3	cloves garlic, finely chopped	3
2 tbsp	finely chopped fresh ginger	25 mL
1 tbsp	curry powder	15 mL
1 lb	lean ground beef	500 g
1 tbsp	tomato paste	15 mL
1 tbsp	lime juice	15 mL
1 cup	water	250 mL
1 tbsp	mango chutney	15 mL
	Salt and freshly ground pepper to taste	
8	sheets phyllo dough	8
1 cup	melted butter	250 mL

1. In a heavy pot, heat the vegetable oil. Sauté the onion, garlic and ginger until the onion is golden around the edges, about 7 to 8 minutes.

2. Add the curry powder. Sauté for 1 minute. Add the ground beef and continue to cook until the beef loses its pink color. Add the tomato paste, lime juice, water, mango chutney, salt and pepper. Cover and simmer for 1 hour.

3. Preheat the oven to 400°F (200°C).

4. Brush one sheet of phyllo with melted butter and cut lengthwise into six strips. (Use a damp tea towel to cover the remaining phyllo to prevent it from drying out.)

5. Put 1 tbsp (15 mL) filling in the bottom corner of each strip. Fold the dough containing the filling across to the edge, forming a triangle. Continue folding the triangle back and forth to the end of the strip. Place on a buttered baking sheet and brush with melted butter. Repeat until the filling is finished.

6. Bake for 15 minutes, or until the pastry is golden.

Makes about 4 dozen triangles

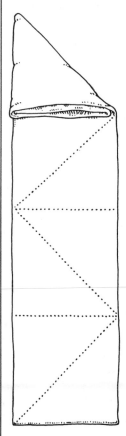

Pastry-wrapped hors d'oeuvres freeze well. The pastry can be phyllo, puff or shortcrust. Other wrappers suitable for freezing include bread, won ton skins and egg roll skins.

12
December

The hustle and bustle of holiday cooking, entertaining, partying and gift-buying calls for energy and perseverance. This is the month for rich, exciting meals balanced with simple homey dishes, culminating in a magnificent Christmas feast.

In season
clementines
kumquats
mandarins
navel oranges
tangerines

Holidays
Hanukkah
Christmas
New Year's Eve

Menu
Réveillon Supper for Six

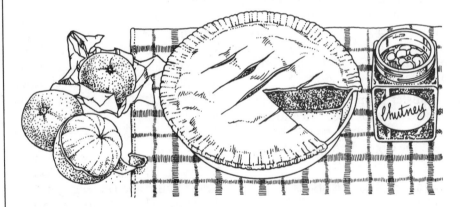

BONING BIRDS

Boning a chicken breast or a whole chicken is an easy technique to learn. Although boned breasts are easily available, they're cheaper if you bone the breasts yourself, and you get to keep the bones for stock. And sometimes a recipe calls for a boned chicken breast with the skin left on (often the boned breasts you buy are skinless). As for a whole chicken, most butchers today don't want to take the time to do it, except at a prohibitive price. But there is nothing as spectacular as a whole boned bird borne in on a huge platter and sliced in seconds to provide juicy, gorgeous-looking pieces.

Chicken Breasts

• Choose either whole or half breasts. If you wish to remove the skin, slip your fingertips under the skin and loosen from the meat. Then pull the skin off.

• For whole breasts, make a slit cut in the V where the shoulder bones meet. Holding the breasts skin side down, press up from underneath; the

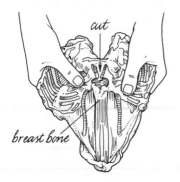

breast bone should loosen. Pull the breast bone away from the breast with your fingers. Cut the breasts in half.

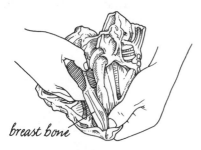

• Holding onto the rib and shoulder bones of one breast, scrape the flesh away from the remaining rib bones, pulling them off as they free. Feel for the attached shoulder bone and scrape the flesh from it. Cut through the ball joint to remove the bone com-

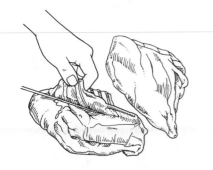

pletely. Feel for the wishbone and remove it. Repeat with the second breast. You will now have two boned chicken breasts.

Whole Birds

This is no more complicated than boning the breast; the technique of scraping the meat from the bones is the same. A large turkey takes no more time than a chicken. In fact, it is simpler, because the bones are easier to feel and loosen.

• Remove the neck bone if it is still on the chicken.
• Cut off the wing tip and first joint. Use for stock.
• Turn the bird breast side down with the ends of the legs facing you. Using a sharp knife, slit the bird from the neck to the tail along one side of the backbone but not through the

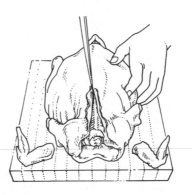

backbone. Scrape the meat from the rib bones, working as close to the bones as you can. Use your fingers to loosen the meat if necessary.

A boning knife is a sharp pointed knife with a narrow, flexible blade about 6 inches (15 cm) long. A sharp paring knife can be used instead. The point is needed to get behind the sockets of bones to release them.

If you are not sure of the configuration of the meat you are boning, always remember to scrape the meat away from the bones and cut through any ball joints you come to. Eventually you will end up with a boned bird.

Trussing needles are long saber-like darning needles. They are sharp enough to pierce through meat and skin. The ''thread'' is usually unwaxed butcher twine or kite string.

the wing. Cut through all the ball joints and remove the bones.

A boned chicken or turkey is easy to carve, and can sit contentedly in a 200°F (100°C) oven for 45 minutes without becoming excessively dry. It also freezes well uncooked.

Boned birds can be stuffed and frozen. Defrost them in the refrigerator, then bake according to directions. Bone out your Christmas turkey in early December, stuff it and freeze. It makes Christmas day a snap.

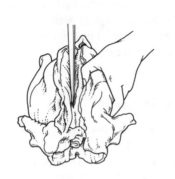

• When you come to the place where the thigh bone is nestled in a hollow in the carcass, insert the knife behind it and cut through the ball joint until it separates from carcass. Continue scraping until the ribs and backbone are free of meat.

• Repeat on the other side (turn the chicken around if that is easier), then cut or pull out all the exposed bones.

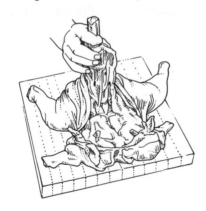

• At the neck end of the breastbone, the shoulder bones form a V shape. Cut through the center of the V, making sure you don't cut through the skin on the other side. Holding the breasts skin side down, press up from underneath; the breast bone should loosen. Scrape the flesh off the breastbone, shoulder bone and first joint of

• Holding onto the end of the thigh bone, cut around the sinews of the thigh bones, then scrape the meat down the bone to the ball joint. Cut through the ball joint; the thigh bone should come away, leaving the bone in the drumstick.

• To take out the drumstick bone, cut around the leg sinews, then push the meat down to the knuckle (ankle).

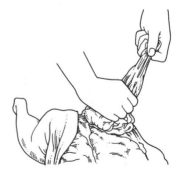

Pull out the leg bone and cut it off. Repeat on the other side.

• You can cut off the wing bones now if you wish, or leave them attached.

• Spread the meat out evenly and check for any bones that might remain. The chicken is now ready for stuffing.

Duck

Duck seems to be one of those things that people don't cook; they prefer to eat it in restaurants because of the fattiness and the difficulty with carving. But duck is far better eaten at home. Home cooking best ensures the release of fat and the crisp skin that is the glory of this succulent dish.

I have come up with a foolproof method for cutting up and cooking a duck. It eliminates carving and ensures a luscious, tasty bird every time.

• If the duck is frozen, defrost for 24 hours in the refrigerator.

• With a heavy chef's knife, slice through the breastbone. Continue to cut through on both sides of the backbone, giving you two half ducks and one backbone. Freeze the backbone for stock or discard.

• Slice through the ball joint between the thigh and breast on each side. You will have four pieces now — two breasts and two legs with the thighs attached. Trim away any fat and prick the skin with the tines of a fork.

• Rub 2 tbsp (25 mL) soy sauce on the duck skin, set on a rack with a baking sheet underneath and refrigerate for 24 hours to allow the skin to dry out.

Crispy Roast Duck

One duck should feed four, but if people have large appetites it may only feed two. Serve with lemon-scented roast potatoes (see page 18), cabbage with juniper berries and garlic (see page 178) and applesauce. Remember to let the duck skin dry out for 24 hours before cooking for the crispest results.

4	cloves garlic, peeled	4
1	duck, cut in four pieces	1
	Salt and freshly ground pepper to taste	

1. Preheat the oven to 450°F (230°C).

2. Insert a garlic clove under the skin of each duck quarter. Season with salt and pepper.

3. Place the duck legs on a rack in a roasting pan. Roast for 10 minutes.

4. Turn the heat down to 400°F (200°C) and add the breasts to the rack with the legs. Roast for a further 30 minutes.

5. Remove the pan from the oven and let the duck sit for 5 minutes before serving.

Serves 2 to 4

Duck legs take longer to cook than breasts, so they should go into the oven first.

Duck Breasts with Black Currant Sauce

Duck breasts can now be bought in some supermarkets and meat stores. The first time I ate them in France, I thought I was being served a steak by mistake, because they were so meaty. If you cannot find them, buy a whole duck, bone it out, roast the legs and serve them at another meal or with the duck breasts and some sauce if the duck is small. If you want to cut down the fat, instead of sautéing, grill the duck breasts for about 5 minutes on each side.

If fresh black currants are not in season, you can find dried ones at health food stores, or substitute frozen blueberries. If cassis is unavailable, use black currant syrup.

4	single duck breasts, boned	4
	Salt and freshly ground pepper	
1 tbsp	vegetable oil	15 mL
1/3 cup	butter	75 mL
1/2 cup	dry red wine	125 mL
2 cups	chicken or duck stock	500 mL
2 tbsp	cassis	25 mL
1/4 cup	black currants	50 mL

1. Preheat the oven to 200°F (100°C).

2. Sprinkle the breasts with salt and pepper. Heat the oil and 2 tbsp (25 mL) butter in a large frying pan on medium heat.

3. Add the breasts, skin side down. Sauté until the skin is brown, about 4 minutes. Turn over and sauté on the second side for 4 minutes, or until the breast meat is pink. Keep warm in the oven.

4. Discard all the fat from the frying pan. Return the pan to the heat and add the red wine. Bring to a boil, scraping up any bits stuck to the bottom of the pan. Reduce to 2 tbsp (25 mL).

5. Stir in the stock and cassis. Reduce until the sauce thickens slightly, about 2 minutes. Remove from the heat and whisk in the remaining butter.

6. Taste for seasoning, adding salt and pepper as needed. Add the black currants.

7. Slice the duck breasts on the diagonal and place on plates. Pour over the sauce.

Serves 4

Boned Capon with Prunes

A magnificent main course for a special dinner party. Serve with whole mushrooms sautéed with baby onions and prunes.

1 cup	pitted prunes	250 mL
1 cup	dry red wine	250 mL
2 tbsp	vegetable oil	25 mL
1	Spanish onion, chopped	1
1 1/2 lb	ground pork	750 g
1 tbsp	dried marjoram	15 mL
1 tsp	dried thyme	5 mL
2 tbsp	finely chopped parsley	25 mL
	Grated rind of 1 orange	
1 cup	fresh breadcrumbs	250 mL
1	egg	1
1 tsp	salt	5 mL
1/2 tsp	freshly ground pepper	2 mL
1	5- to 6-lb (2.5 to 3 kg) capon, boned	1
Sauce:		
2 tbsp	all-purpose flour	25 mL
4 cups	chicken stock	1 L
1 tsp	tomato paste	5 mL
	Prune-cooking liquid	
	Salt and freshly ground pepper to taste	

There are several different species of duck available today. The white Pekin duck and the Muscovy are the most common. The Pekin duck is more fatty and has a thicker skin and less meat than the Muscovy, but it is more tender and more tasty.

Capons are castrated male chickens, which grow bigger breasts after castration.

1. In a small pot, simmer the prunes in the wine for 15 minutes.

2. Preheat the oven to 375°F (190°C).

3. Heat the oil in a frying pan on medium-high heat. Add the onions and sauté until softened, about 2 minutes.

4. In a large bowl, combine the pork, onions, marjoram, thyme, parsley, orange rind, breadcrumbs, egg, salt and pepper. Fry up a little stuffing and adjust the seasonings to taste.

5. Lay the bird flat, flesh side up, tucking in any loose pieces of flesh. Spread the filling over the whole bird.

6. Drain the prunes and reserve the liquid. Place the prunes down the center of the filling.

7. Fold in the two sides of the capon with the skin overlapping slightly. With a trussing needle and string or skewers, sew the skin together.

8. With your hands, form the capon into a long, even-sized roll. Tie in three or four places to help the bird keep its shape.

9. Place on rack and bake for 1½ hours, or until the juices run clear. Let the capon sit on a platter while you are making the sauce.

10. To make the sauce, drain the fat from the roasting pan, leaving 2 tbsp (25 mL).

11. On high heat, stir the flour into the fat and cook, stirring, until it turns a pale gold color, about 1 to 2 minutes.

12. Add the chicken stock, tomato paste and prune-cooking liquid. Bring to a boil, turn the heat to low and simmer for 10 minutes. Season with salt and pepper. Serve with the capon.

Serves 10 to 12

Baked Chicken Breasts Dijon

This coating also works well on firm-fleshed fish such as monkfish. Serve with French fries and a salad.

¼ cup	Dijon mustard	50 mL
2 tbsp	finely chopped parsley	25 mL
1 tbsp	soy sauce	15 mL
1 tbsp	lemon juice	15 mL
1 tsp	dried thyme	5 mL
½ tsp	freshly ground pepper	2 mL
3	whole boned chicken breasts	3

1. Preheat the oven to 400°F (200°C).

2. In a small bowl, combine the mustard, parsley, soy sauce, lemon juice, thyme and pepper.

3. Brush the chicken breasts on both sides with the mustard mixture.

4. Place the chicken on a lightly oiled baking dish large enough to hold the breasts in one layer. Bake for 15 to 20 minutes, or until the coating is lightly browned and the juices run clear. Serve hot or cold.

Serves 6

Sautéed Mushrooms with Onions and Prunes
In a frying pan, heat 2 tbsp (25 mL) butter. Sauté 20 small onions with 1 tsp (5 mL) granulated sugar until browned. Cover the pan and cook for 10 minutes, or until the onions are soft. Add 8 oz (250 g) whole small mushrooms and 16 pitted prunes. Sauté together until the mushrooms soften, about 5 minutes. Serves 10 to 12.

Chicken Breasts Perigord

This flavorful and elegant chicken is stuffed with a scented combination of fresh and dried mushrooms. Because the breasts are stuffed under the skin, the stuffing moistens the chicken meat and keeps it juicy. Use either dried porcini or dried Chinese mushrooms; they have the most flavor. The sauce can be made ahead of time and the breasts stuffed a few hours before baking.

6	dried mushrooms	6
¹/₂ cup	boiling water	125 mL
2 tbsp	butter	25 mL
4	shallots or green onions, chopped	4
8 oz	mushrooms, finely chopped	250 g
1 tsp	dried tarragon or basil	5 mL
3 tbsp	fresh breadcrumbs	45 mL
¹/₃ cup	whipping cream	75 mL
3 tbsp	finely chopped parsley	45 mL
	Salt and freshly ground pepper to taste	
6	single boned chicken breasts, with skin on	6
Sauce:		
¹/₂ cup	chopped onions	125 mL
¹/₄ cup	dry red wine	50 mL
¹/₂ cup	mushroom-soaking liquid	125 mL
3 cups	chicken stock	750 mL
2 tbsp	port or Madeira	25 mL
1 tbsp	arrowroot or cornstarch	15 mL
1 tbsp	cold water	15 mL
	Salt and freshly ground pepper to taste	

1. Soak the mushrooms in boiling water for 20 minutes. Drain the mushrooms, reserving the soaking water and the mushrooms separately. Chop the mushrooms.

2. Preheat the oven to 375°F (190°C).

3. Heat the butter in a frying pan over medium-high heat. Add the shallots and dried and fresh mushrooms. Sauté until all the liquid has evaporated, stirring occasionally, about 4 minutes. Stir in the tarragon, breadcrumbs, cream and parsley. Cook until the cream has reduced and the filling is thick. Season well with salt and pepper.

4. Divide the filling in six portions. With your fingertips, make a pocket between the skin and the flesh of each chicken breast. Stuff the filling under the skin of the chicken breasts. Season the breasts with salt and pepper and place in a buttered baking dish large enough to hold the breasts in one layer.

5. Bake for 30 to 40 minutes, basting occasionally, until the juices run clear.

6. To make the sauce, in a frying pan, combine the onions and wine. On high heat, bring to a boil and reduce until you have 1 tbsp (15 mL) liquid.

7. Pour in the mushroom liquid, reduce to 2 tbsp (25 mL), then add the chicken stock and continue to boil until the stock is reduced by half. Add the port and simmer for another 2 minutes, or until the sauce is smooth and strongly flavored.

8. Combine the arrowroot and cold water and stir into the sauce, simmering until the sauce thickens slightly, about 2 minutes. Season with salt and pepper and add any juices from the chicken. To serve, pour the sauce over the chicken breasts.

Serves 6

CLEMENTINES, MANDARINS AND TANGERINES

In December, look for clementines, mandarins and tangerines piled high in the fruit bins. Clementines are the smallest variety, but what they lack in size they make up for in taste and texture. Look for the clementines grown in Morocco under the trade name Maroc — they are the sweetest. Mandarins and tangerines come from Japan, Spain, Florida and California. All these fruits have in common a skin that peels like a zipper, and a fine juicy, sweet taste.

• Look for a bright, rich color. Don't worry about small green areas around the stem.

• The fruit should feel heavy for its size and slightly puffy.

• To keep for longer than a day or two, refrigerate them.

• All these fruits are wonderful eaten raw, but their juices also make a good base for sauces for fish or chicken, or as the topping of a fruit tart.

Sautéed Orange Roughy with Mandarin Sauce

Substitute boneless chicken breasts, scallops or shrimp. I like to use orange roughy because its firm texture and mild taste pair well with the sauce. The fish is imported, frozen, from New Zealand. Defrost overnight in the refrigerator.

1 tbsp	butter	15 mL
1 lb	orange roughy	500 g
	Salt and freshly ground pepper to taste	
2 tbsp	finely chopped fresh dill	25 mL
1/2 cup	mandarin juice	125 mL
1/2 cup	whipping cream	125 mL

1. Heat the butter in a frying pan on medium-high heat. Pat the fish dry, season with salt and pepper and sprinkle with 1 tbsp (15 mL) dill.

2. Place in the frying pan and fry for 2 minutes, or until the flesh is colored. Turn over and fry on the second side.

3. Pour in the mandarin juice and bring to a boil. Pour in the whipping cream and reduce until the sauce thickens slightly. Sprinkle with the remaining dill and serve immediately.

Serves 2 to 3

Although mandarin is actually the collective botanical name for clementines, tangerines and mandarins, mandarin usually refers to the seedless fruit, while a tangerine is the fruit with seeds. Clementines are usually seedless and smaller than either mandarins or tangerines.

Two small clementines contain only about 40 calories.

Mandarin Grape Tarts

Use seedless fresh mandarins or clementines. Red and green seedless grapes look colorful in these tarts as well. The pastry is easy to pat into small muffin tins or individual tartlet tins. Double the pastry and have extra tarts in the freezer for unexpected visitors!

The kumquat (tiny orange), native to China and edible whole, makes a better table decoration than an eating experience. It's full of seeds and bitter-tasting. Creative bartenders enhance the taste of certain cocktails by thinly slicing kumquats and dropping them into drinks.

1 cup	all-purpose flour	250 mL
³/₄ cup	ground almonds	175 mL
¹/₂ cup	granulated sugar	125 mL
¹/₃ cup	unsalted butter, cold	75 mL
1	egg yolk	1
3 tbsp	orange juice	45 mL
¹/₂ cup	marmalade	125 mL
¹/₂ cup	red currant jelly	125 mL
1	small bunch seedless green or red grapes	1
2	mandarins, peeled	2

1. In a bowl, stir together the flour, almonds and sugar. With a pastry blender or two knives, cut in the butter until it is crumbly. Blend in the egg yolk and orange juice. Wrap and refrigerate for 1 hour.

2. Preheat the oven to 350°F (180°C).

3. Press the pastry into 2³/₄ × 1-inch (7 × 2.5 cm) muffin tins. Line the pastry with foil and weigh down with pie weights or beans*. Bake for 10 minutes. Remove from the oven, take out the foil and weights and cook for a further 3 minutes. Remove the tarts from the pan while warm.

4. In two separate pots, warm the marmalade and jelly until just melted.

5. Place 1 tsp (5 mL) red currant jelly in each of half the pastry shells. Place marmalade in the remaining shells. Place grapes on the red currant tartlets, and orange sections on the marmalade tartlets. Brush the fruit lightly with the appropriate remaining glaze.

Makes 20 tartlets

Mandarin Posset

Posset is the old English term for a creamy dessert. It takes minutes to make and is always a hit. Decorate with mandarin sections, if desired. Or pile the posset into a baked pie shell coated with chocolate for an unusual and delectable presentation.

	Grated rind and juice of 4 mandarins	
¹/₄ cup	granulated sugar	50 mL
1 cup	whipping cream	250 mL
2 tbsp	orange liqueur	25 mL
2 tbsp	grated bittersweet chocolate	25 mL

1. Mix together the mandarin rind, juice, sugar and whipping cream.

2. In an electric mixer or by hand, beat together until the cream thickens and holds its shape. Fold in the orange liqueur.

3. Pile into Champagne flutes or wine glasses. Top with grated chocolate.

Serves 4

*See *Lucy Waverman's Cooking School Cookbook*, page 93.

Clementine Custard Pudding

This recipe tastes wonderful and is so easy to make. The texture is cakey on top and custard-like underneath. Use orange or lemon rind and juice if clementines are unavailable.

2 tbsp	unsalted butter	25 mL
¹/₂ cup	granulated sugar	125 mL
2 tsp	grated clementine rind	10 mL
3	eggs, separated	3
¹/₄ cup	clementine juice	50 mL
1 cup	light cream	250 mL
3 tbsp	all-purpose flour	45 mL
pinch	salt	pinch
1 tbsp	icing sugar	15 mL

1. Preheat oven to 350°F (180°C).

2. With an electric mixer or in the food processor, beat the butter until light. Gradually beat in the sugar until light and fluffy. Beat in the rind, then the egg yolks, one at a time.

3. Combine the clementine juice and cream. Stir the flour into the batter alternately with the cream, mixing well after each addition.

4. In a separate bowl, beat the egg whites and salt until soft peaks form. Fold into the clementine mixture.

5. Pour into a buttered 4-cup (1 L) soufflé dish. Place in a baking pan half-filled with hot water.

6. Bake for about 35 minutes, or until the top is set; underneath will still be liquid. Sift icing sugar over top. Serve hot.

Serves 4

OYSTERS

Oysters have long been associated with Christmas, usually as a first course before an elegant Christmas dinner, or on the half shell as a special treat for oyster lovers.

There is an old story about only eating oysters when there is an "R" in the month. "Not true today," says Rodney Clarke, one of P.E.I.'s foremost oystermen who has campaigned vigorously to make Canadians aware of the exquisite briny taste of his native P.E.I. Malpeque oysters. Before the days of refrigeration, and because European oysters carry their young in their gills in the summer, traditionally oysters weren't fished commercially in the summer. But this has changed, and now oysters are available twelve months of the year.

Other things have changed for our oysters, too. Heavy demand over the past few years has depleted our Maritime oyster beds, and the price of oysters is steadily increasing. Because P.E.I. fishermen have looked at mariculture (the artificial breeding of oysters) with a considerable lack of interest, their natural oyster beds are overpicked. But mariculture is the only way to ensure constant supplies of excellent oysters. In Nova Scotia, and now to a lesser extent in P.E.I., mariculture oyster farms are being developed. The young oysters are bred in hatcheries in non-polluted, ionized water. They are then transferred to "finishing school" or treated warm ocean water where they grow more quickly and take on the traditional briny Malpeque characteristics. These farmed oysters are plump, juicy, sweet and a tad less

The Christmas feast traditionally includes roast turkey (see page 170), cranberry sauce (see page 166) and fruit cake (see pages 179 to 182). If you have not managed to make your Christmas cake in advance, try the Five-Day Christmas Pudding (see page 180).

salty than naturally fished oysters (at a recent oyster-tasting that I attended, all the tasters preferred the maricultured oysters to the "natural" ones!).

Belons, the French oysters, are now being cultivated in our colder waters in Nova Scotia. They have a shorter shelf-life than the Malpeques and a stronger salt flavor with a heavier aftertaste.

• The most important guide to buying good oysters is to trust your fishmonger to tell you the truth about freshness.

• A good oyster feels like a solid, heavy weight in your hand.

• An oyster should have a good teardrop shape and a rounded cup, or top shell.

• Choose oysters that have been out of the water for less than five to seven days.

• If oysters are very fresh, they will last for a week in the coldest part of a home refrigerator, with a wet cloth over them.

• To open or shuck an oyster, place it cup side down on a rough cloth. Insert a short oyster knife near the hinge and work in with a twisting motion. Twist off the flat shell. Slip the oyster down your throat. Eat 'em raw with their juice and a squeeze of lemon.

An oyster knife is a squat knife with a strong steel blade and a short handle. The pointed end of the knife slips into the muscle of the oyster and the blade levers it apart. If you don't have an oyster knife, open oysters by the oven method rather than risk breaking your other knives.

Easy Oven Method for Opening Oysters
Bake oysters at 400°F (200°C) for 2 minutes. Slip a knife in. The shells should open easily.

Pesto Baked Oysters

A great hors d'oeuvre for the Christmas season. Pesto can be bought in jars, or you might have some in the freezer, left over from the summer. Substitute clams, mussels or oyster mushrooms for the oysters, if desired.

24	shucked oysters	24
24	croustade shells	24
1/2 cup	pesto (see page 121)	125 mL
1/4 cup	grated Parmesan cheese	50 mL

1. Preheat the oven to 375°F (190°C).

2. Place the oysters in the croustade shells. Top with 1 tsp (5 mL) pesto. Sprinkle with Parmesan.

3. Bake for 5 to 7 minutes, or until the oysters curl slightly. Serve immediately.

Serves 6 as an appetizer; 12 as an hors d'oeuvre

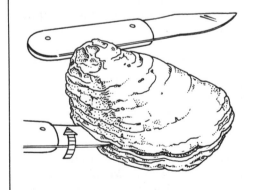

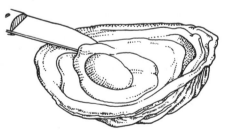

Original Oysters Rockefeller

Antoine's, a restaurant in New Orleans, developed this rich and elegant oyster recipe. Rock salt helps the oyster shell to sit steady on a baking sheet. If you do not have any, use crumpled foil.

24	oysters on the half shell	24
1 cup	butter	250 mL
1/3 cup	finely chopped parsley	75 mL
1/4 cup	finely chopped celery	50 mL
4	shallots, finely chopped	4
1	clove garlic, finely chopped	1
2 cups	chopped watercress leaves	500 mL
1/3 cup	chopped fresh fennel	75 mL
1/3 cup	dry breadcrumbs	75 mL
1 tbsp	Pernod or anisette	15 mL
	Salt and freshly ground pepper to taste	

1. Preheat the oven to 450°F (230°C). Completely cover a baking sheet with rock salt. Arrange the oysters on top.

2. In a frying pan on medium-high heat, melt the butter. When the butter sizzles, add the parsley, celery, shallots and garlic. Cook for 3 minutes. Add the watercress and fennel and cook for a further minute.

3. Place the mixture in a food processor and puree with the breadcrumbs and Pernod. Season with salt and pepper.

4. Put 1 tbsp (15 mL) sauce on each oyster. Spread to the rim of the shell.

5. Bake for 4 minutes, or until the sauce bubbles.

Serves 4 to 6 as an appetizer

Slap Jack Chowder

This elegant soup is best made with oysters; however, other shellfish such as mussels or shrimp can be substituted. Rodney Clarke, master oysterman from P.E.I., used this recipe at the Cooking School to demonstrate how quickly oysters cook. If fresh oysters are unavailable, frozen can be used, but don't use canned.

2 tbsp	butter	25 mL
2	red onions, chopped	2
1/4 cup	finely chopped parsley	50 mL
1 tbsp	soy sauce	15 mL
1 tsp	dried thyme	5 mL
1	bay leaf	1
1/2 tsp	salt	2 mL
1/2 tsp	freshly ground pepper	2 mL
dash	Tabasco	dash
2 cups	fresh shucked oysters and oyster liquor (approximately 25 oysters)	500 mL
2 cups	milk	500 mL
1/2 cup	light cream	125 mL
1/2 cup	dry white wine	125 mL
2 cups	grated Cheddar cheese	500 mL

1. In a frying pan, melt the butter on medium heat. Cook the onion and parsley until the onion is softened, about 2 minutes.

2. Stir in the soy sauce, thyme, bay leaf, salt, pepper and Tabasco.

3. Add the oysters and their liquor and cook, stirring, over low heat for 5 minutes, or until the edges curl.

4. Stir in the milk and cream. Bring to a simmer but do not boil. Simmer for 2 minutes.

5. Add the wine and cheese and stir until melted. Remove from the heat and serve immediately.

Serves 4

Croustade Shells
With a cookie cutter, cut 2 1/2-inch (6.5 cm) rounds from thinly sliced white bread. Brush both sides with melted butter and press into small muffin cups. Bake at 300°F (150°C) for 20 to 25 minutes, or until golden-brown. Use as casings for savory fillings.

Réveillon Supper for Six

French Canadians celebrate Le Réveillon on Christmas Eve. Traditionally they go to midnight Mass, come home, eat supper and then open presents. Réveillon is a joyous occasion to share with friends and family. There is music, dancing and singing, and often the celebrations go on until dawn (there is no traditional Christmas dinner in French-speaking homes).

The traditional food of old Quebec adapts wonderfully to any Christmas Eve celebration. Everything is prepared ahead of time and only needs to be reheated before serving.

Réveil means "awakening," referring to the French-Canadian Christmas Eve tradition of putting the kids to bed and then waking them up to attend Mass and present-opening.

Helen Gougeon's Pea Soup

Tourtière

Apple Pear Chutney

Pickled Beets

Cole Slaw*

Syrup Pudding

*See *Lucy Waverman's Cooking School Cookbook*, page 146.

Helen Gougeon's Pea Soup

This is an authentic French Canadian pea soup (made with salt pork, not a ham bone) from Helen Gougeon, journalist and cookbook author. If you use split peas, do not presoak them. Some people use the green peas because the color is so attractive, but traditionally the soup calls for yellow peas.

1 lb	dried yellow peas	500 g
1 tbsp	butter	15 mL
1	large onion, chopped	1
1 tbsp	coarse salt	15 mL
1 lb	salt pork	500 g
12 cups	water	3 L
1 tsp	dried savory	5 mL
	Salt and freshly ground pepper to taste	

1. Wash the peas, removing any that are wrinkled. Soak overnight in water to cover. Drain.

2. In a large pot, melt the butter. Sauté the onion until softened slightly, about 2 minutes. Add the peas, salt, salt pork, water and savory. Bring to the boil, cover and simmer for 1½ hours, or until the salt pork is tender. Remove the pork. (Chop up the salt pork and put it back into the soup, or slice it thinly and serve it as a main course with warm bread and pickles.)

3. Continue to cook the soup, covered, until the peas are tender, about 30 minutes longer.

4. Remove 2 cups (500 mL) peas from the soup and press through a sieve or puree. Stir back into the soup. (This gives a richer, less watery texture.) Taste for seasoning, adding salt and pepper as needed.

Serves 6

Tourtière

The true French Canadian meat pie has a lard-based pastry, but you can substitute a basic shortcrust* if you prefer a lighter crust. If the potato is omitted, the filling will be less dense. Tourtière is traditionally served with pickled beets or other pickles and a salad.

Pastry:

1³/₄ cups	all-purpose flour	425 mL
¹/₂ tsp	salt	2 mL
¹/₄ tsp	baking powder	1 mL
¹/₃ cup	lard	75 mL
¹/₄ cup	butter	50 mL
¹/₄ cup plus 1 tbsp	ice water	65 mL

Filling:

1¹/₂ lb	ground pork	750 g
1	onion, chopped	1
2 tsp	dried savory	10 mL
¹/₄ tsp	ground cloves	1 mL
1 tsp	freshly ground pepper	5 mL
1¹/₂ tsp	salt	7 mL
¹/₄ cup	water	50 mL
pinch	allspice	pinch
2 tsp	dried thyme	10 mL
1	bay leaf	1
1	potato, cooked and mashed	1

1. To make the pastry, sift the flour with the salt and baking powder. With your fingertips, cut in the lard and butter until the mixture resembles coarse meal. Stir in the ice water. Form into a ball. Wrap in waxed paper and chill for 30 minutes.

2. Place all the filling ingredients except the potato in a pot. Mix well. Simmer, covered, for 45 minutes, stirring occasionally, until the pork is cooked. Add the mashed potato and mix well to eliminate any lumps. Taste for seasoning, adding salt, pepper or spices as needed. Cool.

3. Preheat the oven to 375°F (190°C).

4. Divide the pastry in half. Roll out half to fit a 9-inch (23 cm) pie plate. Add the filling. Cover with the remaining pastry. Make three or four incisions on top of the pastry to allow steam to escape.

5. Bake for 45 minutes, or until the pastry is golden. Serve hot.

Serves 6

Hanukkah

In December, the Jewish Festival of Lights, or Hanukkah, is celebrated for eight days. The holiday celebrates the victory of a small band of tenacious Jews who fought the pagan Syrians for the right to worship God with their own religious rituals. After their victory, they dedicated the Jewish temple by lighting the sacred oil lamp, but there was only enough oil for one day. Through a miracle, the oil lamp burned for eight days — enough time for the Jews to find more oil. Today Hanukkah is commemorated by lighting the eight-pronged menorah candlestick for eight days.

*See *Lucy Waverman's Cooking School Cookbook*, page 94.

Apple Pear Chutney

This chutney is not the traditional tomato chili sauce served with tourtière, but it has a wonderful flavor and is also delicious with cold ham and turkey for after-Christmas leftovers. Cook the chutney until it is a dark rich color. Sterilize jars in the oven at 225°F (108°C) for 15 minutes, pack with the chutney and seal with wax or sealing lids. It should keep, refrigerated, for a year. Whatever you don't use, give away as Christmas presents.

Stem ginger is a preserved ginger stored in syrup. It has a hot/sweet taste. If you can't find it, use 2 tbsp (25 mL) chopped fresh ginger.

	Rind and juice of 1 lemon	
3 cups	brown sugar	750 mL
4 cups	white vinegar	1 L
4	whole dried chilies, or 1 tbsp (15 mL) crushed dried chilies	4
4	cloves, tied in cheesecloth	4
6	pears, peeled and chopped	6
3	large green apples, peeled and chopped	3
1	large onion, chopped	1
1¹/₂ cups	raisins	375 mL
4	pieces stem ginger in syrup, chopped	4
3	cloves garlic	3

1. Bring the lemon rind and juice, brown sugar, vinegar, chilies and cloves to a boil in a large pot. Add the pears and apples. Remove from the heat, cover and let sit overnight.

2. Add all the remaining ingredients and bring to a boil. Turn the heat to low and simmer for 2 to 3 hours, until the chutney is thick.

Makes about 8 cups (2 L)

Syrup Pudding

A traditional French Canadian dessert. Serve with a large dollop of ice cream to cut the sweetness.

¹/₂ cup	unsalted butter	125 mL
1 cup	granulated sugar	250 mL
2	eggs	2
1¹/₂ cups	all-purpose flour	375 mL
1¹/₂ tsp	baking powder	7 mL
¹/₂ tsp	salt	2 mL
¹/₂ cup	milk	125 mL
1 tsp	vanilla extract	5 mL
3 cups	brown sugar	750 mL
2¹/₂ cups	water	625 mL

1. Preheat the oven to 350°F (180°C).

2. In a medium bowl, beat the butter until very smooth. Add the granulated sugar and beat until fluffy. Beat in the eggs one at a time.

3. In a separate bowl, sift the flour, baking powder and salt. Beat half the flour mixture alternately with milk into the butter/sugar mixture, then beat in the remaining flour. Stir in the vanilla.

4. In a pot, bring the brown sugar and water to boil. Boil for 2 minutes.

5. Pour the batter in a large clump onto a greased 11 × 7-inch (3-L) baking dish. Pour over the syrup.

6. Bake for 50 to 60 minutes, or until a toothpick comes out clean. Serve warm.

Serves 6

Index